Federico García Lorca

Four Key Plays

The Audience • *Blood Wedding*
Yerma • *The House of Bernarda Alba*

Translation and Introduction by
MICHAEL KIDD

Hackett Publishing Company, Inc.
Indianapolis/Cambridge

Copyright © 2019 by Hackett Publishing Company, Inc.

All rights reserved
Printed in the United States of America

22 21 20 19   1 2 3 4 5 6 7

For further information, please address
Hackett Publishing Company, Inc.
P.O. Box 44937
Indianapolis, Indiana 46244-0937

www.hackettpublishing.com

Cover design by Rick Todhunter
Interior design by Elizabeth L. Wilson
Composition by Aptara, Inc.

Library of Congress Cataloging-in-Publication Data

Names: Garcâia Lorca, Federico, 1898-1936, author. | Kidd, Michael, 1968– translator, writer of introduction. | Garcâia Lorca, Federico, 1898–1936. Pâublico. English. | Garcâia Lorca, Federico, 1898–1936. Bodas de sangre. English. | Garcâia Lorca, Federico, 1898-1936. Yerma. English. | Garcâia Lorca, Federico, 1898–1936. Casa de Bernarda Alba. English.
Title: Four key plays / Federico Garcâia Lorca ; translated, with an introduction, by Michael Kidd.
Description: Indianapolis : Hackett Publishing Company, Inc., [2019] | Includes bibliographical references.
Identifiers: LCCN 2018038706 | ISBN 9781624667763 (cloth) | ISBN 9781624667756 (pbk.)
Subjects: LCSH: Garcâia Lorca, Federico, 1898–1936—Translations into English.
Classification: LCC PQ6613.A763 A2 2019 | DDC 862/.62—dc23
LC record available at https://lccn.loc.gov/2018038706

The paper used in this publication meets the minimum requirements of American National Standard for Information Sciences—Permanence of Paper for Printed Library Materials, ANSI Z39.48–1984.

∞

Federico García Lorca

Four Key Plays

For Nico

*Who can say, my son,
what the water brings
with its flowing skirts
and its chambers of green?*

The door to the theater never closes.

—Federico García Lorca

CONTENTS

Acknowledgments	viii
Preface	ix
Introduction	xi
Biographical Sketch	xi
1. The Taste of Earth (1898–1909)	xi
2. The Smell of Mystery (1909–1919)	xiii
3. Capital Gains (1919–1928)	xiv
4. Highs and Lows (1928–1929)	xvii
5. Far from Home (1929–1930)	xix
6. New Hope (1930–1933)	xxii
7. International Celebrity (1933–1935)	xxiv
8. Poisoned Well (1935–1936)	xxvi
9. Return to Earth (Summer 1936)	xxviii
Critical Guide	xxx
1. Lorca's Place in Spanish Theater	xxx
2. Performance History and Reception of Lorca's Plays	xxxv
3. Signature Elements of Lorca's Theater	xxxviii
4. The Four Plays in Brief	xliv
Translator's Note	lii
The Audience: Drama in Five Tableaux	1
Blood Wedding: Tragedy in Three Acts and Seven Tableaux	45
Yerma: Tragic Poem in Three Acts and Six Tableaux	109
The House of Bernarda Alba: Drama about Women in the Villages of Spain	157
Appendix 1: Variations from García-Posada's Text	210
Appendix 2: Professional Debuts of Lorca's Major Plays	212
For Further Reading	214

ACKNOWLEDGMENTS

This project came about as the result of a collaboration with the Theater Department of Augsburg College (now University), which performed my translation of *The House of Bernarda Alba* in the fall of 2013. I would like to begin by thanking all those involved in the production including the department chair, Darcey Engen; the director, Dario Tangelson; the stage designer, Michael Burden; and the wonderful all-student cast. Thanks also to Doug Green and Sarah Myers for allowing me into their drama classes to discuss the translation. It was a privilege to test the words of Bernarda and company in the actors' mouths and to discuss the plays with such bright students, which then led to the idea of a volume of Lorca translations. Augsburg provided the sabbatical during which I accomplished the writing, for which I am also grateful.

I am fortunate to count myself a member of a reading group with whom I share both fiction and nonfiction. Becky Boling, Scott Carpenter, and Greg Johnson offered valuable critiques of several of the translations and most of the introductory materials. Other readers and correspondents who provided encouragement and helpful suggestions along the way include Christopher Maurer, Lee Jacobus, and Leslie Stainton.

I am indebted to my editor at Hackett Publishing Company, Rick Todhunter, who believed in the project from the beginning and was willing to return to it three years after an impasse over copyright threatened to derail it.

Finally, my son Nico read the Biographical Sketch in full and made many useful suggestions. ¡Gracias, hijo!

PREFACE

This anthology brings together four key plays by Federico García Lorca (1898–1936), Spain's greatest modern dramatist, providing reliable translations into standard American English. The plays chosen for inclusion reveal the two poles of Lorca's dramatic output: his experimental "impossible theater," represented by *The Audience* (1930), and his successful commercial theater, represented by *Blood Wedding* (1932), *Yerma* (1934), and *The House of Bernarda Alba* (1936). While the latter three are the author's best-known plays and are often anthologized alone, they give an incomplete picture of Lorca's dramatic corpus. As Paul Julian Smith notes: "If the 'impossible' theatre was, as García Lorca declared, destined for the future, we are now that audience, and we have an ethical responsibility to respond to its challenge, a responsibility denied to earlier generations of scholars and theatre-goers. Such a burden cannot leave us indifferent, intellectually or aesthetically" (Smith 2010, p. 34). Taken together, the four plays translated in this collection reveal the astonishing range of Lorca the playwright at the height of his creative powers.

The Spanish text used as the basis of all four translations is that of Miguel García-Posada in *Obras completas II: Teatro* (Círculo de Lectores/Galaxia Gutenberg, 1997), abbreviated throughout as *OC*. I have explained the few instances I diverge from the source text in Appendix 1. In my bibliographical references I use a modified version of the *MLA Handbook*, eighth edition, placing the date directly after the author's name to facilitate citing authors with multiple publications. Unless otherwise noted, all translations from the Spanish in the introductory materials are my own.

INTRODUCTION

Biographical Sketch

The life of Federico García Lorca—or simply Lorca, as he is commonly referred to—has invited passionate description. Handsome, charismatic, romantic, a born poet. Private, stubborn, melancholic, terrified of death. Gypsy connoisseur, avant-garde genius, gay icon, left-wing martyr. The greatest Spanish writer since Cervantes. Though all these characterizations border on clichés, none is entirely without merit. Who was the man who inspired such awe?[1]

1. The Taste of Earth (1898–1909)

Lorca was born on June 5, 1898, in Fuente Vaqueros, a tiny village in the heart of the southern Spanish province of Granada. Rich in cultural history, Granada was ruled by ancient Romans, Germanic Visigoths, and nearly eight centuries of Moorish kings before it fell permanently into Christian hands at the close of the Middle Ages. The myth and reality of Granada, and of the broader southern region known as Andalusia, would come to figure heavily in Lorca's literary imagination.[2]

In addition to the place, the year of Lorca's birth weighs heavily in Spanish history. One month before he was born, the United States declared war on Spain, partly in response to the sinking of the U.S.S. *Maine* in Havana Harbor. Lasting only four months, the Spanish-American War resulted in a decisive U.S. victory that had profound consequences for the once mighty Spanish Empire including the loss of its last overseas colonies: Cuba, Puerto Rico, and the Philippines. The disillusionment that took root at home led to a loose association of progressive

---

1. In the summary that follows, I have drawn heavily from Lorca's two greatest biographers, Ian Gibson and Leslie Stainton (Gibson 1989 and Stainton 1999). I have cited additional references where appropriate, especially regarding details that have emerged since the publication of Gibson's and Stainton's works. In fairness to Lorca, it should be noted that he preferred to be called simply Federico: "If you could understand how strange and cold it sounds to me to be called Lorca! I'm Federico, but I'm not Lorca" (*OC* 3, p. 773).
2. Granada is the name of both the province and the provincial capital. Lorca was born in the province, but his family moved to the provincial capital in 1909 (see section 2, "The Smell of Mystery," below).

writers and intellectuals known as the Generation of 1898.[3] Lorca would come into literary consciousness during the course of this generation's intellectual activity, as its luminaries fervently—and very publicly—debated topics such as Spanish identity and Spain's place in Europe.

One man who actually profited from the Spanish-American War was Lorca's father, also named Federico. A town clerk in Fuente Vaqueros, in 1895 he purchased several tracts of rich farmland outside the village, where he established a successful sugar beet plantation. When the loss of Cuba cut off Spain's Caribbean sugar supply, Lorca's father quickly became a wealthy man. In contrast, Lorca's mother, Vicenta, who was the elder Federico's second wife (the first had died childless), was a schoolteacher of modest means. What they each brought to the relationship was a remarkably open mind and a deep cultural refinement. Vicenta had earned her teaching degree at the age of twenty-one and was commended by a state education official for her excellent pedagogy, leaving the profession only when she became pregnant with Lorca (Guerrero 2009). The elder Federico came from several generations of prodigious musical, artistic, and literary talent. As was common in Spain at the time, both parents were Catholic, Vicenta being the more devout of the two; both rejected religious zealotry and fundamentalism. After firstborn Lorca, the couple had four more children: Luis (1900), Francisco (1902), María de la Concepción (1903), and Isabel (1909).[4]

As a result of his parents' wealth, status, and progressive orientation, Lorca lived a privileged early childhood in tiny Fuente Vaqueros, playing freely in the village streets and surrounding countryside and cavorting with friends, siblings, and more than forty first cousins. An extremely impressionable child, he showed a precocious talent for the arts. Music was an early affinity: he was reportedly humming tunes and memorizing songs by the age of four. Theater, too, proved a strong attraction, and he frequently pulled those around him into homemade skits, masques, and faux religious rituals. Reading material from the family library included classics such as Miguel de Cervantes and Victor Hugo. Lorca would remember these carefree years in Fuente Vaqueros with an aching sense of loss. The bucolic setting in particular left a deep impression on him. "My earliest childhood memories taste of earth," he stated in an interview as an adult, adding

---

3. The moniker was coined by one of the group's members, José Martínez Ruiz (better known as Azorín), in an essay in 1913. Following his example, Spanish literary history has insisted on grouping writers into "generations" named for the year of an event considered foundational to the consciousness of the group. Lorca's generation, for reasons to be explained below, is known as the Generation of 1927.
4. Luis died before the age of two. Francisco was nicknamed Paco and María de la Concepción, Concha.

that without this "agrarian complex" he would not have been able to write *Blood Wedding* or *Yerma* (*OC*, vol. 3, pp. 526–27).

When Lorca was eight, his father moved the family across the River Cubillas to the village of Asquerosa, perhaps because it was closer to his sugar beet plantation. Though it was a similar rural setting, Lorca found the name of the village disturbing, and he avoided using it even later in life.[5] The idyll of Fuente Vaqueros had been shattered.

2. The Smell of Mystery (1909–1919)

An even bigger change came in the spring of 1909, a few months before Lorca's eleventh birthday, when his family moved to the provincial capital of Granada.[6] The city's stunning vistas and rich cultural history made a deep impression on young Federico. He was particularly captivated by the ancient Moorish citadel known as the Alhambra, a spectacular relic of the advanced civilization of medieval Islam, whose ultimate defeat by the Catholic monarchs, Ferdinand and Isabella, struck Lorca as a devastating loss. "I believe that being from Granada predisposes me," he would tell an interviewer as an adult, "to identify with those who have suffered persecution: gypsies, blacks, Jews . . . Moorish converts to Christianity. All Granadans carry them within us. Granada smells of mystery, something that can't be, yet is" (*OC*, vol. 3, p. 378).

That fall, after partially failing the entrance exam, Lorca began attending the city's General and Technical High School, taking supplemental classes at a private academy. A central contradiction of his intellectual character emerges at this point. On the one hand, in his formal studies, he was unmotivated at best, lazy and stubborn at worst. Much of his high school's traditional curriculum flummoxed him, particularly mathematics and foreign languages. He received his diploma in 1914 only after retaking the math section of the graduation exam. On the other hand, in his spare time he devoured difficult writers such as Plato, Ovid, Shakespeare, Voltaire, and Darwin, freely charging titles to his father's account at the local bookstore. In music, Debussy was a personal favorite, and under the guidance of a private instructor, he composed several pieces that left his listeners thinking piano might be his true vocation.[7]

---

5. The name of the village means "repulsive" or "creepy," a sharp contrast to the poetic Fuente Vaqueros (Cowherd Fountain). Asquerosa has since been renamed Valderrubio. Lorca preferred to use the name of the family estate, known as Daimuz.
6. The family would continue to spend summers at the Daimuz estate in Asquerosa until purchasing, in 1926, the property known as the Huerta de San Vicente.
7. Unfortunately, the pieces seem to have been lost.

Lorca's lackluster high school performance was repeated in his college career. At the insistence of his parents, he enrolled in the University of Granada in the fall of 1914, where he pursued dual tracks in humanities and law. But he seldom attended class and missed many final examinations, preferring to wander Granada's narrow streets and lively cafés. On one occasion, when he did show up for class, he was ejected for laughing at the professor.

In fact, Lorca's college years were marked by the old contrast between mediocre official performance and rich private life. He had a talent for finding the people and activities that were most likely to spark his creativity. He joined the Granada Arts Club in 1915, where, as he played the piano one day, he met a progressive young law professor named Fernando de los Ríos. The founder of Granada's Socialist Party, de los Ríos would become a key influence in Lorca's life, reemerging at crucial moments.

Another significant figure was a humanities professor, Martín Domínguez Berrueta, who followed the then-unusual practice of taking his students on extended field trips. Lorca signed up for four of his expeditions across Spain in 1916–1917. In addition to sightseeing, he met some of the most distinguished Spanish writers of the period, including Antonio Machado and Miguel de Unamuno. The travels with Berrueta set his imagination whirling, and when his beloved piano teacher died in 1917, he channeled his creativity into words. The result was his first book, published at his father's expense: a philosophical travel memoir called *Impressions and Landscapes* (1918). It was a rambling work (the longest prose piece Lorca would ever complete) that was riddled with mechanical errors, but its sincerity and passion earned it a pair of sympathetic reviews in the local press. A writer was born.

A key extracurricular development during this period was Lorca's association with a group of young men known as the Rinconcillo (Little Corner), so named because of their meeting spot at the back of the Café Alameda. The group had evolved from the editorial activities of the monthly magazine *Granada* but quickly expanded to include many of the city's young writers and artists. Their creative support proved vital to Lorca, who, by the time he published *Impressions and Landscapes*, had all but dropped out of the university. When several members of the Rinconcillo moved to Madrid, they urged Lorca to follow. After lobbying his parents for permission, he set off for the capital in the spring of 1919.

3. Capital Gains (1919–1928)

In Madrid, Lorca moved into the Residencia de Estudiantes, a male student hostel of a type that had never before existed in Spain. Modeled on the Oxbridge college system, the innovative Residence was designed to cultivate the country's brightest young minds from across the arts, sciences, and humanities. Lorca's obvious talents gained him easy admission to the hostel even though, having left the University of Granada far behind, he was not an active student at the time. On and off, he would live on the premises for the better part of a decade.[8]

The Residence's intimate setting, gifted occupants, and impressive guest speaker program—H. G. Wells, Albert Einstein, Marie Curie, and John Maynard Keynes all made an appearance—provided a fertile environment for the development of the young poet's imagination. At the same time, two mentorships added to the mix. In Madrid, Spain's foremost poet, Juan Ramón Jiménez (who would go on to win the Nobel Prize in Literature in 1956), took Lorca under his wing; in Granada, the distinguished musical composer Manuel de Falla did the same.

In one of his absences from the Residence, Lorca returned to the University of Granada, determined to satisfy his parents and graduate. Though he failed his final exam in mercantile law, a lenient professor passed him on the retake. He received his diploma in 1923: nine years after beginning. But his limp across the formal finish line belied, once again, an astonishingly productive private life, for by the time he earned his diploma he had shepherded his first play, *The Butterfly's Evil Spell*, through to production; published his first poetry collection, *Book of Poems*, and made substantial progress on three others; and, with Falla's collaboration, organized a music festival on the gypsy deep song (*cante jondo*) and staged a private puppet production.[9]

No sooner had Lorca graduated from the University of Granada than Spanish history took an ominous turn. Following a period of economic malaise and social unrest, General Miguel Primo de Rivera led a successful military coup against the country's parliamentary government, and King Alfonso XIII attempted to legitimize the rebellion by naming him prime minister. Originally promising to rule for only ninety days, the general soon declared martial law and dissolved parliament. The Left was outraged, including most of the writers and intellectuals of Lorca's generation. When the dictator sought to suppress Catalan (a Romance language spoken in the northeastern region of Catalonia), Lorca himself, who typically eschewed organized politics, signed a manifesto of protest.

---

8. What the Residence required in terms of residency is not entirely clear. Its records were destroyed during the Civil War, making it difficult to give a thorough accounting of Lorca's movements during his association with the institution. He clearly spent long stretches there but also returned home frequently, where he tended to spend the summers. His name appears on a roster from the University of Madrid in 1920, but there is no indication that he ever attended class there. For an extraordinary collection of photos of Lorca at the Residence, see Fernández-Montesinos 1991.

9. See Critical Guide, pp. xxxii–xxxiii, for details on Lorca's fascination with puppets.

Lorca's newfound sympathy for the Catalan language was probably no accident. An eccentric young Catalan painter had recently enrolled in Madrid's Royal Academy of Fine Arts and moved into the Residence, where Lorca, who had returned to the hostel after graduating, met him in February 1923. Within a couple of years, Lorca and Salvador Dalí had become almost inseparable and, along with surrealist filmmaker Luis Buñuel (whom Lorca had met at the Residence the year before Dalí's arrival), formed an avant-garde coterie known as much for pranks and outlandish behavior as for artistic brilliance. By the time Lorca visited Dalí at the seaside Catalan resort of Cadaqués, during Easter 1925, he was in love. The following year he published an intimate and highly admired poem, "Ode to Salvador Dalí," that exalted the "olive-voiced" painter. Dalí's feelings toward Lorca were more complicated. He seems to have sincerely admired Lorca's talent and been flattered by his advances, but he had a malicious streak that led him to toy with the poet's affections. It is unknown to what extent their physical relationship developed, though speculation has been intense.[10]

What is clear is that the two men left a deep and lasting imprint on each other's work. Lorca's second book of poetry, *Songs*, published in May of 1927, included several poems that allude to his passion for the painter. In June of the same year, Dalí designed the set for the Barcelona premiere of *Mariana Pineda*, Lorca's historical drama that would mark the beginning of his long collaboration with the theater company of Catalan actress Margarita Xirgu.[11] Dalí also encouraged Lorca's emerging talent as a visual artist, leading to an exhibit of his drawings that opened in Barcelona within twenty-four hours of the *Mariana Pineda* premiere. Meanwhile, Dalí had begun writing poetry and, soon after the drawing exhibit closed, published a Catalan prose poem on Saint Sebastian—like Mariana Pineda, a martyr figure—that he dedicated to Lorca. Lorca would publish the poem, in Spanish translation, in the first issue of the avant-garde literary magazine *gallo* (rooster), which he helped to found.

At the height of the collaboration between the two men, in that feverish summer of 1927, something ruptured. In August Lorca abruptly left Cadaqués, where he'd been staying with Dalí and the latter's sister since the final performance of *Mariana Pineda*. "I behaved like an ass toward you," Lorca told him

---

10. See, for example, Edwards 2009 and Gibson 2009.
11. Recounting the story of a Granadan folk heroine executed during the reign of Ferdinand VII, *Mariana Pineda* was the second of Lorca's plays to reach the stage, after *The Butterfly's Evil Spell*. More commercially oriented than the latter, it was, not surprisingly, more successful, reopening in Madrid in October. The other two plays Lorca had completed by this point—*The Shoemaker's Prodigious Wife* and *The Love of Don Perlimplín and Belisa in the Garden*—would not be staged until the early 1930s.

in a subsequent letter. "I see it all clearly now and am truly sorry" (*OC*, vol. 3, p. 1010). One can only speculate about what Lorca is alluding to in his letter. Whatever the cause, the breach between the men would only grow.

The year 1927 was a momentous one for Lorca not only because of his stormy friendship and collaboration with Dalí. It was also the three hundredth anniversary of the death of baroque poet Luis de Góngora, who until that point had been much maligned for his supposed rhetorical excesses. The year before, Lorca had given a lecture at Granada's Athenaeum in which he extolled, among other characteristics of Góngora's poetry, its ingenious use of metaphor. The positive response to the lecture inspired Lorca and a group of like-minded poets to organize a tercentenary tribute to Góngora, with events and public lectures scheduled throughout 1927. The celebrations culminated in December when Lorca reprised his presentation from the previous year before an audience at the Residence, followed by a three-day symposium in Seville.

Henceforth known as the Generation of 1927, the poets mobilized by the Góngora tercentenary fit perfectly into what philosopher José Ortega y Gasset had defined, two years earlier, as "dehumanized" art: in short, an art that glorified artistic process at the expense of content. In painting, Ortega had argued, Pablo Picasso was the chief representative of the new aesthetic; in music, it was Igor Stravinsky; in theater, Luigi Pirandello. And in poetry, a new name could now be added to the list: Federico García Lorca.

The point seemed to be confirmed the following year with the publication of *Gypsy Ballads*, a poetry collection in which Lorca channeled the marginalized world of Andalusia's Romany population. "Green flesh, green hair, / with eyes of cold silver," intones the collection's most famous poem, "Ballad of the Sleepwalker" (*OC*, vol. 1, p. 420). Lorca had begun the book in 1924 following the success of the deep song festival he organized with Manuel de Falla in Granada, and he published it in July 1928 thanks to the sponsorship of another old mentor, Juan Ramón Jiménez. Soon afterward, during what was perhaps Lorca's final sojourn at the Residence, a steady stream of ecstatic reviews hailed the author of *Gypsy Ballads* as the greatest poet of his generation. Sales of the book soared, forcing a bewildered Lorca to contemplate the unthinkable: that a poet might actually make a living from his poetry.

4. Highs and Lows (1928–1929)

Flush from the success of the Góngora tercentenary, *Gypsy Ballads*, and the first issue of *gallo*, Lorca found himself riding high in the first half of 1928. That same spring, a young sculptor named Emilio Aladrén, whom Lorca had first met in

1925, completed a plaster bust of the poet's head.[12] By the summer, despite still harboring feelings for Dalí, Lorca was entangled in a passionate relationship with Aladrén. By August, however, his personal correspondence indicates he was in a deep depression. "I am recovering from a great struggle and need to get my heart in order," he says in one letter. "I feel very isolated and still have extremely sad moments. I am less and less sure what love is. The more passionate I feel, the less I understand it" (*OC*, vol. 3, p. 1069).

Things only grew worse. In early September a highly personal, seven-page critique of *Gypsy Ballads* arrived in the mail from Catalonia. The sender: Salvador Dalí, who was now in the tow of the nascent surrealist movement. Dalí confessed to admiring several poems in *Gypsy Ballads* but objected to most of them as too conventional and folkloric, too rational, too human. In other words, a betrayal of the principles Lorca had espoused at the Góngora tercentenary. In the same letter, Dalí also managed to allude, in an unflattering way, to Lorca's relationship with Aladrén.

Lorca laughed off Dalí's attack, but it clearly affected him. Though he consistently refused to align himself with any artistic movement, later that same month he published two prose poems, "Submerged Swimmer" and "Suicide in Alexandria," that certainly seemed like attempts at surrealism. They appeared in the Catalan avant-garde journal *L'Amic de les Arts* (*Friend of the Arts*), following a surrealist text by Dalí (who sat on the journal's editorial board) and accompanied by an extraordinary drawing of Lorca's that showed a pair of male lovers locked in an embrace: perhaps a representation of the "final embrace" alluded to in "Submerged Swimmer." In two lectures he delivered in Granada in October, Lorca made it clear that he was beginning to embrace the unconscious as a primary source of artistic inspiration: a central tenet of surrealism.

In January 1929, Dalí began collaborating on a film script with Luis Buñuel, his and Lorca's old buddy from the Residence. Buñuel was aghast at rumors he'd heard of Lorca's sexuality, and it seems that one goal of his collaboration with Dalí was to undermine the painter's already strained friendship with Lorca.[13] In a literary magazine on February 1, the two men revealed their project: a silent surrealist piece called *Un Chien Andalou* (*An Andalusian Dog*). Though Buñuel later denied it, the film's title seemed to allude to a pejorative nickname given at the Residence to Lorca and other Spaniards from the south, and that is certainly how

---

12. Unfortunately the piece survives only in photos.
13. Perhaps Buñuel also had simple revenge on his mind. As early as 1926, he had asked Lorca to collaborate on a film with him but was rebuffed.

Lorca interpreted it.[14] He could not escape the feeling that Dalí had betrayed him.

To make matters worse, Lorca's relationship with Aladrén was now unraveling: the sculptor, it turned out, had fallen for a woman. Then, in February, on the day scheduled for the premiere of *The Love of Don Perlimplín and Belisa in the Garden*, which Lorca had begun four years earlier, the Queen Mother died and theaters were shuttered in mourning. Rehearsals continued in secret but were quashed by the police. A final blow came when Dalí rejected one of Lorca's letters he'd promised to publish in *L'Amic de les Arts*; instead, the issue featured a full-page interview with Buñuel.

The loss of both Dalí and Aladrén together with the cancelation of *Don Perlimplín* took a heavy toll on Lorca, already exhausted by the demands of his growing celebrity. By Easter 1929—the last week in March—he was close to a nervous breakdown. After writing his ambitious "Ode to the Most Holy Sacrament," he marched as an anonymous penitent in Granada's Holy Wednesday procession. Hidden beneath the traditional tunic and cone-shaped hood and carrying one of three heavy crosses, he walked barefoot in the candlelit procession, reported by one witness to have lasted four hours.

Homosexuality was a deeply taboo topic in the Spain of 1929. Though the elder Federico and his wife Vicenta were relatively enlightened and Lorca adored them, it would have been unthinkable for him to confide in them, or in any of his siblings or extended family, about the secrets that tormented him. Yet it did not take a confession to reveal the poet's deteriorating mental state. Clearly alarmed, his parents became convinced that a drastic change of scenery was in order. Opportunity presented itself in the form of Lorca's old law professor from the University of Granada, Fernando de los Ríos, who had been invited to give a seminar in New York that summer. It was agreed that Lorca would accompany him. Hatched in desperation, it was a plan that would transform Lorca as both an artist and a man.

5. Far from Home (1929–1930)

Lorca and de los Ríos arrived in New York aboard the S.S. *Olympic* on June 25, 1929, after a calm six-day crossing. The great metropolis made an immediate and profound impression on Lorca: "Paris and London are like tiny villages compared

---

14. "Buñuel has made a tiny little shit of a film called *An Andalusian Dog*—and I'm the Dog," he is recorded as saying (qtd. in Gibson 1989, p. 229). The "little shit of a film" went on to become one of the most famous pieces in early film history.

to this pulsing, maddening Babylon," he reported in a letter to his family three days after arriving. All of Granada, he added, would fit into three of its skyscrapers (*OC*, vol. 3, pp. 1104–5). His own residence was on the ninth floor of Furnald Hall at Columbia University in Harlem, where he had enrolled in a summer program with the pretext of studying English language and literature, though it is not clear how much he learned beyond basic vocabulary. As in the case of his high school and college years in Granada, his extracurricular activities in New York proved much more fruitful than his formal studies.

Lorca had an uncanny talent for inserting himself into pivotal places and moments, and New York in 1929 was no exception. In the first place, it was the tail end of the Harlem Renaissance, and the poet's residence at Columbia placed him in a privileged position to engage with the phenomenon. Befriended by the novelist Nella Larsen, he was immediately fascinated by African American culture and spent many evenings in the jazz clubs, cabarets, and revues of Harlem, the only neighborhood he considered free of New York's decadence. The soulful singing of African Americans, he explained to his family, was comparable only to the deep song of the gypsies (*OC*, vol. 3, p. 1114). His sympathy for their plight and his mythification of their "mighty captive king, clothed in a janitor's overall" (*OC*, vol. 1, p. 519) would become a central theme of the collection *Poet in New York*.[15]

Another crucial event of 1929 was the Wall Street crash. In this case as well, Lorca seemed to stumble into the middle of it all. In a remarkable letter to his family, he described how he witnessed the panic personally, relating a chaotic scene of shouting and wailing, of people fainting in the street, of a friend of his who lost fifty thousand dollars, of a banker who threw himself from the sixteenth floor of the Hotel Astor (*OC*, vol. 3, pp. 1148–49). It was as if Lorca were living in the flesh the principles espoused by surrealism: the juxtaposition of incongruous images, the unleashing of pure instinct, the absence of moral authority. Perhaps that explains his confession, in the same letter, that he observed the catastrophic spectacle with cold-blooded detachment and was "very pleased to have witnessed it" (ibid.). The experience seemed to crystallize his view of New York as a soulless jungle of glass and steel, a dystopian metropolis of rootless beings and mechanized monstrosities. In his most iconic self-portrait from the period, he appears as a ghostly, disembodied head surrounded by fantastical creatures and drab skyscrapers.

Lorca's arrival in New York also coincided with the final flowering of the so-called Pansy Craze, just before the Great Depression ushered in a new, austere morality. As revealed in a pioneering study, gay men and women in 1920s

---

15. Written over the course of Lorca's stay in New York, the complete collection of poems was published only after his death.

New York, far from closeted or marginalized, enjoyed an autonomy and visibility that would not be seen again until the post-Stonewall period.¹⁶ Their freedom must have taken Lorca's breath away, and it marks a turning point in his understanding of his own sexuality, which he would gradually come to see as legitimate and inborn. Of course, it was not an entirely intellectual process. An acquaintance who introduced him to the gay American poet Hart Crane tells of leaving him at Crane's apartment—at Lorca's request—with a roomful of drunken sailors. But nor was it entirely physical, for Lorca's sensual experiences always turned up in his art. Following the Hart Crane episode, for example, sailors became a common motif in Lorca's drawings. One eye-opening color sketch from the New York period shows a burly, bearded man with his arm around an effeminate sailor as a woman in a bride's dress protests from a balcony in the background.

In his written work, too, the temptation to explore sexuality in ever more daring ways seems to have sent Lorca's creativity into overdrive. An avant-garde film script titled *Trip to the Moon*, which he wrote with the Mexican American artist Emilio Amero, consists of seventy-two disjointed, often graphic, descriptions that suggest the frustrations of same-sex desire (the parallels with *Un Chien Andalou* are often striking).¹⁷ And in "Ode to Walt Whitman," from *Poet in New York*, Lorca attempts a complex and often ambivalent recuperation of the New York icon's homosexual identity.

Lorca remained in New York, aside from a pair of excursions to Vermont and the Catskill Mountains, until March of 1930. At that point he boarded a train for Miami and a boat to Cuba, taking advantage of the opportunity to see a little of "Spain's America." Lodging in a room at the Union Hotel in Havana, he gave a series of talks, sponsored by the Hispano-Cuban Institute for Culture, that turned him into a minor celebrity on the island. Social invitations and interview requests filled his calendar. What was to have been a brief lecture tour turned into a three-month stay during which he met most of the nation's young writers and intellectuals, took part in Easter week celebrations, went on a crocodile hunt in the countryside, frequented racy cabarets, drank Cuban rum, smoked Cuban cigars, listened to Cuban rumba (there is no report of the flatfooted poet ever dancing), and basked in the Cuban sun. But it was not all fun and games, for the most daring of his surviving plays (and the first in this volume) dates from this period. *The Audience*, a Dada-style drama in which a closeted gay director is nearly murdered

---

16. Chauncey 1994; see especially pp. 301–29.
17. Catalan filmmaker Frederic Amat produced a faithful, nineteen-minute version of the script in 1998. See Karageorgou-Bastea 2003 for an analysis.

for his controversial staging of *Romeo and Juliet*, was written partly on stationery from the Union Hotel.[18]

On June 12, Lorca set sail for Spain a changed man: more confident, more audacious, more forgiving of himself, and, importantly, more critical of Spain's—and especially Granada's—petty provincialism and bourgeois values. Fittingly, he finished his paean to Walt Whitman, that "dear old man, as lovely as fog, / who moaned like a bird / with its sex pierced by a needle" (*OC*, vol. 1, p. 564), on the sea voyage home. Along with *The Audience*, it would provide the greatest evidence of the transformation he had undergone in the Americas.

6. New Hope (1930–1933)

Lorca returned to a country holding its breath. In January of 1930, when the poet was still living in New York, General Miguel Primo de Rivera, who had seized power in 1923, lost the confidence of King Alfonso XIII and fled to Paris, where he died less than two months later. In an attempt to placate the popular sentiment that had risen against Primo, the king appointed a more moderate general as his replacement, but Alfonso had already discredited himself by backing Primo's coup to begin with. Support for a lay republic soared, and Lorca's former professor and New York travel partner, Fernando de los Ríos, was jailed in December 1930 for leading anti-monarchical demonstrations. The liberal leanings of Lorca and his family made them natural republican sympathizers.[19]

In this tense atmosphere, Lorca slipped back into a seemingly normal routine. The same month that de los Ríos was jailed, he delivered a pair of lectures in the northern cities of Gijón and San Sebastián, where he had a brief reunion with Emilio Aladrén. Back in Madrid, he attended the premiere of his farce *The Shoemaker's Prodigious Wife*, which was again produced by Margarita Xirgu's company. In January of the new year, he began renting an apartment in the capital with his brother Paco. That spring he published his *Poem of the Deep Song*, which he had begun as early as 1921.

But the political situation progressed beyond anyone's ability to ignore, and Lorca once again stumbled into the epicenter. Caught in a huge Republican

---

18. It is likely that Lorca conceived of the play in New York, as it shares many formal and thematic characteristics with *Poet in New York* and *Trip to the Moon*. The date at the end of the handwritten manuscript, August 22, suggests that he finished it upon his return to Spain. (The four plays of this volume are more fully discussed in the Critical Guide below.)
19. It should be noted, in the context of modern Spain and much of Europe, that the terms *republic* and *republican* (capitalized when they refer to specific countries or parties) imply a democratically elected form of government in contrast to hereditary monarchy.

demonstration in the middle of Madrid on election day 1931, he fell to the ground and injured a finger.[20] It was a memorable scene, but the election results were more so: in all the major cities, Republicans trounced their pro-monarchy opponents. Though the elections were technically local, they were interpreted as a referendum on the crown. The king saw the handwriting on the wall and, as Primo de Rivera had done a year before, fled the country. Two days later, on April 14, 1931, citizens across the country—Lorca included—poured into the streets to celebrate the declaration of the Second Spanish Republic.[21] De los Ríos was released from jail the same day and named minister of justice in the provisional government. A tense national drama had given way to a fragile hope.

The new government invested heavily in education, establishing, among other initiatives, a division of "Teaching Missions" designed to spread the message of liberal democracy to Spain's impoverished countryside. The instrument: concerts, films, art exhibitions, public libraries, teacher training, and, crucially, plays. It did not take long for Lorca, who that summer was finishing his dreamlike play *Five Years from Now*, to understand the implications of the Teaching Missions. By the end of the year he had, along with a group of students from the University of Madrid, proposed the idea of a traveling theater troupe that would perform the classics of Spanish drama—Cervantes, Lope de Vega, Calderón de la Barca—to the poorest villages in Spain. Fernando de los Ríos promised government support, a promise he kept, upon being named minister of education, in the form of a 100,000-peseta annual subvention. La Barraca (The Shack) theater troupe was in business. With Lorca as artistic director (and occasionally as actor), it offered its first public performance—two Cervantes interludes and a third attributed to him (erroneously) at the time—in the main square of Burgo de Osma on July 10 of the following year. The troupe would continue performing, to the delight of rural audiences and the horror of the right-wing press, until the Civil War forced its suspension in 1936.[22]

---

20. A witness later recounted Lorca's dramatic rendering of the incident: "He began to tell us in a loud voice what had happened, with a verbal exuberance, precise details, a vocabulary and a mimicry that were absolutely fantastic. He expressed his terror in words that gushed from his mouth, and such was the emotion he generated in the café that someone made him get up on one of the marble tables so that everyone present could hear the account he had begun. I can honestly say that in all the work of García Lorca I have found nothing that could equal what, in a seemingly inextinguishable flood of words, he said in only a few minutes, turning from one side to the other" (qtd. in Gibson 1989, p. 312).
21. The First Republic was a short-lived affair in 1873–1874. Its failure led to a restoration of the Bourbon monarchy that produced Alfonso XIII.
22. Leslie Stainton provides a useful summary of a typical day in La Barraca's routine: "The troupe arrived by truck and selected a performance site—often in a square backed

The early years of La Barraca were among the happiest of Lorca's life, with positive ramifications for his career as a playwright. To begin with, the countless rehearsals—eighty alone, it is reported, for the debut of *Life Is a Dream*—earned him valuable experience as a director. He also completed his first tragedy (and the second play of this volume) during this period. The story of a rural Spanish bride swept away by her former love, *Blood Wedding* was not intended for La Barraca. It premiered instead in Madrid's Teatro Beatriz in March 1933, before an audience filled with many of Spain's greatest living writers. The thunderous applause the performance received marked a turning point: the fame of Lorca the playwright had eclipsed that of Lorca the poet. Icing on the cake came the following month in Madrid with the staging of *Don Perlimplín*, which had been shut down by Primo de Rivera's police in 1929.

A final development from the theater troupe's early years is a personal one. In the summer of 1933, Lorca met a young engineering student, Rafael Rodríguez Rapún, who had joined La Barraca a few months earlier and was now its secretary. While he did not identify as homosexual, Rodríguez Rapún was swept away by Lorca's charisma and soon became the third great love—after Dalí and Aladrén—of the poet's life.

7. International Celebrity (1933–1935)

As Lorca's new romance blossomed, in faraway South America the Argentinian actress Lola Membrives opened her production of *Blood Wedding* in Buenos Aires. In August the actress' husband and business partner wrote to Lorca to inform him that the play had conquered the Argentinian capital in a matter of hours and earned the playwright the astonishing sum of 3,500 pesetas.[23] But there was more: the company was inviting Lorca to Buenos Aires to coincide with the second run of the show in the fall (spring in Argentina).

Lorca arrived in the Americas for the second—and last—time on October 13, 1933. Including a two-week trip to the Uruguayan capital of Montevideo in

---

by a picturesque church or civic building. As they unpacked, a town crier would roam the streets, announcing their presence. At curtain time residents brought chairs and cushions into the square and settled down to watch Lorca's young actors perform. After the production, which generally lasted ninety minutes, company members dismantled the stage and stored their equipment. The following day, enthusiastic reviews usually appeared in the local press. The actors bought copies to take home" (Stainton 1999, p. 303). For an exhaustive study of La Barraca, written by an actor in the troupe, see Sáenz de la Calzada 1976.
23. According to Gibson 1989, p. 357, the amount was equivalent to the yearly salary of a Spanish miner or metalworker at the time.

February, he would remain in South America until late March 1934. The royal welcome he received began with the triumphant second opening of *Blood Wedding* at the end of October. Taking advantage of the author's presence, Membrives went on to produce *The Shoemaker's Prodigious Wife* in December and *Mariana Pineda* in January. Both were received enthusiastically, and Lorca's celebrity status soared. Lodging at the Hotel Castelar in the center of Buenos Aires, he gave lectures and interviews and met with the continent's most distinguished writers. He immediately hit it off with Chilean poet (and eventual Nobel Prize winner) Pablo Neruda, whereas his madcap sense of humor seems only to have irritated Argentina's most famous writer, Jorge Luis Borges, who stalked out of their encounter.

Though he managed to continue sketching in Buenos Aires, including a group of illustrations he drew to accompany a poetry collection of Neruda's, Lorca's busy social agenda left little time for writing. In principle, his two-week trip to Montevideo was intended to carve out the breathing room necessary for him to finish his latest play, *Yerma*. Yet it was not to be, and he did not complete any significant new literary work during his South American sojourn.[24] Nonetheless, his theatrical successes lined his pockets with cash, allowing him to wire ten thousand pesetas to his father back in Spain and to shower his mother with gifts. So long the beneficiary of their indulgence, he was eager to share his new earnings.

He also had cause to worry about them. From the safety of Buenos Aires, he followed the political situation back home with alarm. The fragile Republic was holding, but the political pluralism it enabled was threatening to undo it. The fascist Falange Party was founded in October 1933, and in November, the broad Catholic alliance CEDA captured the largest number of seats in the national election, ushering in a right-wing government that promised to roll back many of the previous regime's progressive reforms. Anarchist strikes and uprisings followed in December, and bombs were set off across the country including in Lorca's Granada. In an ominous sign, the new government reinstated the death penalty.

Lorca thus returned, in April 1934, to a country once again on tenterhooks. Several activities, nevertheless, kept him occupied. First, he resumed his liaison with Rodríguez Rapún, and both men continued touring with La Barraca, which now required defending the troupe's existence to the press given that its subvention was in jeopardy under the new government. Second, Lorca's friend Pablo Neruda arrived from South America as the newly appointed Chilean ambassador

---

24. He did manage to revise and stage, in a 1:30 a.m. production five days before his departure, his farce *Don Cristóbal's Puppet Show*, a project that stretched all the way back to his collaboration with Falla in the early 1920s.

to the Second Republic, kicking off a long summer of alcohol binges and wild late-night parties. Third, Lorca began assembling a collection of sensual poems, inspired in his readings of Arabic poetry, that he called *The Tamarit Divan*.[25]

Also that summer, a bullfighter and writer whom Lorca had met during the Góngora tercentenary in Seville, Ignacio Sánchez Mejías, emerged from retirement. On August 11, he was gored in the thigh and died of gangrene two days later. Lorca, who had worshiped Mejías' machismo, was shaken to the core. By October he had written his longest poem, much of it composed in Neruda's apartment. The elegiac *Lament for Ignacio Sánchez Mejías*, in which the speaker pleads with the moon to appear—"for I can't bear to see the blood / of Ignacio spilt upon the sand" (*OC*, vol. 1, p. 618)—went on to become one of his most popular works.

Lorca's biggest literary accomplishment of 1934 was the completion of his second tragedy (and the third play of this volume), *Yerma*. He declined an invitation from Pirandello to a conference in Rome in order to attend rehearsals, and the play premiered in Madrid at the end of December, with Margarita Xirgu as the protagonist. The tragedy of a mannish, infertile woman in rural Spain, *Yerma* aroused intense hostility from the Right, which did its best to poison the opening performance. As the curtain went up before another audience of eminent literati, jeers of "Queer!" were hurled from the upper gallery. The hecklers were ejected and the play continued, and when the final curtain came down over two hours later, the applause was deafening.

8. Poisoned Well (1935–1936)

Yerma's premiere in Barcelona, in the fall of 1935, garnered even greater success than the Madrid performances. Lorca would now have appeared on almost any shortlist of Spain's most famous living writers. But he had earned himself powerful enemies in the process, as he recognized in a letter to his parents: "Of course the Right will use all of this to continue its campaign against Margarita [Xirgu] and me, but it doesn't matter. It's almost preferable that way, so everyone ends up showing their cards. Because of course it's impossible to be *neutral* in Spain these days" (*OC*, vol. 3, p. 1270).

His words proved eerily prophetic, as the country's political polarization continued at an alarming pace. The conservative alliance that had come to power in 1933 was voted out in the national election of February 1936, defeated by the Popular Front, a broad left-wing coalition of Republicans, socialists, communists,

---

25. Like *Poet in New York*, this collection would not be published until after his death.

anarchists, and labor activists. The PF's one-percent victory in the popular vote outraged the traditional bases of the Right, who now called themselves Nationalists: the Roman Catholic Church, the monarchists, and, crucially, the army. Rumors of a military coup swirled. The political center—the "neutral" space that Lorca referred to in his letter—had indeed crumbled.

Somehow, Lorca managed to stay focused on his work, partly through a gradual retirement from the punishing schedule of La Barraca.[26] Important literary achievements during this period include two original dramas. *Doña Rosita the Spinster* tells the lonely story of a turn-of-the-century Granadan woman who, as the title implies, never marries; it premiered in Madrid to favorable reviews in late 1935. *The Dream of Life* is a play that, along with *The Audience* and *Five Years from Now*, Lorca referred to as his "impossible theater." Though he expressed on several occasions a considerably high opinion of these works, saying that they contained his "true purpose" (*OC*, vol. 3, p. 631), he recognized the difficulties inherent in bringing them to the stage. He hoped, nonetheless, to see *The Dream of Life* performed that fall.[27]

Among Lorca's final poetic endeavors is the erotically charged collection *Dark Love Sonnets*, addressed to an unnamed male lover who seems to have been the last of the poet's life: "I hide you with my tears, hounded / by a voice of penetrating steel," he writes. Speculation about the identity of the lover has centered on Rodríguez Rapún (though he had, like Aladrén, jilted Lorca for a woman); Dalí (with whom Lorca had a warm final encounter in September 1935); and, perhaps most convincingly, an aspiring young actor named Juan Ramírez de Lucas, whom Lorca met in Madrid in 1935 and with whom, it seems, he hoped to flee to Mexico.[28]

Lorca's most important work from this period—and in the opinion of many critics, his masterpiece (Ruiz Ramón 1992, p. 207)—is the last play collected in this volume. *The House of Bernarda Alba* tells the story of a tyrannical widow's attempts to control every aspect of her daughters' lives in a rural setting similar to that of *Blood Wedding* and *Yerma*, a stifling "riverless village where one lives in fear of drinking from a poisoned well" (p. 165). Lorca finished a draft of the play on June 19, 1936, two weeks after his thirty-eighth birthday. He gave several

---

26. He formally withdrew from the group at the end of 1935, having presided over more than two hundred free performances of classical Spanish drama. The troupe soldiered on under a new artistic director.
27. As it turned out, all three "impossible plays" went unperformed in Lorca's lifetime.
28. Ramírez de Lucas died in 2010 at the age of ninety-three, leaving behind a previously unknown collection of love letters from Lorca in which the failed escape plan was revealed (Castilla and Magán 2012a, 2012b, 2012c).

readings of the work to friends, explaining that he intended to revise the second and third acts.

The anticipated revisions would never happen. A month later, in the midst of a hot summer full of labor strikes, demonstrations, and political assassinations, Nationalist army garrisons across Spanish Morocco rose up against the Republican government. The imprisoned leader of the Falange Party, José Antonio Primo de Rivera (son of the exiled dictator), declared his support for the uprising. The next day, July 18—Lorca's saint's day, which the writer was spending with his family in Granada—Nationalist troops took control of Las Palmas in the Canary Islands. By that evening the city of Seville—150 miles from Granada—had fallen. The Spanish Civil War was underway.

9. Return to Earth (Summer 1936)

Up till this moment, Lorca had seemed to live a charmed existence, consistently inhabiting the right places at just the right times (his idyllic childhood in Fuente Vaqueros, his Residence years in Madrid, his New York sojourn) and benefiting from friendships with talented and powerful people (de los Ríos, Buñuel, Jiménez, Falla, Dalí, Neruda). In June and the first two weeks of July 1936, as the country spiraled toward anarchy, his luck seemed to hold in the relative safety of Republican Madrid and the comfort of his family apartment.[29] It was here that he finished *The House of Bernarda Alba* and enjoyed the cosmopolitan company of friends such as Pablo Neruda, Carlos Morla Lynch, and Rafael Martínez Nadal.[30] It was here that he felt free to insult Granada's middle class in an interview with the press (*OC*, vol. 3, p. 637). And it was here that he hatched the plan to flee to Mexico with his new love, Juan Ramírez de Lucas (see n. 28).

But by mid-July of 1936, the nineteen-year-old Ramírez de Lucas had been unable to gain permission from his parents to travel abroad with the thirty-eight-year-old playwright. Meanwhile, on July 12, right-wing icon José Calvo Sotelo was assassinated in a savage act of political retaliation. The conflagration that everyone feared seemed to be imminent. Wealthy residents fled the capital; refugees choked the highways to France and Portugal. Lorca himself was terrified, telling Martínez Nadal that "these fields are going to be strewn with corpses" (qtd. in Martínez Nadal 1974, p. 14). He asked Ramírez de Lucas to go back

---

29. His parents had purchased an apartment in Madrid at the end of 1932, though they continued to spend summers in Granada.
30. Like Neruda, Morla Lynch was a Chilean diplomat and writer. Martínez Nadal, also a writer, was an old friend of Lorca's from the Residence years. The three men were among Lorca's closest friends.

home, to Albacete, to lobby his parents for permission to leave the country; in the meantime Lorca would return to Granada to wait out the uncertainty with his family.

So it was that Lorca arrived in Granada on July 14, only three days before the Nationalist uprising in Morocco. Hopeful that the rebellion would be quickly quashed, he was dumbstruck to see the speed with which it spread. After a three-day skirmish, Granada surrendered to the Nationalists on July 23. Soldiers soon began rounding up "undesirables"—Republican politicians, prominent left-wing sympathizers, trade union officials—and throwing them into prison. Among the detainees was the former Republican mayor of the city, Manuel Fernández Montesinos. He was also Lorca's brother-in-law.

The remainder of July and the beginning of August were punctuated, almost every day before dawn, by the sound of gunfire as truckloads of prisoners were driven to the city cemetery and shot execution style. In this hostile environment, Lorca's last hope was his hometown friend, the poet Luis Rosales, whose family was prominent in the Falange movement. Surely, Lorca thought, he would be safe if he took refuge in the Rosales home. He moved in on August 11.

But his charmed existence had come to an end. In the early morning of August 16, Lorca's brother-in-law was executed. The news reached Lorca, still in the Rosales house, by telephone. He was undone with pity but also fear. And with good reason. That afternoon, despite strenuous protests from the Rosales family members, he was removed from their home and locked in a room in the Civil Government building. The arresting officer cited Lorca's provocative writings and supposed communication with the Soviet Union through a secret radio, though his sexuality almost certainly played a role.[31] Two or three days later, at around three in the morning, he was taken from his cell and executed on the outskirts of Granada, his body tossed into an unmarked grave that has yet to be located.

The last words known to come from Lorca's hand took the form of a cruel ransom note his captors had him write to his father, demanding a thousand pesetas for his release. The elder Federico immediately paid the ransom to the extortionist who had delivered the note, not knowing that his son was already dead. He is said to have carried the note in his wallet until his own death, in exile in New York, nine years later.

---

31. A week earlier the Falange had searched Lorca's home, and one of the officers referred to him as "the little queer friend of Fernando de los Ríos" (qtd. in Gibson 1989, p. 451). There is some dispute as to whether there was a warrant for Lorca's arrest. If there was, it has never been found.

Critical Guide

When Federico García Lorca met his untimely end in 1936, he left behind an enormous creative corpus that ranged across prose (including a voluminous personal correspondence), poetry, theater, a film script, drawings, musical compositions, and scores of fragments and unfinished titles. Many of the works, including some for which he is now well known, had yet to be performed or published, a process complicated by several factors that will be discussed below. In keeping with the scope of this volume of translated plays, I will focus my critical survey on Lorca's theater with occasional references to his poetry (it is particularly difficult in Lorca's case to separate the two genres). Rather than furnishing my own interpretation of the plays—which would be merely one reading among many—I aim to provide the tools that will enable students, directors, and theatergoers to interpret Lorca for themselves.

1. Lorca's Place in Spanish Theater

Public playhouses made their first appearance in Spain in the late Renaissance, signaling the emergence of drama as a secular art form, independent of venues such as churches, courts, palaces, and universities.[32] The popular *comedia* (not to be confused with the Italian *commedia dell'arte*) flourished between the years of 1580 and 1660, a period frequently referred to in Spanish literary history as the Golden Age. The typical *comedia* was a three-act play written entirely in verse, with happy and often moralizing endings and little regard for the classicizing formulas admired in France and Italy. Indeed, in both spirit and substance, early modern Spanish drama is closer to its Elizabethan counterpart than to developments elsewhere on the Continent.[33] Writers from this period, such as Lope de Vega, Tirso de Molina, and Calderón de la Barca, produced some ten thousand original plays (approximately two thousand of which survive today), many of them highly admired and enormously influential.[34] The enduring vitality of Golden Age drama

---

32. Drama in these venues continued to exist, however, alongside the public theaters.
33. A major difference is that Spanish playwrights, unlike the English, tended to avoid tragedy.
34. Among the many standouts by Lope de Vega: *Sheep's Fount, The Knight from Olmedo, The Silly Dame, Peribáñez and the Commander of Ocaña,* and *Justice without Vengeance*. By Tirso de Molina: *The Lady-Killer of Seville* (origin of the Don Juan legend) and *Damned for Doubting*. By Calderón de la Barca: *The Steadfast Prince, Devotion to the Cross, Secret Vengeance for Secret Offense, The Honor Surgeon, Life's a Dream, The Wonder-Working Magician, The Self-Defaming Painter,* and *The Mayor of Zalamea*. Cervantes, better known as the

formed a wellspring to which Lorca would return, three hundred years later, in his quest to revitalize Spain's moribund theatrical tradition. What had happened in the meantime? The prodigious creativity that fueled the *comedia* seems to have exhausted itself somewhere in the second half of the seventeenth century. Between the death of Calderón in 1681 and the birth of Lorca in 1898, there are scarcely half a dozen Spanish plays of any transcendence (one of them being a romantic rewriting of Tirso's *Lady-Killer*). A notable exception toward the end of the nineteenth century is novelist Benito Pérez Galdós, whose fine dramatic output includes several of his novels adapted for the stage. For the most part, however, by the time of Lorca's birth, Spanish theater had become mired in a set of conventions that allowed expression only through, in the words of one literary historian, "a thick protective screen of morality and conformism" (Shaw 1972, p. 78). The world portrayed in this theater was by and large that of its bourgeois spectators, whose drawing rooms, polite dialogue, and traditional gender roles were reflected in performances and set designs that fell squarely within the naturalistic tradition. As another literary historian notes, "What good taste would not admit was any attempt to puzzle or worry the audience, or to reflect any moral or social values other than those of the bejewelled matrons of the orchestra stalls" (Brown 1972, p. 111).

Such was the theatrical moment into which Lorca was born. While several members of the Generation of 1898—Unamuno and Azorín, for example—recognized and accurately diagnosed the problem, they proved largely powerless to remedy it.[35] An important innovator in the early twentieth century is Galician-born playwright Ramón María del Valle-Inclán. In a remarkable trilogy, *The Savage Dramas* (1907–1922), Valle-Inclán employs archetypal protagonists, emotive language, and epic sets that strain against the petty specificity of bourgeois theater. In his most admired work, *Bohemian Lights* (1920), he takes a turn toward social criticism, coining the term *esperpento* to describe the degenerate, distorted tragic form he was seeking to cultivate. Significantly, Valle-Inclán wrote most of his plays to be read rather than staged, and neither *The Savage Dramas* nor *Bohemian Lights* was performed during his or Lorca's lifetime (both men died in 1936).

---

author of *Don Quixote*, also wrote for the theater, but in contrast to the previous three he followed a more classical formula, which proved much less successful.
35. See Biographical Sketch, pp. xi–xii, for a discussion of the Generation of 1898. Unamuno and Azorín, along with other members of the group, signed a letter of protest against the awarding of the 1904 Nobel Prize in Literature to José de Echegaray, whom they considered the chief proponent of bourgeois theater. They also tried their own hand at theater, largely unsuccessfully.

It is safe to say, then, that by the time Lorca began writing his first play, in 1920, little in the Spanish theater scene appeared to have shifted from the late nineteenth century. Even by 1935, with the Spanish avant-garde in full swing—enriched by contributions not only from Lorca and Valle-Inclán but from additional innovators such as Jacinto Grau, Max Aub, and Rafael Alberti—Lorca's own words suggest a deep pessimism regarding the character of Spanish theater: "As long as actors and playwrights remain at the mercy of exclusively commercial companies that operate free of any literary standard or governmental control, then actors and playwrights—indeed, all of theater—will sink further and further into mediocrity, with little hope of salvation" (*OC*, vol. 3, pp. 255–56).

As a result, a central concern of Lorca's dramatic experiment—perhaps *the* central concern—is his opposition to the commercial interests of mainstream theater and to the bourgeois values that propped it up.[36] His defiance manifests itself across his corpus, both in the serious subject matter he chooses and in his anti-naturalistic approach to stagecraft. It begins with his very first production, *The Butterfly's Evil Spell* (1920), which audaciously dramatizes the unnatural love of a cockroach for a butterfly. Inspired by the Ballets Russes that toured Spain in the teens, the play's vivid color scheme, movements, and poetic language signal the playwright's symbolist leanings and multi-sensual approach to stagecraft. The performance at the avant-garde Teatro Eslava, which Lorca carefully oversaw, emphasized abstract set designs, futuristic costuming, and a lyrical musical score from Edvard Grieg. It was an ambitious shot across the bow of contemporary theater that was, predictably, unsuccessful at the box office; but it established the twenty-two-year-old playwright as a force to be reckoned with.

Lorca initially intended *The Butterfly's Evil Spell* to be performed with puppets rather than human actors. While that wish did not materialize, he remained fascinated with puppet theater, which had long been a popular art form in Spain and was beginning to influence avant-garde writers such as Valle-Inclán and Jacinto Grau as well as European artists including Maurice Maeterlinck and Gordon Craig. Puppet theater allowed Lorca to introduce serious themes into a seemingly innocuous form, while the use of marionettes in place of human actors liberated him from the staging demands of naturalistic drama and encouraged him to embrace the artifice of theater. He tested the waters as early as 1923, when, in collaboration with Manuel Falla, he staged a private puppet production at his family home in Granada on the Feast of the Epiphany (January 6). The triple performance included a short play attributed to Cervantes, a medieval mystery play,

---

36. See Fernández Cifuentes 1986 for an extensive analysis. This book remains the best global study of Lorca's theater, though it is, unfortunately, inaccessible to English-only readers.

and, finally, Lorca's adaptation of an Andalusian folktale, *The Girl Who Waters the Basil and the Over-Inquiring Prince*. With music from Claude Debussy and stage decorations by Lorca himself, the production was a logical vehicle for the author's modernist aesthetic.

The three "impossible plays"—*The Audience* (1930), *Five Years from Now* (1930), and *The Dream of Life* (1936)—showcase Lorca's avant-garde stagecraft at its most mature: a feast of the senses that encompasses music, dance, color, lighting, movement, and sound. *The Audience*, for example, portrays three white talking horses that also play trumpets (Tableau 1), a dancing male couple bedecked in grapevines and tiny bells (Tableau 2), a moonlit resurrection of Shakespeare's Juliet (Tableau 3), a naked red man with a crown of blue thorns (Tableau 4), and a slow rain of white gloves (Tableau 5). The set is compared both to a primitivist painting (p. 29) and to the "silvery tint" of a movie screen (p. 35). *Five Years from Now*, which is Lorca's longest play, is filled with the pale blue light of dreams, with whimsical scenery of clouds and angels, and with singing mannequins. *The Dream of Life*, though incomplete, shows characteristics similar to the others, especially in its lighting. The uncompromising themes of the impossible plays along with their dreamlike, often hallucinatory imagery and multi-sensual approach to stagecraft represent Lorca's most defiant stand against mainstream theater.

Significantly, however, Lorca did not completely reject the commercial theater. His first overture toward it came in 1927 with *Mariana Pineda*, a play that followed an essentially Romantic template (specifically, that of Spanish dramatist Eduardo Marquina) complete with drawing room settings and a maudlin plot of a revolutionary heroine betrayed by love. Yet the conventional elements of *Mariana Pineda* are challenged by its avant-garde visual cues. Even the play's subtitle reflects Lorca's subversive intent. On the one hand, *Popular Ballad in Three Prints* promises the easy entertainment of a folksong. On the other, it frustrates familiar notions of theater by stressing the simple, static quality of a nineteenth-century print. Accordingly, the stage directions in the prologue specify that "the scene will be framed by a yellowish border, as in an antique print" (*OC*, vol. 2, p. 84), while the "grays, whites, and ivories" of Act 2 are compared to those of a lithograph (ibid., p. 115). Salvador Dalí's set for the Barcelona premiere, on which Lorca closely collaborated, stressed these pictorial qualities by exploiting the proscenium arch as if it were indeed the frame of a print.[37] The result was a stage-within-a-stage illusion (Rodrigo 1975, p. 100), with one critic describing the performance as

---

37. The emphasis on the visual in *Mariana Pineda* and its use of the word "print" (*estampa*) anticipates Lorca's use of the word "tableau" (*cuadro*) in place of the more traditional "scene" (*escena*), which occurs in three of the plays collected in this volume: *The Audience*, *Blood Wedding, and Yerma*. See Translator's Note, pp. lii–liii.

the pretext for "a series of pictorial connections and visual designs" (qtd. in Plaza Chillón 1998, p. 155). Even at its outset, Lorca's pact with the dialogue-heavy commercial theater was a tenuous one.[38]

Lorca's artistic direction of his traveling theater troupe, La Barraca, reveals the same uneasy compromise. On the one hand, the works he chose for performance were among the most commercially successful in the history of Spanish theater, including many of those mentioned above (see n. 34). On the other, the generous subvention provided by the Republican government freed him from commercial constraints and allowed him to experiment by channeling the period's most avant-garde approaches to the visual and performing arts. In addition to finding models in likely suspects such as Buñuel, Dalí, and Picasso, he drew inspiration from Pirandello, Piscator, Maeterlinck, Stanislavsky, Russian ballet, Chinese theater, and the New York theater scene. Accordingly, Remedios Sánchez García notes the balletic influences and stylized sets of cardboard and watercolors in La Barraca's productions (Sánchez García 2012, pp. 209–10). As a concrete example, a performance of the religious version (*auto sacramental*) of *Life Is a Dream* staged the opening clash of the four elements as if it were a ballet: with Earth costumed in white and burnt sienna, Air in gray and purple, Water in blue and green, and Fire in yellow, orange, and red, the elements fought over a crown of laurel leaves. Lorca himself played the Shadow, cloaked in flowing dark tulle and wearing a large two-horned hat with a black veil (Plaza Chillón 2001, p. 222; Sáenz de la Calzada 1976, pp. 52–53).

Lorca's own description of his staging of Calderón's secular play *The Wonder-Working Magician* for La Barraca neatly encapsulates the delicate balance between tradition and avant-garde that he sought to strike in all his work: "On the first night we'll give a traditional, realistic performance and on the second a simplified, stylized one; one as new as the latest experiment and one as old as the most ancient staging technique of set and gestures. We'll see which one the audience prefers" (*OC*, vol. 3, p. 390). Slowly but surely, then, he developed an approach to writing and staging plays that allowed him to stay true to his artistic principles while pleasing crowds in ever greater numbers. It was an approach that would produce *The Shoemaker's Prodigious Wife* and *Doña Rosita the Spinster* and culminate in *Blood Wedding* and *Yerma*, all four of which follow a fairly realist paradigm albeit with numerous lyrical elements and modernist visual registers. By the time of his last play, *The House of Bernarda Alba* (unperformed at the time of his death), Lorca would be boasting to a friend of his "pure realism" (see below, p. l).

---

38. See Edwards 2010, pp. 47–48, for more on the dual nature of *Mariana Pineda*.

Nevertheless, it was always clear where his preferences lay. Just a few months before his death, he quipped to an interviewer: "My true purpose lies in these [impossible] plays. But to make a name for myself and earn a certain amount of respect, I've done other things" (*OC*, vol. 3. p. 631). Let us turn, then, to the name he made for himself with his plays.[39]

2. Performance History and Reception of Lorca's Plays

Seven of Lorca's plays debuted in professional venues during his lifetime, as detailed in Appendix 2. Given the biases of the Spanish stage during this period, it is not surprising that the least commercial of the plays, *The Butterfly's Evil Spell*, was also the most poorly received. Loud protests punctuated the duration of the performance (Gibson 1989, pp. 98–99), and while a review by noted poet Manuel Machado acknowledged Lorca's talent for writing "extremely beautiful" verse, it chided him for "confusing drama with lyric poetry" (quoted in Gil 1973, p. 471). Stung by the cold reception, Lorca would wait seven years before staging his next play (*Mariana Pineda*).

At the other end of the spectrum lies *Blood Wedding*. In a glowing review following the Madrid debut, Antonio Espina praised the universal qualities of the work and compared its author to the great playwrights of classical Greece and the Spanish Golden Age (quoted in Gil 1973, p. 481). The play earned Lorca an international reputation, premiering in Buenos Aires in July 1933 (and reopening there in October) and, under the title *Bitter Oleander*, in New York in 1935. The city that Lorca had entered as a stranger in 1929 was now hosting the performance of his most famous play.[40]

Yerma met with a similar reception from the liberal press, confirming the assessment of Lorca as the leading playwright of his generation. Perhaps the greatest Spanish theater critic of the period, Enrique Díez-Canedo, began his review thus: "We have a new dramatic poet. Those who might have wavered after *The Shoemaker's Prodigious Wife* or *Blood Wedding* will no longer be able to deny it"

---

39. In what follows, I will mostly leave aside Lorca's reputation as a poet, though it roughly parallels the trajectory of his theater: great acclaim during his lifetime; a period of repression and censorship during the Franco period even as his international reputation continued to grow; and, finally, a convergence of domestic and international criticism, in the late twentieth and early twenty-first centuries, into a consensus that regards Lorca as among the finest poets of his era. For the impact of Lorca's poetry on the United States in particular, see Mayhew 2009.

40. *Bitter Oleander* received mixed reviews in New York owing in part, it would seem, to a poor translation (Stainton 1999, p. 301).

(quoted in Gil 1973, p. 486). But the conservative press attacked the play as immoral and called attention to the number of homosexuals in the audience at the premiere (Stainton 1999, p. 383). It was the beginning of Lorca's role as a polarizing figure, a proxy in the fight between liberal and conservative Spain. Even the conservatives, however, were forced to recognize the popularity he had achieved.[41]

Between *The Butterfly's Evil Spell* on the one hand and *Blood Wedding* and *Yerma* on the other lie the four additional plays that were professionally staged during Lorca's lifetime. Of these, it was again the least commercial—the audacious farce *Don Perlimplín*—which met with the most muted reception (and, as with *Yerma*, a somewhat polarized one). The other three—*Mariana Pineda*, *The Shoemaker's Prodigious Wife*, and *Doña Rosita the Spinster*—fell on the spectrum between modest and decisive success.[42]

After Lorca's death, performance and publication of his plays in Spain were severely hampered both by the new military dictatorship (1939–1975), which had conspired in his murder, and, equally importantly, by his family and heirs, who were uncomfortable with bringing to light such intimate works as *The Audience* (and, in poetry, *The Dark-Love Sonnets*). Tellingly, *The House of Bernarda Alba* was first performed not in Madrid or Barcelona but in Buenos Aires, in 1945. In Spain, nevertheless, Lorca's reputation was already far beyond what any domestic censorship regime, much less a single family, could contain. By 1943, even the Falangist magazine *Alerta* was referring to him as "probably one of the best lyric poets of our period" and praising his plays (quoted in London 2001, p. 907). A slow trickle of performances followed, though often with severe curtailments and, even then, not without controversy.[43] Franco allowed the publication of a heavily censored version of Lorca's "complete works" in the 1950s, and in 1966, on the thirtieth anniversary of the poet's death, the conservative daily *ABC*—then the most widely read paper in Spain—published an "homage" to Lorca, confirming his remarkable rehabilitation (Gibson 1973, p. 158).

Upon General Franco's death in 1975 and the establishment of parliamentary democracy in 1978, Lorca's reputation as a playwright only grew in his home country. In 1981 director Carlos Saura released his flamenco-based cinematic

---

41. See Barga 1935 for more on the contemporary reaction to *Yerma*.
42. Stainton 1999 provides good summaries of the critical reactions to *Mariana Pineda* (pp. 161–62), *Shoemaker* (pp. 265–66), *Don Perlimplín* (pp. 316–17), and *Doña Rosita* (pp. 415–16). For additional detail see Vilches de Frutos and Dougherty 1992a, pp. 37–72, 79–86, and 105–12.
43. *Bodas de sangre* was performed privately in Barcelona in 1946, while a staging of *Yerma* in Madrid in 1947 ran into trouble (London 2001, p. 907). A single performance of *The House of Bernarda Alba* was allowed in Madrid in 1950, but press reviews were banned (Quinto 1986, *passim*).

adaptation of *Blood Wedding* to widespread acclaim. Interest was further fueled by the fiftieth anniversary of Lorca's death (1986), a year that witnessed the first rehearsals of *The Audience* in Spain.[44] The 1980s were also the decade in which the first serious scholarly editions of Lorca's plays began to appear in Spain, both in single editions and in volumes of collected and "complete" works.[45] Publication of the primary works fueled in turn a flowering of critical studies, with Lorca becoming perhaps as studied in classrooms and lecture halls as he was performed in theater houses. The establishment in Madrid of the García Lorca Foundation (1984) added to the institutional momentum.

Outside Spain, appreciation of Lorca's theater has followed a parallel track. In the United States, while only two doctoral dissertations were written on Lorca in the 1950s and nine in the 1960s, twenty-five appeared in the 1970s, nineteen in the 1980s, and similar numbers in the following decades.[46] In American undergraduate programs, *The House of Bernarda Alba* has achieved canonical status: in a Spanish-language textbook now in its seventh edition (Friedman et al. 2012) and in two English-language anthologies (Bedford and Norton) widely used in literature and theater departments. Both *House* and *Blood Wedding* have been performed countless times on the stages of American collegiate theaters.[47] Even Sony Pictures attempted to jump on the Lorca bandwagon with its U.S. release of *The Disappearance of García Lorca* (1997).[48]

In 1998—the centenary of Lorca's birth—a series of symposia, homages, and performances around the world included a Japanese production, in Tokyo, of *Blood Wedding* and an Arabic adaptation, in Egypt, of *Yerma* (Doggart 2010, p. 19). That same year, Spain's conservative prime minister and former Falangist,

---

44. The performance opened in January 1987 at the Teatro María Guerrero in Madrid. For an analysis, see Delgado 2008, pp. 160–63; Edwards 2003, pp. 55–60; and Smith 1998, pp. 122–36. As with *The House of Bernarda Alba*, the first professional performance of *The Audience* had taken place outside Spain, in Poland in 1984 (Delgado 2008, p. 160).
45. Spanish publishers that contributed to the boom in Lorca editions include Cátedra (Letras Hispánicas) and Castalia (Clásicos de Castalia). Caution is always appropriate in speaking of Lorca's "complete" works, even in the post-censorship period, as new titles and correspondence have continued to trickle forth.
46. I have not separated out dissertations on Lorca's theater in particular, nor would it be possible to do so in all cases (as some dissertations cross various genres). Instead, I see the total number of dissertations as a reasonable barometer of academic interest in Lorca, which would, of course, include interest in his plays. The data were returned by an online search of the *MLA International Bibliography*.
47. My own translation of *House*, performed at Augsburg College (now University) in the fall of 2013 (dir. Dario Tangelson), gave rise to this volume.
48. Directed by Marcos Zurinaga and starring Andy Garcia as García Lorca, the film debuted outside the United States the year before.

José María Aznar, proclaimed, "Today Spain calls itself Federico" (Thompson 2010, p. 9). Meanwhile, Lorca was overtaking Brecht in the United Kingdom as the most staged foreign playwright of the 1990s (Johnston 1993, p. 21). In the new century, Lorca's reputation as a playwright seems unassailable, spawning countless adaptations. Major new performances of *Blood Wedding* have seen the work adapted to a dysfunctional Greek world set in a postindustrial space (Athens Greek Festival, 2014), to a barren American setting with music from Rick Sims (Chicago's Lookingglass Theatre, 2016), and to a dance-based production stripped of all Spanish references (Philadelphia's Wilma Theater, 2017).[49] With Lorca's complete works in the public domain as of January 2017 and the hundredth anniversary of his death on the horizon, his star is likely only to rise, forever bound to the myth that emerged from the circumstances of his death. As Sarah Wright notes in a recent retrospective, "Part of the attraction of attending a production of one of Lorca's plays springs from a desire on the part of the audience and director to revisit the trauma of his untimely death in a process of collective mourning" (Wright 2007, p. 40).

3. Signature Elements of Lorca's Theater

Lorca was an extremely innovative artist, not only in the wide array of genres he cultivated but also in the great variety encompassed within each genre, especially poetry and drama. No two of his plays or verse collections fit the same mold. Nevertheless, the tension between tradition and experimentation that runs throughout his work produces a fairly consistent set of thematic preoccupations and creative approaches. In what follows I will highlight some of the most significant of these, concentrating on examples from the plays translated in this volume with occasional references to others.

Frustrated Desire

At the top of the list belongs the theme of unfulfilled longing or frustrated desire, commonly manifested in scenarios of tragic or impossible love. "There's no force on earth like desire," comments the Old Woman in *Yerma* (3.1, p. 141). Indeed, the number of characters who suffer or die as a result of such conflicts stretches across Lorca's dramatic corpus: Curianito the Cockroach, Mariana Pineda, the Shoemaker, Perlimplín, Gonzalo, the Bride, Yerma, Doña Rosita, and Adela. While critics such as Daniel Eisenberg view Lorca's homosexuality—which expresses

---

49. For reviews of these performances, see Stavrakopoulou 2015, Jones 2016, and D. Fox 2017.

itself openly only in *The Audience*—as a sort of secret key to interpreting all these scenarios, such readings risk fetishizing the author's sexual identity and reducing his achievement to a clumsy roman à clef.[50] Instead, desire in Lorca forms part of a broad human pattern that, as Jacques Lacan has shown, is constituted by a radical lack.[51] In other words, unfulfilled longing is a core experience of human identity, not something that can be avoided by simply following "the call of instinct instead of yielding to socio-economic pressures" (Gibson 1989, p. 341). It is this sense of frustration and alienation that characterizes human relationships—of all sexual configurations—in the work of Lorca.

Fate and Blood

Related to the idea of unfulfilled longing is the motif of fate. Lorca admired ancient Greek drama and adapted its concept of fate to the Spanish context, where it haunts his characters and propels them toward tragedy. "The issue here is people who can't accept their fate," comments one of the washerwomen about the protagonist's sterility in *Yerma* (2.1, p. 128), a defect that seems predetermined by her very name.[52] Martirio's story of Adelaida reveals a similar worldview: "No, but history repeats itself. I see it all as a terrible cycle. Adelaida is marked by the fate of her mother and grandmother: both wives to the man who fathered her" (*House*, Act 1, p. 170). In the latter passage, fate has fused almost indistinguishably with blood, which is also seen as conditioning one's behavior from birth. The association is particularly strong in *Blood Wedding*, whose protagonists are swept toward each other by forces beyond their control, whether outer (fate or nature) or inner (blood). "They were fooling each other and in the end their blood won out," notes one of the woodcutters (3.1, p. 88). The Bride, for her part, describes Leonardo's pull on her as "a dark river swirling with leaves" and "an ocean breaker" (3.2, pp. 104, 105).

Social Oppression

Marginalized characters are another common element of Lorca's work. Like fate, they are closely related to the theme of frustrated desire. Among the most

---

50. "It seems probable that . . . Lorca centered his plays which were produced on women because he couldn't write as he wished about men" (Eisenberg 1991, p. 122).
51. "Desire as such [for Lacan] proceeds out of this radical finitude or lack and seeks to cover it by generating an endless metonymic chain of substitute signifiers, an endless displacement" (Muller and Richardson 1982, p. 321).
52. In Spanish, *yerma* is the feminine form of an adjective meaning "uninhabited" or "uncultivated."

prominent examples are Lorca's female protagonists, frequently represented as victims of the violence that erupts from rigid societal expectations. This is the case with Yerma, whose obsession with childbearing propels her tragedy: "This fixation of yours is driving you mad. You don't think as you should, and you insist on beating your head against a rock," Juan tells her (2.2, p. 134). In *Blood Wedding* it is the case with the Bride, ostracized as a "loose, weak, indecent woman" for "go[ing] in search of a bed warmed by another man's wife" (3.2, p. 105); it is also the case with Leonardo's wife, widowed by the tragedy and left with no option other than "weeping as you grow old" (3.2. p. 101); and it is the case with the Groom's Mother, reduced to licking up her first son's blood (2.2, p. 79) and, upon the death of the second, to carving "a cold ivory dove from my sleep" (3.2, p. 103). Finally, the suffocating village life of *The House of Bernarda Alba* takes a heavy toll on almost every member of the all-woman cast: the head domestic Poncia, who complains that "fate has bound me to this nunnery!" (Act 2, p. 183); the daughters, whose stunted existence—"like cups in a china closet," according to Poncia (Act 3, p. 201)—pits them against each other and claims Adela's life; the grandmother, whose dementia relegates her to a closet; and even Bernarda, who seems to feel forced into her domineering role "to uphold common decency" (Act 1, p. 168).

In addition to gender, Lorca's characters are subject to societal pressure on account of their sexual identities, whether real or perceived. The slightest bit of nonconformity is considered pathological. One of the washerwomen links Yerma's sterility to her suspiciously masculine behavior: "That's the way of these barren macho women. When they could be making lace or apple preserves, they prefer to climb up to the rooftop or wade barefoot through the river" (2.1, p. 127). When Magdalena suggests that she prefers to "break my back at the mill" rather than get married, Bernarda's reply leaves no room for doubt: "Needles and thread for the women, whips and mules for the men. That's the way of all decent people" (*House*, Act 1, p. 166). The pressure to conform assumes its most obvious homophobic dimension in *The Audience*, where a closeted theater director's production of *Romeo and Juliet* provokes a riot when it is discovered that "Romeo was a thirty-year-old man and Juliet a fifteen-year-old boy" (Tableau 4, p. 35). That such a casting decision is actually faithful to Elizabethan theatrical practice adds a thick layer of irony to the cast's apparent lynching at the hands of the outraged spectators.[53]

---

53. In addition to these examples from his theater, it is worth noting that Lorca's poetry is full of marginalized groups including Romany characters in *Gypsy Ballads* and African Americans in *Poet in New York*. In a public lecture from 1922, moreover, he traces the Andalusian deep song, which he cultivated in his collection of that title, back to classical

Revolt and Revolution

Flowing logically from the previous point, the theme of rebellion—political, social, artistic—is a favorite of Lorca's. Well known for his left-wing sympathies, the playwright expressed on a number of occasions deep admiration for the Russian Revolution and Soviet culture.[54] While he never advocated for open revolution in Spain and remained aloof from political organizations, he clearly believed in the responsibility of the artist, who, "as an observer of life, cannot remain indifferent to social issues" (*OC*, vol. 3, p. 600). Such was the primary impulse behind La Barraca, which Lorca described as "the great ideal of educating the people of our beloved Republic by giving them back their theater" (*OC*, vol. 3, p. 390).

While *Mariana Pineda*'s protests against the repressive regime of Ferdinand VII are Lorca's most direct thematization of *political* rebellion, *Blood Wedding*, *Yerma*, and *House* all offer abundant examples of *social* rebellion. The women of these plays—for in every case women dominate the cast of characters—are not simply victims of the socioeconomic forces that subjugate them; they also take concrete measures to challenge, block, or destroy those forces. Thus the Bride deserts the respectable Groom at the altar to abscond with her former beau Leonardo. Yerma, frustrated by her husband's cavalier attitude toward her inability to conceive, strangles him to death during a pagan fertility rite. And, in a dramatic scene with an obvious political reading, Bernarda's youngest daughter Adela "grabs the staff from her mother and breaks it in two," exclaiming "That's what I think of the tyrant's rod" (Act 3, p. 207).

While *The Audience* presents a much different social scenario, it is no less revolutionary in its implications. The sexually closeted Director overcomes his initial misgivings to stage a version of *Romeo and Juliet* that challenges the provincial, bourgeois values of the audience, alluded to at one point as "people who vomit when they see the underside of an octopus and . . . grow pale if they hear the word 'cancer' spoken in just the right tone" (Tableau 1, p. 6). Though Lorca consistently rejected literary labels, the use of art as a weapon against bourgeois society together with the irrational nature of the language points to the Dadaist nature of *The Audience*. Ironically, the "revolution" eventually comes from the

---

Arabic and Persian sources, noting that it is the expression of an "utterly oppressed people" (*OC*, vol. 3, p. 50).
54. In April 1933 he signed a manifesto in support of the Bolshevik Revolution (Stainton 1999, p. 319). In an interview in 1935, he stated: "The USSR is impressive. Moscow is the counterbalance to New York. I am very eager to become personally acquainted with Russia given the fantastic commitment of the Russian people" (*OC*, vol. 3. pp. 597–98). Such sympathies may have given rise to the absurd rumor, cited upon his arrest, that he was a Soviet spy.

weak-stomached audience members, who, pushed past their breaking point by the suggestive content of the play, stage a riot in which they demand the head of the Director. It is yet another eerie instance of Lorca's art anticipating his life.

FOLKLORIC ELEMENTS

Lorca's childhood experiences in the Andalusian countryside, where he was exposed to popular wisdom and traditions stretching back centuries, left a profound impression on him as a writer. Though he bristled at being pigeonholed as some sort Southern Spanish bard—an insecurity that was probably exacerbated by his friendship with Dalí, Buñuel, and others from the Residence, who referred to him as an "Andalusian dog" (see n. 14)—there is no doubt that he consistently incorporated elements of Spanish folklore into his work, especially in verse collections such as *Book of Poems*, *Poem of the Deep Song*, and *Gypsy Ballads*. In his drama, too, there is no shortage of folkloric language and motifs. Of the four plays represented in this collection, only *The Audience* escapes the pattern. *Blood Wedding*, *Yerma*, and *House*, for their part, are all deeply rooted in the superstitions and folk traditions of southern Spain.[55] The heavily lyric dimension of the first two is particularly conducive to folkloric language in the form of popular songs and lullabies. In *Yerma*, furthermore, characters such as the Old Woman of 1.2, the chorus of washerwomen in 2.1, and the folk healer Dolores in 3.1 espouse an earthy, fatalistic wisdom that culminates in the sensual fertility dance of the final scene. In *Blood Wedding*, the chorus of woodcutters in 3.1 provides a similar function, while the personified figures of the Moon and Death in 3.1 channel popular notions of fate in highly poetic form. And while *The House of Bernarda Alba* unfolds on a more realist plane than the other two, it nevertheless incorporates stylized folkloric language in the prayer for the deceased (Act 1, p. 164), in the chorus of harvesters (Act 2, p. 184), and in the delusional lullabies that María Josefa sings to her "child" (Act 3, pp. 203–5).

---

55. Many commentators speak of the three plays as Lorca's "rural trilogy" or "trilogy of the land," but Lorca himself, in an interview from July 1933 (*OC*, vol. 3, pp, 418–19), included only *Blood Wedding* and *Yerma* in that grouping. (In the same interview he referred to the third part of the trilogy as *The Destruction of Sodom*, while in others he called it *The Daughters of Lot* [e.g., *OC*, vol. 3, pp. 545, 548]. In December of 1935 he announced that *The Destruction of Sodom* was "almost finished" [*OC*, vol. 3, p. 552]. Unfortunately, the play exists today only in a short initial fragment.) Whether conceived of as a trilogy, it is true that *Blood Wedding*, *Yerma*, and *House* are defined in large part by their rural settings.

Metaphor

Lorca's admiration for Luis de Góngora's use of metaphor led him to organize the baroque poet's tercentenary celebration in 1927, which both rehabilitated Góngora's reputation among critics and inaugurated the avant-garde cohort of poets, known as the Generation of 1927, to which Lorca belonged (see Biographical Sketch, p. xvii). In his keynote lecture, Lorca praised Gongora's "new method of seizing upon metaphors and giving them expression" (*OC*, vol. 3, p. 57), citing examples such as "green voices," "winged song," and "feathered organs" (ibid., p. 59). Metaphor in Góngora, Lorca concludes, "unites two competing worlds by means of an equestrian leap of the imagination" (ibid., p. 60). Indeed, nothing better describes Lorca's own extraordinary use of metaphor than this equestrian leap of the imagination. It is his greatest talent as a poet, the closest thing to a Lorcan "fingerprint." From the alluring "parchment moon" of *Gypsy Ballads* (*OC*, vol. 1, p. 416) to the shocking "pickled trees" and "saliva harps" of *Poet in New York* (ibid., p. 527), Lorca's metaphors consistently probe the limits of the mind's ability to make symbolic connections.

In his plays, frequent verse forms such as lullabies, nonsensical rhymes, prayers, ritualized chanting, choral songs, and lyrical interventions from symbolic characters serve as natural vehicles for the type of avant-garde metaphors Lorca cultivated. Thus one finds the Buffoon Shepherd's "sky full of [chairs]" in *The Audience* (Soliloquy of the Buffoon Shepherd, p. 38); Girl 1's "Wounds of wax, / pain of myrtle" in *Blood Wedding* (3.2, p. 99); Washerwoman 4's "dreamless birds" in *Yerma* (2.1, p. 130); and María Josefa's "tiny ant [who] will guard his door" in *House* (Act 3, pp. 203 and 205).

Yet far from limited to the verse forms in Lorca's plays, such language extends to the heart of his prose. *The Audience* is saturated with the most baffling of metaphors, from the all-important "theater beneath the sand" (pp. 5, 23, and 40) to the Bell Figure's "whip made of orchid stamens" (Tableau 2, p. 11) to the White Horse's "ash in the form of apples" (Tableau 3, p. 21) to Juliet's "meningitis masks" (Tableau 3, p. 20) to the Director's "barometer hair" (Tableau 4, p. 33) to the stage directions' call for a "slow rain of white gloves" (Tableau 5, p. 43). In *Blood Wedding*, the Bride cites a string of opaque metaphors in describing Leonardo's effect upon her: "And I'd run to your son and he was like a little boy with a sip of cool water, while the other would send me flocks of birds that would block my way and leave my wounds poulticed in frost" (3.2, p. 104). In *Yerma*, Washerwoman 4 compares Juan's sisters to "those vines that spring up on tombstones. Smeared with wax and twisted in on themselves. I bet they cook their food with lamp oil" (2.1, p. 126).

As Lorca's most realistic play, *The House of Bernarda Alba* generally avoids the opaque in favor of the striking, replacing metaphor with the more rational simile: a parish priest's voice is "like a clay pitcher filling slowly with water" (Act 1, p. 161); field-workers are "dark like well-seasoned trees" (Act 2, p. 183); and a sexually excited young man is "wound up tight like an ear of wheat" (Act 2, p. 183). In the final sequence, nonetheless, the dementia-stricken María Josefa escapes from her closet and confronts her granddaughter Martirio in a rich soliloquy:

> When my neighbor had a child I'd take her chocolate, and then she'd bring me some, and so it went always, always, always. You'll have white hair, but the neighbors won't come. I have to go, but I'm afraid the dogs will bite me. Will you help me leave the countryside? I don't like the country. I want houses, but open houses where the women lie in their beds with their little ones and the men sit outside in their chairs. Pepe el Romano is a giant. You're all smitten with him. But he's going to gulp you down because you're just grains of wheat. No, not grains of wheat. Tongueless frogs! (Act 3, p. 205)

The language of madness, which Lorca had begun to experiment with in *Yerma*, enables the irrational "equestrian leaps" that he loved within a perfectly rational—and commercial—framework. It is a formula that allows him to have his metaphorical cake and eat it too. One can only speculate where he would have taken it had he survived.

4. The Four Plays in Brief

This section provides succinct backgrounds on each of the plays including when and how they came into being (and, in the case of *The Audience*, how it survived); brief comments on content; and instructive observations from Lorca. It avoids plot summaries and extensive interpretation, though the previous section, "Signature Elements of Lorca's Theater," provides some thematic orientation. Debut performances are catalogued in Appendix 2. The reader may also wish to peruse the relevant sections of the Biographical Sketch, referenced at the beginning of each segment.

The Audience (1930)

(See also: Biographical Sketch, "Far from Home," pp. xix–xxii.)

This play survives in a single handwritten copy, whose physical characteristics and extraordinary textual history are worth exploring at some length.

Several pages of the manuscript are scribbled on stationery from the Union Hotel in Havana, which suggests that Lorca wrote part of it when he lodged there during his visit in the spring of 1930. It is likely that he at least conceived of the idea during his stay in New York, as the language and imagery bear striking parallels to *Poet in New York*, which he began in the fall of 1929, and *Trip to the Moon*, which he wrote over several days during the same period. Whatever the case, the play was nearing completion by July of 1930, for at that point, back in Spain, Lorca wrote to his friend Rafael Martínez Nadal, in an almost certain allusion to *The Audience*: "I've written a play that I'd love to read to you in the company of Miguel. The theme is *openly* homosexual. I think it's my best poem" (*OC*, vol. 3, p. 1171).[56] The last page of the manuscript is dated August 22, 1930, and Martínez Nadal reports having heard Lorca read a complete draft in the home of Carlos Morla Lynch in late 1930 or early 1931 (Martínez Nadal 1974, p. 19).

At this point, the transmission of the manuscript becomes as convoluted as its plot. Lorca published two extracts in the literary magazine *Los Cuatro Vientos* in 1933, where they appear with the subtitle "From a Play in Five Acts" (Paco 2002, p. 116). Martínez Nadal states that when he asked Lorca why he did not publish the entire play, he responded, "Because I am correcting and polishing it" (Martínez Nadal 1974, p. 19). Martínez Nadal further explains that Lorca read a revised version of the play at a restaurant in Madrid in July 1936 and that, several days later, when he had decided to leave for Granada, he gave Martínez Nadal a package with instructions to burn the contents should he not survive (Martínez Nadal 1974, p. 16). Opening the packet later at home, Nadal realized it contained a draft of five scenes from *The Audience*, though he wonders in a footnote if it was not actually six (Martínez Nadal 1974, p. 17).

The inconsistencies and unanswered questions in Martínez Nadal's account of how he came to possess Lorca's manuscript have led some to cast doubt, perhaps rightly, on his credibility.[57] It is unclear, for example, why Lorca would have given Martínez Nadal the first draft of the play instead of one of the more polished versions he read at the Morla Lynch home and in the restaurant. At any rate, the first draft is the only copy we now possess, and we have no account of its existence other than the one offered by Martínez Nadal, who explains that instead of burning it he entrusted it to an unnamed friend when he himself fled Spain, shortly after Lorca's death, to exile in London. Regaining possession of it in 1958,

---

56. Lorca sometimes referred to his plays as "poems," a practice that reflected his love of Spanish classical theater, in which all playwrights were known as *poetas*. The quoted passage is noteworthy as Lorca's only documented use of the word "homosexual" (the emphasis on "openly" is his). The identity of "Miguel" is unknown.

57. For example: Gibson 1989, p. 444.

he began to lobby Lorca's family for permission to publish a facsimile edition. After releasing a book-length study prefaced with the details mentioned above, Martínez Nadal published the long-awaited facsimile edition in 1976.

Now available in digital format on the webpage of Spain's National Library, the manuscript is a chaotic mess, scrawled in both ink and pencil over sixty-two pages of different types and sizes. Some sheets have writing on both sides and others on only one. Heavily line-edited with additions and deletions throughout, the text is interspersed with doodles and the apparent beginning of another play titled *Sampson*. There are six independent units: five longer pieces, each with its own page numbering, and a two-page poetic monologue with no page numbering. Two of the longer pieces are labeled as tableaux (Cuadros 5 and 6), one of which (Cuadro 5) is missing its final page.[58] There is debate about the intended sequence of the six units, which the play's internal logic is insufficient to determine. Most critics accept Martínez Nadal's ordering given that he professed to have heard Lorca read the play.[59]

There is also uncertainty about the definitive number of scenes. The two extracts published in *Los Cuatro Vientos* indicate they come from "a play in five acts," while the first page of the manuscript announces a "Drama in Twenty Tableaux and a Murder." In an interview from October 1930, Lorca refers to the play having "six acts and a murder" (*OC*, vol. 3, p. 372), and what appears to be the last scene of the manuscript (because it ends with the date of completion) is titled Tableau 6. In reviewing the conflicting information, many critics believe the manuscript is missing what would correspond, in most orderings, to Tableau 4. Miguel García-Posada, the editor of the Spanish text on which I have based my translation, titles the longer units Tableaux 1–5 and places the Soliloquy of the Buffoon Shepherd between 4 and 5.[60] I have deferred to his judgment.

The Frankenstein-like nature of the manuscript could not serve as a more appropriate vehicle for the contents of *The Audience*. Even if we knew for certain that we possessed the entire text in the correct sequence, it is difficult to

---

58. The missing page has been reconstructed from Cuadro 5's publication in *Los Cuatro Vientos*. For Lorca's use of the word "tableau" (*cuadro*) instead of "scene," see Translator's Note, pp. lii–liii.
59. One particularly vexing question concerns the placement of what editors, following Martínez Nadal, call the Soliloquy of the Buffoon Shepherd (Lorca did not give the unit a title). Martínez Nadal places the soliloquy between the last two tableaux of his ordering, though he suggests it might fall between the first two (Martínez Nadal 1974, p. 22).
60. Following Martínez Nadal, García-Posada does not accord the soliloquy the status of a tableau, presumably because of its short length. Given, however, the extremely experimental nature of *The Audience*, it seems at least possible that Lorca could have considered the soliloquy a tableau unto itself, possibly intending it as the supposedly missing Tableau 4.

imagine that our understanding of it would be much enhanced. For while the play's substance—its irrational language and anti-bourgeois sentiments—might be described as Dadaist, its form is essentially cubist: a decentered, kaleidoscopic structure that operates through the repetition and accumulation of images rather than through anything approaching a linear plot.[61] The sprawling cast of characters includes humans, horses, and disembodied costumes. Everything is held together by two inextricable themes, sexual identity and theater, both engaged in a constant play between the authentic (homosexual desire and the theater beneath the sand) and the counterfeit (heterosexual posing and the open-air theater). Yet even this opposition is ultimately unsettled by the vertiginous interplay of the terms, so that ultimately the only constant that emerges is performance itself: "The door to the theater never closes," Man 2 tells Juliet (Tableau 3, p. 27). Indeed. And nothing opens the door to the turmoil of García Lorca's private world more than this extraordinary play.

Blood Wedding (1932)

(See also: Biographical Sketch, "New Hope," pp. xxii–xxiv.)

Lorca's first tragedy—to adopt the term he applied to this play—was inspired by real-life events. In late July of 1928, in the town of Níjar (southeast Spain), a young bride-to-be escaped on horseback with a cousin and former lover while her groom waited at the altar of a farmhouse. By apparent coincidence, the groom's inebriated brother, who was not among the wedding party, came across the renegade lovers and murdered the man in an act of retaliation for his family's stained honor. The case received sensational press coverage as the details unfolded over the course of a week. Lorca, who read about it in the newspaper *ABC* while living at the Residence in Madrid, is reported to have exclaimed to his friends: "Read this article! You couldn't make up such a story!" (Josephs and Caballero 1986, pp. 27–28).

The story incubated for four years in Lorca's imagination, where, little by little, the tawdry details metamorphosed into the plot and setting of a highly stylized poetic tragedy. Thus it is that the real-life bride's farmhouse becomes a cave dwelling; the families are transformed into feuding clans with a history of blood vengeance; the brother's chance encounter with the escaped couple blooms into a

---

61. A. A. Anderson 1992b identifies all of Lorca's impossible theater with the German expressionism of the 1920s. While there are various artistic movements of the period with which the author's work might be identified—Dadaism, cubism, expressionism, symbolism, surrealism, futurism—it is worth noting that he did not affiliate himself directly with any of them.

full-scale search party with interventions from the Moon and Death; and the final outcome is conditioned by the maneuverings of a silent, inescapable fate.[62]

Despite the many lyrical elements, the story unfolds quickly and dramatically, infused with a raw urgency befitting "the heat of a man and a woman," to use the Maid's felicitous phrase (2.1, p. 67). The plot requires no special explanation, its simplicity and elegance in stark contrast to the labyrinthine twists and funhouse distortions of *The Audience*. The language, too, is remarkably natural and accessible, exhibiting such an impeccable sense of rhythm in both verse and prose that the spectator would be forgiven for confusing the two. As Lorca noted, "Free and unembellished prose can reach great expressive heights, permitting us an effortlessness impossible to achieve in the rigidities of metrical verse" (*OC*, vol. 3, p. 411). It is easy to understand how *Blood Wedding* rocketed its author to international fame.

Yerma (1934)

(See also: Biographical Sketch, "International Celebrity," pp. xxiv–xxvi.)

With *Blood Wedding*'s success, Lorca began to conceive of a trilogy of plays set in rural Spain, the Spain of his idyllic childhood and of his tours with La Barraca. But setting was only one important element in the trilogy. The other was genre, as he explains in an interview:

> I am close to finishing *Yerma*, my second tragedy. The first was *Blood Wedding*. *Yerma* will be the barren woman's tragedy. The topic, as you know, is classic. But I intend to give it a new twist. A tragedy with four main characters and choruses, the way tragedies are meant to be. A return to tragedy is imperative. Our dramatic tradition demands it. (*OC*, vol. 3, p. 536)

And in another:

> *Yerma* is a tragedy. I have attempted to remain faithful to the classical precepts. The key, of course, is the chorus, which underlines the actions of the protagonists. There is no plot in *Yerma*. What I wanted to make was a tragedy, pure and simple. (*OC*, vol. 3, p. 583)

---

62. The scene with the Moon and Death was Lorca's personal favorite from the play: "The realism that presides until that moment in the tragedy breaks down and disappears, giving way to poetic fantasy, which of course suits me like a fish in the water" (*OC*, vol. 3, p. 412). The fantasy occurs even at the level of the text, where the stage directions note that the Beggar Woman "does not appear in the Dramatis Personae" (3.1, p. 91).

Lorca's classification of *Yerma* as a tragedy in the classical sense might seem puzzling given his insistence that it has no plot, and much ink has been spilt on the question of whether he in fact lived up to classical models such as Aristotle.[63] Pedantry aside, what Lorca seemed to want to channel from Greek tragedy was a symbolic dimension that would communicate the weight of ancient traditions and mysteries, of a terrifying sacred power that he felt to be completely lacking in the popular bourgeois drama. Having already experimented with this symbolic dimension in the figures of the Moon and Death in *Blood Wedding*, he was ready to take it further in *Yerma*.

One element that helps him achieve his goal is the poetic language of the chorus, which he intended to give a "more intense development" (*OC*, vol. 3, p. 548) than in *Blood Wedding*.[64] Another is the presence of characters such as the Old Woman of 1.2, whose earthy sexuality and scandalous atheism would seem to identify her with the Old Pagan Woman in the cast of characters.[65] A third is the consistent imagery around the ancient elements of earth, air, fire, and water, the latter associated with the fertility that Yerma craves: "I just laid on my back and started singing. The children came like water," the Old Woman states, adding a few lines later: "Men are there to give us pleasure, girl. They're supposed to unbraid our hair and bring us water to drink in their own mouths" (1.2, pp. 119, 120). All these elements converge in a final, bacchanalian scene as the Old Woman reappears, the chorus participates in the fertility ritual, and Yerma refers to herself as "a dry field wide enough for a thousand teams of oxen to plow" (3.2, p. 153).

Such are the characteristics that not only make *Yerma* unique but that also provoked outrage among Lorca's conservative critics. The tragedy may be not so much the play itself but the role it played in Lorca's undoing.

---

63. "The Plot, then, is the first principle, and, as it were, the soul of a tragedy" (Aristotle 1961, p. 63). See Cannon 1962, Lott 1965, Sullivan 1972, and R. Anderson 1982 for evaluations of *Yerma* as tragedy.

64. The main choral intervention in *Blood Wedding* comes in 2.1, in which the Bride awakens. *Yerma* 2.1 is devoted exclusively to the washerwomen, who sing in the manner of a chorus, while the fertility ritual of the final scene (3.2) is punctuated by a chorus of women pilgrims.

65. As in many of Lorca's plays, the Dramatis Personae do not correspond precisely to the characters that appear in the text (see n. 62, and the Translator's Note, p. liv). There is no Old Pagan Woman in any of the scenes, though there are several Old Women (in 1.2, 3.1, and 3.2).

The House of Bernarda Alba (1936)

(See also: Biographical Sketch, "Poisoned Well," pp. xxvi–xxviii.)

Lorca had a draft of his best-known play by the spring of 1936. Though set in rural Spain, it was not intended as the third installment of the trilogy that began with *Blood Wedding* and *Yerma*. That spot was reserved for a play titled *The Destruction of Sodom* or *The Daughters of Lot*, which has not survived (see n. 55).

Significantly, he referred in the new play's subtitle not to a tragedy but rather to a "drama," which did not mean, however, that it would be free of calamity. Instead, as suggested above, tragedy for Lorca seems to have involved, more than anything, a symbolic dimension constituted through formal elements such as a chorus and heavily poetic language. These are precisely the elements lacking in *House*. Lorca's friend Adolfo Salazar recounts how Lorca explained the play to him: "Not a single drop of poetry! Reality! Pure realism!" (Doménech 2008, p. 205). As if to emphasize the point, he tagged the following stipulation onto the cast of characters: "The author wishes to communicate that these three acts bear the intent of a photographic documentary" (p. 158). Not surprisingly, the play presents few conceptual challenges.

The subtitle indicates that the play is not merely a drama but a "drama about women in the villages of Spain." Even for an author who was known for his women characters, the all-female cast of *House* (over fifteen roles in all) is striking. When asked about this predilection in an interview (before he wrote *House*), Lorca seemed surprised by the question and replied: "Well I've never thought of it that way.... It's just that women have more passion, they're less cerebral, more human, more corporal; what's more, an author would have great difficulty staging his plays if all the heroes were men. There's a lamentable shortage of actors... good actors anyway" (*OC*, vol. 3, pp. 501–2).

As for the woman at the center of the play, Bernarda was based on a childhood memory of Lorca's. Doña Frasquita Alba Sierra lived in the village of Asquerosa, across the street from young Federico and next door to his cousins, with whom she shared a well. She indeed had five daughters (and a pair of sons), who, according to Lorca, walked through the village like shadows, silent and cloaked in black. Though Lorca remembered Doña Frasquita as domineering, she was outlived by her second husband, so she could not have ruled tyrannically over her daughters in widowhood as Bernarda did.[66] It would, of course, be churlish to expect absolute fidelity to history in a play. Few great artists, if any, work that way.

---

66. For more on Doña Frasquita and her family, see Gibson 1989, pp. 436–37, and Stainton 1999, pp. 430–31.

As was Lorca's custom, he gave several private readings of the script as he wrote, spellbinding his listeners with his innate dramatic flair. When he finished the first draft, according to his friend Adolfo Salazar, he broke down in tears, convinced that his career as a playwright was just beginning (Doménech 2008, p. 206).

The draft was dated June 19, 1936. Lorca's intention was to revise Acts 2 and 3 (Stainton 1999, p. 431). Two months later he was dead.

TRANSLATOR'S NOTE

Traduttore, traditore goes the old Italian axiom. Translator, traitor. Cliché but no less true: every translation is an act of betrayal committed against the original. Lawrence Venuti goes a step further and identifies it with violence.[1] But in the case of a literary text that one holds close to the heart, it is also an act of love. Such is the dilemma in translating as great a writer as Federico García Lorca: how to least violate a loved one.

Most translators, myself included, aim for a balance between accuracy and readability. Both terms are worth interrogating. *Accuracy* is certainly a worthy goal, perhaps the most important duty of a translator. But to be properly understood, it must be dislodged from the myth of the "literal translation," which presumes that there is one true rendering from which all others stray. If that were the case, an algorithm should be able to produce it; yet with all the coding genius of Silicon Valley at its disposal, Google Translate still produces gibberish in many cases. Perhaps it's just a matter of finding a sufficiently sophisticated algorithm, but count me dubious. Two languages can never line up in a one-to-one correspondence; if they did, they would be one language rather than two. To rephrase the old Italian adage discussed above, then, there is no such thing as a "literal translation," only differing degrees of betrayal.

To cite a small example: if one types "el público" into Google Translate, out comes "the public." It's hard to argue with the literal quality of this "translation." In fact, most Lorca specialists writing in English refer to the first play in this collection as *The Public*.[2] Such a translation is not "wrong," but is it the most appropriate? In the context of theater, which is paramount to the play in question, I would argue that there is, in fact, a more accurate—though less "literal"—term, and I have thus titled my translation *The Audience*.[3]

Translating *El público* as *The Public*, then, is a case in which tacking too closely to the original ends up offending the principle of accuracy. An opposite case

---

1. "The violence of translation resides in its very purpose and activity: the reconstitution of the foreign text in accordance with values, beliefs, and representations that pre-exist it in the target language, always configured in hierarchies of dominance and marginality, always determining the production, circulation, and reception of texts" (Venuti 1993, p. 209).
2. For example: Martínez Nadal 1974, Jerez-Farrán 2001.
3. It is worth noting, furthermore, that the choice between "the public" and "the audience" involves but a single noun phrase in isolation. When "el público" is embedded in complex syntactic structures with other items such as verb phrases, the notion of literal translations completely breaks down.

involves the translation of Lorca's use of the term *cuadro* as the smallest internal unit of a play, which previous translators have rendered as "scene."[4] In this case, however, the more literal translation of "tableau" does greater justice to Lorca's modernist aesthetic, which involved turning—translating!—pictorial and other fine-arts concepts into theater (see the discussion on Lorca's stagecraft in the Critical Guide, pp. xxxii–xxxv). Translating the word as "scene" erases the distinction the author makes between the standard *escena* in some works and the more artistic *cuadro* in others. In my translations I respect his use of "tableau" in the important unit headings, but in my introductory materials I typically use "scene" when speaking generically (i.e., "In the final scene of *Yerma* . . .").[5]

Readability in a literary text suggests some threshold of pleasure below which the reading becomes joyless and tedious. Of what does this pleasure consist? That is a question for a much longer essay, but I would argue that it includes subtle, deeply entrenched features of language such as syntax (how words fit together), phonemics (how words sound), and rhythm (how stress is distributed across words). To cite a simple example, many basic vocabulary items in Spanish are polysyllabic whereas their English counterparts are monosyllabic. A quick inventory of body parts (fundamental vocabulary for any speaker) confirms this point: *cabeza*: head, *pelo*: hair, *ojos*: eyes, *nariz*: nose, *boca*: mouth, *orejas*: ears, *cuello*: neck, *pecho*: chest, *brazos*: arms, *manos*: hands, and *piernas*: legs. There are obvious exceptions (*shoulders* and *elbows* in English, *pies* in Spanish, etc.), but the basic pattern is indisputable and has important consequences for translation. This is especially the case in verse, where rhythm is paramount; but even with prose, a translator who is consistently inattentive to rhythm will be at greater risk for producing an "unreadable" text. Then again, translating *cabeza* as "cranium" to preserve rhythm would strain against accuracy. It's always a delicate balance and, ultimately, a question of judgment.

There is an additional consideration in the case of translating dramatic texts, where *readability* also means "playability" and "listenability." For actors, the text must be adaptable to the constraints of breath and syntax. For listeners, it must be

---

4. For example: Graham-Luján and O'Connell 1955, Dewell and Zapata 1993, and Edmunds 1997.

5. Lorca was by no means unique in his use of "tableau" as a theatrical term (the Royal Spanish Academy recorded a definition of *cuadro* that captured this meaning even before he was born), but it is safe to say he was in the minority. Even in his own practice, he used "scene" in *The Butterfly's Evil Spell*, in *Mariana Pineda* (though in the latter the larger units—equivalent to acts—were labeled *estampas* or "prints"), and in *The Shoemaker's Prodigious Wife*. In his other plays he used "act," "tableau," or some combination of the two. It is also true that, even when he used the term "tableau" as a unit heading, he often reverted to "scene" in the stage directions. I have followed his inconsistencies for the most part.

graspable in real time and without elucidation, for audience members in a theater do not have the luxury of consulting footnotes, looking up unfamiliar words, or rereading passages. I had the luxury of testing these principles in my translation of *The House of Bernarda Alba* when it was performed at Augsburg College (now University) in the fall of 2013, and I revised accordingly and attempted to apply the lessons learned to the other plays in the volume.

A third principle in translation is *consistency*. If one translates *el público* as "the audience," then one should do so consistently: unless, of course, the context points to a change in meaning, in which case "the public" may become appropriate.

Consistency also means that if one renders a poem in a mostly prose play into verse, then one should use verse for all poems throughout the play. I follow this principle rather scrupulously in the case of Lorca's plays, which are written in a combination of verse and prose: a perceptible distinction that I believe should come through in translation. The thornier question is: How does one translate verse? How to reproduce features such as meter and rhyme (where the latter exists) while preserving accuracy? I have addressed this issue at length in another venue (Kidd 2004), but the short answer is that it cannot be done with any degree of consistency given the fundamental differences in the rhythmic systems of English and Spanish. Nevertheless, I have done my best to render verse as verse through line breaks, rhythm, and a limited use of rhyme.[6]

A final question concerns the case of textual puzzles in the original. For example, Lorca's Dramatis Personae often do not correspond fully to the characters introduced in the plays. Sometimes, however, what seems to be an "error" turns out to be intentional, as in *Blood Wedding*, where the stage directions in 3.1 confirm that the Beggar Woman should not appear in the cast of characters (p. 91). As a translator already engaged in an act of betrayal, I am cautious about "correcting" Lorca in such cases, preferring to defer to the editor of the Spanish text. I occasionally supplement stage directions, usually to indicate an entrance or exit, but I always indicate my interpolations in brackets. The few other changes I have made are explained in Appendix 1.

This, then, is my basic approach to translating Lorca's theater: balancing accuracy and readability as best as possible, with special consideration toward the

---

6. One of the challenges of translating rhyme is that there is no good English equivalent of Spanish assonance, a type of rhyme in which only the vowels coincide. A regular feature of Lorca's poetry, assonant rhyme is much more subtle than full or "perfect" rhyme, whereas the latter, when repeated at length in English, runs the risk of sounding humorous or puerile. I have used full rhyme where the context seemed to justify it; otherwise I have adapted to my purposes Emily Dickinson's sage advice to "tell it slant" or, indeed, employed no rhyme at all.

performance setting; observing consistency where allowed by context; rendering verse forms in a way that sets them apart for the listener; and approaching "errors" in a conservative manner. In conclusion, I would add that there is no substitute for reading Lorca—or any great author—in the original, and I would be thrilled if my translations did nothing more than motivate the reader to learn Spanish in order to do so. In the meantime, I would suggest thinking of them as opera glasses: they can't put you onstage, but hopefully they'll get you close enough to enjoy the show.

The Audience:
Drama in Five Tableaux

DRAMATIS PERSONAE

Director (Enrique)
Servant
White Horse 1
White Horse 2
White Horse 3
White Horse 4
Man 1 (Gonzalo)
Man 2
Man 3
Harlequin Director
Woman in Pajamas
Helen
Bell Figure
Grapevine Figure
Boy
Emperor
Centurion
Juliet
Black Horse
Harlequin Costume
Ballerina Costume
Buffoon Shepherd
Naked Red Man
Male Nurse
Student 1
Student 2
Student 3
Student 4
Student 5
Lady 1
Lady 2
Lady 3
Lady 4
Boy
Thief 1
Thief 2
Prompter
Conjuror
Mother

Tableau 1

(Director's office. The DIRECTOR is seated. He wears a full-dress tuxedo jacket. The set is blue. A large hand is printed on the wall. The windows are X-ray images.)

SERVANT. Sir.

DIRECTOR. What?

SERVANT. The audience is here.

DIRECTOR. Show them in.

([Exit the SERVANT.] Enter four WHITE HORSES.)

DIRECTOR. What do you want?

(The HORSES play their trumpets.)

That would be the case if I were a man capable of sighing. My theater will always be in the open air! But I've lost my entire fortune. Otherwise I would poison the open air. A syringe to pick the scab from the wound would do it for me. Out of my house, horses! The bed for sleeping with horses has already been invented.

(Crying.)

My little horsies.

HORSES. *(Crying.)* For three hundred pesetas. For two hundred pesetas, for a bowl of soup, for an empty flask of perfume. For your saliva, for your fingernail clippings.

DIRECTOR. Out! Out! Out!

(He rings a buzzer.)

HORSES. For anything at all! They used to smell your feet and we were three years old. We would wait in the water closet, we'd wait behind the doors, and then we'd flood your bed with tears.

(Enter the SERVANT.)

DIRECTOR. Give me a whip!

HORSES. And your shoes were stewing in sweat, but we understood that the moon had the same relationship with the apples lying rotten in the weeds.

DIRECTOR. *(To the SERVANT.)* Open the doors!

HORSES. No, no, no. Abominable! You're covered in body hair and you eat whitewash off walls that aren't yours.

SERVANT. I'm not opening the door. I don't want to step into the theater.

DIRECTOR. *(Striking him.)* Open it!

(The HORSES take out large golden trumpets and dance slowly to the rhythm of their song.)

HORSES 1–2. *(Furiously.)* Abominable.

HORSES 3–4. Blenamiboa.

HORSES 1–2. *(Furiously.)* Abominable.

HORSES. Blenamiboa.

(The SERVANT opens the door.)

DIRECTOR. Open-air theater! Out! Get moving! Open-air theater. Get out of here!

(Exit the HORSES. To the SERVANT.)

Go on.

(The DIRECTOR sits behind the table.)

SERVANT. Sir.

DIRECTOR. What?

SERVANT. The audience!

DIRECTOR. Show them in.

(The DIRECTOR changes his blond wig for a black one. Enter three MEN identically dressed in tuxedoes. They have dark beards.)

MAN 1. Mr. Open-Air Theater Director?

DIRECTOR. At your service.

MAN 1. We're here to congratulate you on your latest play.

DIRECTOR. Thank you.

MAN 3. Very original.

MAN 1. And such a beautiful title! *Romeo and Juliet.*

DIRECTOR. A man and a woman who fall in love.

MAN 1. Romeo could be a bird and Juliet could be a stone. Romeo could be a grain of salt and Juliet could be a map.

DIRECTOR. But they will never cease to be Romeo and Juliet.

MAN 1. And in love. Do you believe they were in love?

DIRECTOR. Well . . . that's not for me . . .

MAN 1. Enough! Enough! You've given yourself away.

MAN 2. *(To MAN 1.)* Don't be so impulsive. It's your fault. What do you come to the door of a theater for? You could knock at a forest and it could easily expose the sound of its sap to your ears. But a theater!

MAN 1. It's theaters at which one must knock, it's theaters because . . .

MAN 3. Because then one understands the truth about tombs.

MAN 2. Tombs with spotlights and billboards and long rows of orchestra seats.

DIRECTOR. Gentlemen . . .

MAN 1. Yes. Yes. Mr. Open-Air Theater Director, author of *Romeo and Juliet.*

MAN 2. How did Romeo urinate, Mr. Director? Isn't it nice to watch Romeo urinate? How many times did he throw himself from the tower to find himself trapped in the comedy of his suffering? What happened, Mr. Director, when nothing happened? And what about the tomb? Why didn't you descend the steps of the tomb at the end? You would have seen an angel stealing Romeo's sex organ while leaving another, his own, the one that belonged to him. And if I tell you that the most important main character was a poisonous flower, what would you think? Answer me.

DIRECTOR. Gentlemen, that's not the issue.

MAN 1. *(Interrupting.)* It's the only issue. We'll have to bury the theater because of everyone's cowardice, and I'll have to shoot myself.

MAN 2. Gonzalo!

MAN 1. *(Slowly.)* I'll have to shoot myself to inaugurate the true theater, the theater beneath the sand.

DIRECTOR. Gonzalo . . .

MAN 1. How . . . ?

  (Pause.)

DIRECTOR. *(Defensively.)* I can't. It would ruin everything. It would leave my children blind, and then what do I do with the audience?

What do I do with the audience if I strip the railings from the bridge? I would be devoured by the mask. I once saw a man devoured by the mask. The strongest young men in the city, wielding bloody pikes, were shoving wads of discarded newspapers up his rump, and in America there was once a boy that the mask hanged by his own intestines.

MAN 1. Excellent!

MAN 2. Why don't you say so in the theater?

MAN 3. Could that be the beginning of a plot?

DIRECTOR. An ending at any rate.

MAN 3. An ending brought about by fear.

DIRECTOR. Clearly, sir. You can't expect me to bring the mask onto the stage.

MAN 1. Why not?

DIRECTOR. What about morality? There's only so much spectators can stomach.

MAN 1. There are people who vomit when they see the underside of an octopus and others who grow pale if they hear the word "cancer" spoken in just the right tone. But you know the remedy for all that lies in tinfoil and papier-mâché and glittery mica and, when all else fails, in cardboard, which is readily available, even to those of modest means, as an artistic medium.

(He stands.)

But what you want is to trick us. To trick us so that everything stays the same and it becomes impossible for us to assist the dead. It's your fault that flies descended on the four thousand orange sodas I had ready to go. So I have to start tearing up roots once again.

DIRECTOR. *(Standing.)* I'm not going to argue, sir. What is it you want from me? Do you have a new play to show me?

MAN 1. Can you conceive of any play more novel than the three of us with our beards . . . and you?

DIRECTOR. Me . . . ?

MAN 1. Yes . . . you.

MAN 2. Gonzalo!

MAN 1. *(Looking at the DIRECTOR.)* I still recognize you, and it's as if I'm looking at you that morning you stuffed a swift-footed hare into a little book satchel. And that day you stuck two roses in your ears when you first parted your hair down the middle. And you, do you recognize me?

DIRECTOR. This isn't the way the plot goes. Jesus!

(Shouting.)

Helen! Helen!

(He rushes to the door.)

MAN 1. Well I'm going to bring you onto the stage, like it or not. I've suffered too much because of you. Soon! Bring the screen! The screen!

(MAN 3 brings a folding screen and places it in the center of the stage.)

DIRECTOR. *(Crying.)* The audience will see me. My theater will be destroyed. I produced the best plays of the season, but now . . . !

(The HORSES' trumpets are heard. MAN 1 walks to the back of the stage and opens the door.)

MAN 1. Come inside, with us. There's a place for you in the play. For everyone.

[Enter the HORSES.]

(To the DIRECTOR.) And you, go behind the screen.

(MAN 2 and MAN 3 push the DIRECTOR behind the screen. He comes out on the other side as a BOY, played by an actress, dressed in white satin with a white ruffle around his neck. He carries a small black guitar.)

MAN 1. Enrique! Enrique!

(He buries his face in his hands.)

MAN 2. Don't make me go behind the screen. Let me be. Gonzalo!

DIRECTOR. *(Coldly, as he strums the guitar.)* Gonzalo, I should spit in your face. I want to spit in your face and shred your tuxedo with tiny scissors. Give me some silk and a needle. I want to embroider. I don't like tattoos, but I want to embroider you with silk.

MAN 3. *(To the HORSES.)* Be seated wherever you like.

MAN 1. *(Crying.)* Enrique! Enrique!

DIRECTOR. I will embroider on your flesh, and I will enjoy seeing you sleep on the roof. How much money do you have in your pocket? Burn it!

(MAN 1 lights a match and burns the bills.)

I can never quite make out how the images disappear in the flame. You don't have any more money? What a pauper you are, Gonzalo! What about my lipstick? Don't you have any? What a pain.

MAN 2. *(Timidly.)* I have some.

(He takes a lipstick from under his beard and offers it.)

DIRECTOR. Thank you . . . but . . . so you're here too? Get behind the screen! Behind the screen. You still put up with him, Gonzalo?

(The DIRECTOR shoves MAN 2 behind the screen, and he comes out as a WOMAN dressed in black pajama bottoms with a crown of poppies on her head. In her hand she carries a pair of eyeglasses attached to a blond mustache, which she will place over her mouth at various points in the play.)

MAN 2. *(Coldly.)* Give me the lipstick.

DIRECTOR. Ha, ha, ha! Oh, Maximiliana, Empress of Bavaria! Oh, you evil woman!

MAN 2. *(Placing the mustache over his mouth.)* I would recommend a bit of silence.

DIRECTOR. You evil woman! Helen! Helen!

MAN 1. *(Angrily.)* Don't call Helen.

DIRECTOR. Well why not? She really loved me when my theater was in the open air. Helen!

(Enter HELEN from the left, dressed in ancient Greek style. She has blue eyebrows, white hair, and plaster feet. Her dress, completely open in front, reveals thighs wrapped in tight pink mesh. MAN 2 brings his mustache to his lips.)

HELEN. At it again?

DIRECTOR. Again.

MAN 3. Why did you come out, Helen? Why did you come out if you're not going to love me?

HELEN. Who told you that? But why do you love me so? I'd kiss your feet if you'd punish me and run off with the other women. But you're too fixated on me alone. We're going to have to end this once and for all.

DIRECTOR. *(To MAN 3.)* What about me? Don't you remember me? Don't you remember my ripped-out fingernails? How would I have met the other women and not you? Why did I call you out here, Helen? Why did I call you, my tormenter?

HELEN. *(To MAN 3.)* Go ahead, run off with him! And confess the truth you've been hiding from me. I don't care if you were drunk and use that as your excuse, but you kissed him and slept in the same bed.

MAN 3. Helen!

(He rushes behind the screen and reappears beardless, his face deathly pale, and holding a whip in his hand. He wears leather wrist cuffs with gold spikes.)

MAN 3. *(Striking the DIRECTOR with the whip.)* You're always talking, you're always lying, and I'm going to finish you off without the slightest bit of mercy.

HORSES. Mercy! Mercy!

HELEN. You could beat him for a whole century and I would never believe you.

(MAN 3 approaches HELEN and grabs her wrists.)

You could squeeze my fingers for a whole century and you wouldn't get a single whimper out of me.

MAN 3. We'll see who's boss here.

HELEN. Me. Always me.

(Enter the SERVANT.)

HELEN. Get me out of here now! I want to run away with you! Take me!

(The SERVANT goes behind the screen and comes out unchanged.)

Take me! Far away!

(The SERVANT takes her in his arms.)

DIRECTOR. We can begin now.

MAN 1. Whenever you like.

HORSES. Mercy! Mercy!

(The HORSES play their giant trumpets. The characters remain rigidly in place.)

—SLOW CURTAIN—

Tableau 2

(*Roman ruins. A FIGURE covered completely in red GRAPEVINES sits atop a pillar playing a flute. Another FIGURE, covered in tiny gold BELLS, dances in the center of the stage.*)

BELL FIGURE.   What if I turned into a cloud?

GRAPEVINE FIGURE.   I would turn into an eye.

BELL FIGURE.   And if I turned into dung?

GRAPEVINE FIGURE.   I would turn into a fly.

BELL FIGURE.   And if I turned into an apple?

GRAPEVINE FIGURE.   I would turn into a kiss.

BELL FIGURE.   And if I turned into a breast?

GRAPEVINE FIGURE.   I would turn into a white sheet.

VOICE.   *(Sarcastically.)* Bravo!

BELL FIGURE.   And if I turned into a moonfish?

GRAPEVINE FIGURE.   I would turn into a knife.

BELL FIGURE.   *(Ceasing the dance.)* But why? Why do you torment me? Why won't you follow me, if you love me, wherever I take you? If I turned into a moonfish, you would turn into an ocean wave or a strand of algae or, if you prefer something really far away because you don't want to kiss me, then a full moon. But a knife! You just love interrupting my dance. And dancing is the only way I have of loving you.

GRAPEVINE FIGURE.   When you circle the bed and the items in the house, I follow you, but I'm not going to follow you to the places you want to take me so full of cunning. If you turned into a moonfish I would cut you open with a knife because I'm a man, because I'm nothing more than that, a man, more man than Adam, and I want you to be even more man than I. So manly that the tree branches fall quiet when you pass by. But you're not a man. If I didn't have this flute you'd fly away to the moon, the moon that's covered in lacy little handkerchiefs and drops of woman blood.

BELL FIGURE.   *(Timidly.)* What if I turned into an ant?

GRAPEVINE FIGURE.   *(Exuberantly.)* I would turn into dirt.

BELL FIGURE.   *(More forcefully.)* And if I turned into dirt?

GRAPEVINE FIGURE. *(Weakly.)* I would turn into water.

BELL FIGURE. *(Vibrantly.)* And if I turned into water?

GRAPEVINE FIGURE. *(Swooning.)* I would turn into a moonfish.

BELL FIGURE. *(Trembling.)* And if I turned into a moonfish?

GRAPEVINE FIGURE. *(Standing.)* I would turn into a knife. A knife sharpened across four long springs.

BELL FIGURE. Take me to the bath and drown me. It's the only way you'll see me naked. Do you think I'm afraid of blood? I know how to dominate you. You think I don't know you? I'm so good at dominating you that if I said, "What if I turned into a moonfish?" you would answer "I would turn into a sack of tiny fish eggs."

GRAPEVINE FIGURE. Take an axe and chop off my legs. Let the insects of the ruins come forth. Get out of here. I despise you. I wish you would sink deep down below. I spit at you.

BELL FIGURE. Is that what you want? Goodbye. Fine with me. If I go down through the ruins I will only find more and more love.

GRAPEVINE FIGURE. *(Upset.)* Where are you going? Where are you going?

BELL FIGURE. Don't you want me to go away?

GRAPEVINE FIGURE. *(In a weak voice.)* No, don't go. What if I turned into a little grain of sand?

BELL FIGURE. I would turn into a whip.

GRAPEVINE FIGURE. And if I turned into a sack of tiny fish eggs?

BELL FIGURE. I would turn into another whip. A whip made of guitar strings.

GRAPEVINE FIGURE. Don't whip me!

BELL FIGURE. A whip made of sailing rope.

GRAPEVINE FIGURE. Don't strike my belly!

BELL FIGURE. A whip made of orchid stamens.

GRAPEVINE FIGURE. You'll end up blinding me!

BELL FIGURE. Blind, because you're not a man. *I* am a man. A man so manly that I faint when the hunters wake up. A man so manly that I feel a sharp pain in my teeth when someone snaps a plant stalk, no matter how small. A giant. A giant so gigantic that I can embroider a rose on the fingernail of a newborn baby.

GRAPEVINE FIGURE. I'm upset by the whiteness of the ruins and await nightfall so I can drag myself before your feet.

BELL FIGURE. No. No. Why are you telling me that? You're the one who's supposed to make me do that. Aren't you a man? A man more man than Adam?

GRAPEVINE FIGURE. *(Falling to the ground.)* Oh! Oh!

BELL FIGURE. *(Approaching in a low voice.)* What if I turned into a pillar?

GRAPEVINE FIGURE. Oh, miserable me!

BELL FIGURE. You would turn into the shadow of a pillar, nothing more. And then Helen would come to my bed. Helen, my sweetheart! And you would be stretched out beneath the mattress, bathed in sweat, a sweat that belonged not to you but to coach drivers, fire stokers, and cancer surgeons. And then I would turn into a moonfish and you would be nothing more than a tiny powder case that passes from hand to hand.

GRAPEVINE FIGURE. Oh!

BELL FIGURE. Again? You're crying again? I'll have to faint so the fieldworkers will come. I'll have to summon the Negroes, the enormous Negroes scarred by yucca blades, who struggle day and night in the river muck. Get off the ground, coward. Yesterday I was at the foundryman's house and ordered a chain. Don't turn away from me! A chain. And I stayed up all night crying because my wrists and ankles ached even though I wasn't wearing it.

(The GRAPEVINE FIGURE blows a silver whistle.)

What are you doing?

(He blows the whistle again.)

I know what you want, but I have time to flee.

GRAPEVINE FIGURE. *(Standing.)* Flee if you like.

BELL FIGURE. I'll defend myself with the weeds.

GRAPEVINE FIGURE. Try it.

(He blows the whistle. A BOY dressed in red mesh falls from the roof.)

BOY. The Emperor! The Emperor! The Emperor!

GRAPEVINE FIGURE. The Emperor.

BELL FIGURE. I'll play your role. Don't show yourself. It would cost me my life.

BOY. The Emperor! The Emperor! The Emperor!

BELL FIGURE. Everything we were doing was a game. We were playing. And now I'll imitate your voice and serve the Emperor. You can crouch down behind that big pillar. I never told you that. There's a cow over there cooking food for the soldiers.

GRAPEVINE FIGURE. The Emperor! It's no use. You've snapped the spider's thread and I feel my huge feet becoming tiny and disgusting.

BELL FIGURE. Do you want some tea? Where can I find a hot beverage in these ruins?

BOY. *(On the ground.)* The Emperor! The Emperor! The Emperor!

(A horn blasts and the Roman EMPEROR appears, accompanied by a yellow-robed CENTURION with gray flesh. Behind them are the four HORSES with their trumpets. The BOY approaches the EMPEROR, who takes him in his arms. They disappear among the pillars.)

CENTURION. The Emperor seeks one.

GRAPEVINE FIGURE. I am one.

BELL FIGURE. I am one.

CENTURION. Which is it?

GRAPEVINE FIGURE. Me.

BELL FIGURE. Me.

CENTURION. The Emperor will determine which of the two is one. With a knife or a blast of spit. Damn you and all your kind. It's your fault I'm running back and forth and sleeping on sand. My wife is beautiful like a mountain. She gives birth in four or five places at a time and snores beneath the trees at midday. I have two hundred children. And I will have many more yet. Damn you and all your kind!

(The CENTURION spits and sings. A lengthy scream is heard behind the columns. The EMPEROR emerges wiping his forehead. He takes off a pair of black gloves, then a pair of red gloves, revealing a pair of classically white hands.)

EMPEROR. *(Disdainfully.)* Which of the two is one?

BELL FIGURE. I am, sire.

EMPEROR. One is one and always one. I've beheaded more than forty boys who wouldn't admit it.

CENTURION. (*Spitting.*) One is one and nothing more than one.

EMPEROR. And there aren't two.

CENTURION. Because if there were two, the Emperor wouldn't be out searching the roads.

EMPEROR. (*To the CENTURION.*) Strip them naked!

BELL FIGURE. I am one, sire. He's just a beggar in the ruins, searching for roots to eat.

EMPEROR. Step aside.

GRAPEVINE FIGURE. You know me. You know who I am.

(*He tears off the grapevines, revealing a naked white body made of plaster.*)

EMPEROR. (*Embracing him.*) One is one.

GRAPEVINE FIGURE. And always one. If you kiss me, I will open my mouth so you can thrust your sword down my throat.

EMPEROR. I'll do it.

GRAPEVINE FIGURE. And leave my loving head among the ruins. The head of one that was always one.

EMPEROR. (*Sighing.*) One.

CENTURION. (*To the EMPEROR.*) Not easy, but there you have it.

GRAPEVINE FIGURE. He has it because he will never be able to have it.

BELL FIGURE. Betrayal! Betrayal!

CENTURION. Shut your mouth, you filthy scum! Floor-licker!

BELL FIGURE. Gonzalo! Help me, Gonzalo!

(*The BELL FIGURE pulls at a column, which unfolds into the white screen of the first scene. From behind it emerge the three bearded MEN and the DIRECTOR.*)

MAN 1. Betrayal!

BELL FIGURE. He betrayed us!

DIRECTOR. Betrayal!

(*The EMPEROR remains locked in tight embrace with the GRAPEVINE FIGURE.*)

—CURTAIN—

Tableau 3

(A wall of sand. To the left, a transparent gelatin-like moon is painted on the wall. In the center, an enormous green lanceolate leaf.)

MAN 1. *(Entering.)* This isn't working. After what happened, it wouldn't be fair for me to go back to talking to children and observing the happiness of heaven.

MAN 2. This is an evil place.

DIRECTOR. Did you see the fight?

MAN 3. *(Entering.)* They must have died, both of them. I've never seen such a bloody banquet.

MAN 1. A pair of lions. A pair of demigods.

MAN 2. A pair of demigods if they didn't have anuses.

MAN 1. But the anus is man's punishment. The anus is man's failure, it is his shame and his death. They both had an anus and neither of them could fight against the pure beauty of marble, a marble whose shine preserves intimate desires sheltered by an immaculate façade.

MAN 3. When the moon comes out, the children of the countryside cluster together to defecate.

MAN 1. And behind the reeds, along the pond's moist shores, we found the tracks of the man who persecutes the freedom of the naked.

MAN 3. They must have died, both of them.

MAN 1. *(Exuberant.)* They must have triumphed.

MAN 3. How so?

MAN 1. By being men and not letting themselves get dragged astray by false desires. By being wholly men. Do you think a man can ever stop being a man?

MAN 2. Gonzalo!

MAN 1. They were defeated, and now everything will be a joke and a mockery to people.

MAN 3. Neither of them was a man. And neither are any of you. I'm disgusted by your company.

MAN 1. The Emperor is back there at the edge of the banquet. Why don't you go over and strangle him? I recognize your valor just as I justify your beauty. Why don't you rush over and sink your teeth into his neck?

DIRECTOR. Why don't you do it?

MAN 1. Because I can't, because I won't, because I am weak.

DIRECTOR. But he can, he will, he is strong.

(Raising his voice.)

The Emperor is in the ruins!

MAN 3. He who wishes to smell his breath shall go.

MAN 1. You!

MAN 3. I would need my whip to convince you.

MAN 1. You know I won't resist you, but I despise you for your cowardice.

MAN 2. Cowardice!

DIRECTOR. *(Angrily, looking at MAN 3.)* The Emperor who drinks our blood is in the ruins!

(MAN 3 buries his face in his hands.)

MAN 1. *(To the DIRECTOR.)* That's him, do you recognize him now? That's the brave man who flattens our veins into long fish bones in coffee shops and books. That's the man who loves the Emperor in secret and searches for him in the port taverns. Enrique, take a good look at his eyes. Note the tiny grape clusters that fall from his shoulders. He doesn't fool me. But I'm going to kill the Emperor now. Without a knife, with these fragile hands that are the envy of all women.

DIRECTOR. No, he'll do it! Just wait a bit.

(The MAN sits in a chair and cries.)

MAN 3. I wouldn't be able to show off my cloud-covered pajamas! Oh! You all are unaware that I've discovered a marvelous drink known only to few black men in Honduras.

DIRECTOR. That's where we should be instead of here: a musty swamp. Beneath the slime where dead frogs waste away.

MAN 2. *(Embracing MAN 1.)* Gonzalo, why do you love him so?

MAN 1. *(To the DIRECTOR.)* I will bring you the Emperor's head!

DIRECTOR. That will be a great present for Helen.

MAN 2.   Stay, Gonzalo, and allow me to wash your feet.

MAN 1.   The Emperor's head burns the bodies of all women.

DIRECTOR.   *(To MAN 1.)* But you don't know that Helen can polish her hands with phosphorus and lime. Get out of here with that knife! Helen, Helen, sweetheart!

MAN 3.   Forever my sweetheart! Let no one here mention Helen.

DIRECTOR.   *(Trembling.)* Let no one mention her. It's much better that we serenade ourselves. We can do so by forgetting the theater. Let no one mention her.

MAN 1.   Helen.

DIRECTOR.   *(To MAN 1.)* Shush! Later I'll be waiting behind the walls of the big warehouse. Shush.

MAN 1.   I prefer to finish once and for all. Helen!

(He begins to exit.)

DIRECTOR.   Hey, what if I turn into a tiny jasmine dwarf?

MAN 2.   *(To MAN 1.)* Come on! Don't let yourself be fooled. I'll go with you to the ruins.

DIRECTOR.   *(Embracing MAN 1.)* I would turn into a pill of anisette, a pill that would contain an extract of reeds from every river, and you would be a huge Chinese mountain covered in dainty living harps.

MAN 1.   *(Rolling his eyes.)* No, no. Then I wouldn't be a Chinese mountain. I would be a *bota* of old wine that fills the throat with leeches.

(They fight.)

MAN 3.   We should separate them.

MAN 2.   So they don't devour each other.

MAN 3.   Though it would mean my freedom.

(The DIRECTOR and MAN 1 fight silently.)

MAN 2.   But it would mean my death.

MAN 3.   But I have a slave . . .

MAN 2.   That's because I am a slave.

MAN 3.   But if we're both slaves, we can work together to break our chains.

MAN 1.   I'll call Helen!

DIRECTOR.   I'll call Helen!

MAN 1.   No, please!

DIRECTOR.   No, don't call her. I'll turn into whatever you desire.

(They disappear off to the right, still fighting.)

MAN 3.   We can push them and they'll fall into the well. That way you and I will be free.

MAN 2.   You'd be free. I'd be more a slave than ever.

MAN 3.   It doesn't matter. I'm going to push them. I'm dying to live in my green fields, to be a shepherd, to drink water from the rock.

MAN 2.   You forget that I can be strong when I want to. When I was a boy I yoked my father's oxen. My bones may be covered in tiny little orchids, but I have a layer of muscle that I use when I want to.

MAN 3.   *(Gently.)* It's much better for them and for us. Come on! The well is deep.

MAN 2.   I won't let you!

(They fight. MAN 2 pushes MAN 3 and they disappear across the stage. The wall of sand opens, revealing the tomb of Juliet in Verona. The design is realistic. Rosebushes and ivy. A moon. Juliet is stretched out in the tomb. She wears a white opera dress, open in the front to reveal breasts of pink celluloid.)

JULIET.   *(Jumping from the tomb.)* Please. I haven't come across a girlfriend this whole time, despite passing through over three thousand empty arches. A bit of help, please. A bit of help, please. A bit of help and an ocean of sleep.

(She sings.)

> An ocean of sleep.
> An ocean of blanched earth
> and vacant arches in the sky.
> My dress trailing from the ships,
> trailing through the algae,
> trailing through time.
> An ocean of ceaseless time.
> A beach of lumberjack worms
> and a crystal dolphin in the cherry trees.
> Oh, pure and terminal asbestos! Oh, ruins!
> Oh, archless solitude! Ocean of sleep!

(A clash of swords and voices grows toward the back of the stage.)

JULIET. More and more people every day. They're going to end up invading my tomb and occupying my own bed. I'm not interested in arguments about love or theater. What I want is to love.

WHITE HORSE 1. *(Entering with a sword in its hand.)* To love!

JULIET. Yes. A love that lasts only a moment.

WHITE HORSE 1. I've been waiting for you in the garden.

JULIET. You mean in the tomb.

WHITE HORSE 1. You're as mad as ever. Juliet, when will you understand the perfection of a single day? A day with a morning and an afternoon.

JULIET. And a night.

WHITE HORSE 1. Night is not day. And in a day you will manage to rid yourself of anguish and drive off the impassive marble walls.

JULIET. How?

WHITE HORSE 1. Mount my hindquarters.

JULIET. What for?

WHITE HORSE 1. *(Approaching.)* So I can take you away.

JULIET. Where to?

WHITE HORSE 1. To the dark. In the dark there are soft branches. The winged cemetery has a thousand surfaces of thickness.

JULIET. *(Trembling.)* And what will you give me there?

WHITE HORSE 1. I will give you the most unspoken part of the dark.

JULIET. The day?

WHITE HORSE 1. The shadowy moss. The sense of touch that devours small worlds with its fingertips.

JULIET. Weren't you the one who was going to show me the perfection of a day?

WHITE HORSE 1. To carry you into the night.

JULIET. *(Furiously.)* And what have I got to do with the night, you idiotic horse? What is there for me to learn from its stars or its drunks? I guess I'll have to use rat poison to rid myself of annoying people. But I don't want to kill the rats. They bring me tiny pianos and lacquer brushes.

WHITE HORSE 1.   Juliet, night is not a moment, but a moment can last all night.

JULIET.   *(Crying.)* Enough. I won't listen to you anymore. Why do you wish to carry me away? Deception is the word of love, the broken mirror, the footstep in water. Afterwards you'd leave me in my tomb again, as they all do when trying to convince their listeners that true love is impossible. I'm tired now, and I'm getting up to ask for help. Help against those who theorize about my heart or pry open my mouth with marble forceps. Help to drive them all from my tomb.

WHITE HORSE 1.   The day is a ghost that sits down.

JULIET.   But I have met women killed by the sun.

WHITE HORSE 1.   Understand me well: a single day in order to love every night.

JULIET.   That's what they all say! All of them! Men, trees, horses. I'm perfectly aware of everything you want to show me. The moon pushes softly against uninhabited houses, provokes the collapse of columns, and offers miniature torches to silkworms for boring into the hearts of cherries. The moon slips meningitis masks into bedrooms, fills pregnant wombs with cold water, and, if I'm not careful, hurls fistfuls of weeds at my shoulders. Stop looking at me, horse, with that desire I know so well. When I was a little girl in Verona I would watch the beautiful cows grazing in the meadow. Then I would see illustrations of them in my books, but I always remembered them when walking past butcher shops.

WHITE HORSE 1.   A love that lasts only a moment.

JULIET.   Yes, one minute in which Juliet is alive, overjoyed, free of the penetrating swarm of magnifying glasses. Juliet in the beginning, Juliet on the outskirts of the city.

(The clash of voices and swords reemerges at the back of the stage.)

WHITE HORSE 1.
>   Love. Loving. Love.
>   Love of the slippery slug, glug-glug,
>   antennae wriggling in the sun.
>   Love. Loving. Love.
>   Licking-horse love:
>   a block of salt and a tongue.

JULIET.   Yesterday there were forty of them and I was asleep. They all came: spiders, girls, and a young woman raped by a dog, covering herself with geraniums, but I was not worried. When nymphs speak of cheese, it's usually made from mermaid milk or clover, but now they number four: four boys who tried to outfit me with a little clay phallus and were determined to paint a mustache on my face.

WHITE HORSE 1.
    Love. Loving. Love.
    Ginido and the billy goat gruff,
    the mule and the slippery slug, glug-glug,
    antennae wriggling in the sun.
    Love. Loving. Love.
    Jupiter and the peacock in the hay,
    the horse in the cathedral, hear it neigh.

JULIET. Four boys, horse. It'd been a long time since I'd heard the sound of play, but I didn't wake up until the knives were gleaming.

(Enter the BLACK HORSE, wearing a crest of matching feathers and carrying a wheel in its hand.)

BLACK HORSE. Four boys? Everyone. A land of asphodels and another land of seeds. The dead continue to argue, and the living use scalpels. Everyone.

WHITE HORSE 1. On the shores of the Dead Sea grow beautiful ash apples, but the ash is tasty.

BLACK HORSE. Oh, the freshness! The pulp! The dew! I eat ash.

JULIET. No, the ash isn't tasty. Who speaks of ash?

WHITE HORSE 1. Not ash. I speak of ash in the form of apples.

BLACK HORSE. Form, form! Yearning of blood.

JULIET. Turmoil.

BLACK HORSE. Yearning of blood and ennui of the wheel.

(Enter the THREE WHITE HORSES. They carry long staffs of black lacquer.)

THREE WHITE HORSES. Form and ash. Ash and form. Mirror. And whoever can finish shall deposit a golden loaf of bread.

JULIET. *(Wringing her hands.)* Form and ash.

BLACK HORSE. Yes. You all know already how good I am at beheading doves. When someone says *rock* I hear *air*. When they say *air* I hear *emptiness*. When they say *emptiness* I hear *beheaded dove*.

WHITE HORSE 1.
> Love. Love. Love.
> The moon and the eggshell,
> the egg yolk and the moon,
> the eggshell and the cloud, how swell.

THREE WHITE HORSES. *(Beating the ground with their staffs.)*
> Love. Love. Love.
> Horse dung and the sun,
> the sun and the dead cow, what fun,
> the dung beetle and the sun.

BLACK HORSE. No matter how much you wave your staffs about, things won't happen any other way than how they're supposed to. Damn you! Troublemakers! It's your fault that I'm forced to go searching the forest for resin several times a week, to block out your noise and restore the silence that belongs to me.

> *(Persuasively.)*

> Go, Juliet. I've given you threaded sheets. Now a fine rain will begin to fall, crowned in ivy, that will dampen the skies and walls.

THREE WHITE HORSES. We have three black staffs.

WHITE HORSE 1. And a sword.

THREE WHITE HORSES. *(To Juliet.)* We'll have to pass through your womb to find the resurrection of the horses.

BLACK HORSE. Juliet, it's three in the morning. If you're not careful, people will close their doors and you won't get in.

THREE WHITE HORSES. She still has the meadow and the open mountains.

BLACK HORSE. Juliet, don't pay any attention to them. In the meadow you'll find the field-worker who eats his snot, the gigantic foot that squashes the little mouse, and the army of earthworms that leaves the weeds covered in drool.

WHITE HORSE 1. She still has her firm little breasts, and besides, the bed for sleeping with horses has already been invented.

THREE WHITE HORSES. *(Shaking their staffs.)* And we want to lie down.

WHITE HORSE 1. With Juliet. I was in the tomb on the last night, and I know everything that happened.

THE THREE WHITE HORSES. *(Furiously.)* We want to lie down!

WHITE HORSE 1.   Because we are real horses, stagecoach horses. Our stiff members have shattered wooden mangers and stable windows.

THREE WHITE HORSES.   Take off your clothes, Juliet, and wave your rump in the air so we can whip it with our tails. We need resuscitation!

(*JULIET cringes behind the BLACK HORSE.*)

BLACK HORSE.   Madwoman! Beyond mad!

JULIET.   *(Composing herself.)* I'm not afraid of any of you. You want to lie with me, right? Well now I'm the one who wants to lie with you, but I'll be giving the orders, running the show, riding you, clipping your manes with my scissors.

BLACK HORSE.   Who's passing through whom? Oh, love, love, you need to pierce the dark heat with your light! Oh ocean braced by shadow, oh flower in the dead man's ass!

JULIET.   *(Feistily.)* I'm not a slave girl who gets amber awls plunged into her breasts. Nor am I an oracle for those who tremble with love upon leaving the city. My dream has always been the smell of fig trees and the torso of the wheat harvester. No one passes through me! I pass through you!

BLACK HORSE.   Sleep, sleep, sleep.

THREE WHITE HORSES.   *(They squeeze their staffs. Three spouts of water gush from the tips.)* We urinate on you, we urinate on you. We urinate on you as we urinate on the mares, as the she-goat urinates on the snout of her mate, and as the sky urinates on magnolias to turn them to leather.

BLACK HORSE.   *(To Juliet.)* Back to your spot. No one will pass through you.

JULIET.   Shall I keep quiet then? A newborn baby is beautiful.

THREE WHITE HORSES.   It is beautiful. And it would drag its little tail across the whole sky.

(*MAN 1 and the DIRECTOR enter on the right. The DIRECTOR appears as in the beginning, transformed into a white HARLEQUIN.*)

MAN 1.   Enough, gentlemen!

DIRECTOR.   Open-air theater!

WHITE HORSE 1.   No. We have just inaugurated the true theater. The theater beneath the sand.

BLACK HORSE.   So the truth of tombs may be known to all.

THREE WHITE HORSES.   Tombs with advertisements, spotlights, and long rows of orchestra seats.

MAN 1.   Yes! We've taken the first step. But I know for a fact that three of you are hiding, that three of you are still swimming on the surface.

(The THREE WHITE HORSES cluster together uneasily.)

You're so used to the coach driver's whip and the farrier's forceps, you're afraid of the truth.

BLACK HORSE.   When they've stripped off the last suit of blood, the truth will be a nettle, a devoured crab, or a strip of leather behind glass.

MAN 1.   They must disappear immediately from this place. They're afraid of the audience. I know the truth, I know they don't want Juliet and that they hide a desire that wounds me and that I can read in their eyes.

BLACK HORSE.   Not *a* desire. All desires. Like you.

MAN 1.   I have only one desire.

WHITE HORSE 1.   Just like horses, no one forgets their mask.

MAN 1.   I don't have a mask.

DIRECTOR.   There's nothing more than mask. I was right, Gonzalo. If we poke fun at the mask, it will hang us from a tree like that boy in America.

JULIET.   *(Crying.)* Mask!

WHITE HORSE 1.   Form.

DIRECTOR.   In the open street, the mask buttons us up tight and shades the ill-advised blush that sometimes rises in our cheeks. In the bedroom, when we stick our fingers in our nose or delicately explore our back sides, the plaster of the mask oppresses our flesh to such a degree that we can barely stretch out on the bed.

MAN 1.   *(To the DIRECTOR.)* I've been struggling with the mask in order to see you naked.

(He embraces him.)

WHITE HORSE 1.   *(Mocking.)* A lake is a surface.

MAN 1.   *(Irritated.)* Or a volume!

WHITE HORSE 1.   *(Laughing.)* A volume contains a thousand surfaces.

DIRECTOR. *(To MAN 1.)* Don't hug me, Gonzalo. Your love lives only in the presence of witnesses. Didn't you kiss me enough in the ruins? I despise your elegance and your drama.

(They struggle.)

MAN 1. I show my love for you in front of the others because I abhor the mask and because I've finally managed to rip it off you.

DIRECTOR. Why am I so weak?

MAN 1. *(Struggling.)* I love you.

DIRECTOR. *(Struggling.)* I spit on you.

JULIET. They're fighting!

BLACK HORSE. It's called love.

THREE WHITE HORSES.
> Love, love, love.
> Love of the one for the two
> and love of the three who drowns
> to be one among the two.

MAN 1. I'll strip your skeleton bare.

DIRECTOR. My skeleton has seven lights.

MAN 1. Easy prey for my seven hands.

DIRECTOR. My skeleton has seven shadows.

THREE WHITE HORSES. Stop it, stop it.

WHITE HORSE 1. *(To MAN 1.)* I order you to stop.

(The HORSES separate MAN 1 and the DIRECTOR.)

DIRECTOR. Slave to a lion, I can be friends with a horse.

WHITE HORSE 1. *(Embracing him.)* Love.

DIRECTOR. I'll stick my hands into deep sacks to hurl coins and large quantities of breadcrumbs into the mud.

JULIET. *(To the BLACK HORSE.)* Please!

BLACK HORSE. *(Uneasily.)* Wait.

MAN 1. The time's not yet right for the horses to carry away a naked man that I turned white with my tears.

(THREE WHITE HORSES corner MAN 1.)

MAN 1. Enrique!

DIRECTOR. Enrique? Enrique is over there.

(He quickly removes his costume and throws it behind a column. Beneath it he wears a subtle BALLERINA COSTUME. From behind the column Enrique's costume reappears. It's the same white HARLEQUIN COSTUME with a pale yellow mask.)

HARLEQUIN COSTUME. I'm cold. Electric lights. Bread. They were burning rubber.

(It goes rigid.)

DIRECTOR. *(To MAN 1.)* You won't come with me now? Then with Guillermina the horse-woman!

WHITE HORSE 1. Moon and vixen and tavern bottle.

DIRECTOR. There will be space for you all, and for the ships and the regiments. And if you like, the storks will fit too. I'm a wide woman!

THREE WHITE HORSES. Guillermina!

DIRECTOR. Not Guillermina. I'm not Guillermina. I'm Dominga of the little Negroes.

(He rips off his costume to reveal a leotard covered in tiny bells. He throws the costume behind the column and disappears, followed by the HORSES. The BALLERINA COSTUME emerges from behind the column.)

BALLERINA COSTUME. Gui - guiller - guillermi - guillermina. Na - nami - namiller - namillergui. Let me in or let me out.

(It falls to the ground, asleep.)

MAN 1. Enrique, careful with the stairs!

DIRECTOR. *(Offstage.)* Moon and vixen to drunken sailors.

JULIET. *(To the BLACK HORSE.)* Give me the sleeping potion.

BLACK HORSE. Sand.

MAN 1. *(Shouting.)* A moonfish, I just want you to be a moonfish! I want you to turn into a moonfish!

(He exits violently at the back of the stage.)

HARLEQUIN COSTUME. Enrique. Electric lights. Bread. They were burning rubber.

(Enter on the left MAN 2 and MAN 3. MAN 2 is the WOMAN in black pajamas and poppies from Tableau 1. MAN 3 is unchanged.)

MAN 2. He loves me so much that if he sees us together he could murder us. Let's go. I'll serve you forever now.

MAN 3. You were so lovely beneath the columns.

JULIET. *(To the couple.)* We're closing the door.

MAN 2. The door to the theater never closes.

JULIET. It's raining hard, my girl.

(It begins to rain. MAN 3 reaches into his pocket and takes out his mask with a passionate expression, raising it to his face.)

MAN 3. *(Gallantly.)* Couldn't I stay here and spend the night?

JULIET. What for?

MAN 3. To ravish you.

(He talks to her.)

MAN 2. *(To the BLACK HORSE.)* Did you see a man leave with a black beard and hair, wearing leather shoes that were kind of squeaky?

BLACK HORSE. Never saw him.

MAN 3. *(To JULIET.)* And who better than I to protect you?

JULIET. And who more worthy of love than your girlfriend?

MAN 3. My girlfriend?

(Furiously.)

I'm always missing out because of you all! This isn't my girlfriend. It's a mask, a broom, a sickly lapdog.

(He aggressively strips off the pajamas and wig. MAN 2 appears without a beard, in the outfit from Tableau 1.)

MAN 2. For pity's sake!

MAN 3. *(To JULIET.)* I had him in disguise to protect him from bandits. Kiss my hand, kiss the hand of your protector.

(Enter the PAJAMA COSTUME with the crown of poppies. The face of this character is white and smooth and bulges like an ostrich egg. MAN 3 pushes MAN 2 offstage to the right.)

MAN 2. *[Exiting.]* For pity's sake!

(The PAJAMA COSTUME sits on the stairs and slowly strikes its smooth face with its hands until the end.)

MAN 3. *(He reaches into his pocket and takes out a large red cape, which he places over his shoulders, enveloping JULIET.)*
> Look, love, what envious streaks
> Do lace the severing clouds in yonder East.
> The wind splits the cypress branches . . .

JULIET. That's not how it goes!

MAN 3. . . . and in India visits all women who have hands of water.

BLACK HORSE. *(Shaking the wheel.)* It's going to close!

JULIET. How hard it rains!

MAN 3. Wait, wait. The nightingale is about to sing.

JULIET. *(Trembling.)* The nightingale, my God! The nightingale . . . !

BLACK HORSE. Don't be surprised!

(He seizes her quickly and stretches her out in the tomb.)

JULIET. *(Falling asleep.)* The nightingale . . . !

BLACK HORSE. *(Exiting.)* Tomorrow I'll come with the sand.

JULIET. Tomorrow.

MAN 3. *(Next to the tomb.)* Come back, my love! The wind shakes the maple leaves. What have you done?

(He embraces her.)

VOICE OFFSTAGE. Enrique!

HARLEQUIN COSTUME. Enrique.

BALLERINA COSTUME. Guillermina. Finish already!

(It cries.)

MAN 3. Wait, wait. The nightingale is about to sing.

(A ship's foghorn is heard in the distance. MAN 3 places his mask over JULIET's face and covers her body in the red cape.)

The rain is too heavy.

(He opens an umbrella and exits silently on tiptoe.)

MAN 1. *(Entering.)* Enrique, how did you get back here?

HARLEQUIN COSTUME. Enrique, how did you get back here?

MAN 1. Why are you making fun of me?

HARLEQUIN COSTUME. Why are you making fun of me?

MAN 1. *(Embracing the HARLEQUIN COSTUME.)* You were supposed to come back for me, for my inexhaustible love, after defeating the weeds and the horses.

HARLEQUIN COSTUME. The horses!

MAN 1. Tell me, tell me you've come back for me!

HARLEQUIN COSTUME. *(In a weak voice.)* I'm cold. Electric lights. Bread. They were burning rubber.

MAN 1. *(Aggressively embracing the HARLEQUIN COSTUME.)* Enrique!

HARLEQUIN COSTUME. *(In a weaker and weaker voice.)* Enrique.

BALLERINA COSTUME. *(In a flagging voice.)* Guillermina.

MAN 1. *(Hurling the HARLEQUIN COSTUME to the ground and ascending the stairs.)* Enriqueee!

HARLEQUIN COSTUME. *(On the ground.)* Enriqueeeeee.

(The figure with the egg face strikes itself incessantly. Over the sound of the rain is heard the song of the true nightingale.)

—CURTAIN—

Tableau 4

(At center stage a bed stands on end and facing the audience, as in a primitivist painting. On the bed is a naked red man with a crown of blue thorns. In the background are arches and stairways that lead to the balcony of an elegant theater. To the right stands the front gate of a university. As the curtain rises, a round of applause is heard.)

NAKED MAN. When are you going to finish?

MALE NURSE. *(Entering quickly)* When the raucous dies down.

NAKED MAN. What do they want?

MALE NURSE. They're demanding the death of the director.

NAKED MAN.   What do they say about me?

MALE NURSE.   Nothing.

NAKED MAN.   What about Gonzalo? Do you know what happened to him?

MALE NURSE.   They're searching for him in the ruins.

NAKED MAN.   I want to die. How many cups of blood have you drawn from me?

MALE NURSE.   Fifty. I'm going to give you the vinegar now, and then at eight I'll come with the scalpel and probe that wound on your side.

NAKED MAN.   It's the one with the most vitamins.

MALE NURSE.   Yes.

NAKED MAN.   Did they let the people out from beneath the sand?

MALE NURSE.   On the contrary. The soldiers and engineers are blocking all the exits.

NAKED MAN.   How far to Jerusalem?

MALE NURSE.   Three more stations, if there's enough coal.

NAKED MAN.   Father, take this cup of suffering away from me.

MALE NURSE.   Shut up. This is already the third thermometer you've broken.

(Enter four STUDENTS. They wear black gowns and red hoods.

STUDENT 1.   Can't we saw through the bars?

STUDENT 2.   The alley is full people with weapons. It won't be easy to escape that way.

STUDENT 3.   What about the horses?

STUDENT 1.   The horses managed to escape by breaking through the roof of the set.

STUDENT 4.   When I was locked in the tower I saw them going up the hill together. They were with the director.

STUDENT 1.   Doesn't the theater have an orchestra pit?

STUDENT 2.   Even that is overrun by the audience. It's better to stay put.

(Another round of applause is heard. The MALE NURSE shifts the NAKED MAN on the bed and arranges his pillows.)

NAKED MAN.   I'm thirsty.

MALE NURSE. We've already requested water from the theater.

STUDENT 4. The first bomb from the mob blew the head off the rhetoric professor.

STUDENT 2. To the great joy of his wife, who'll now be working so hard she'll have to attach two faucets to her tits.

STUDENT 3. They say that at night a horse would go with her up to the balcony.

STUDENT 1. She was the one who saw what was happening, through a skylight in the theater, and sounded the alarm.

STUDENT 4. And though the writers grabbed a ladder to kill her, she kept screaming, and the crowd came running.

STUDENT 2. And her name is?

STUDENT 3. Helen.

STUDENT 1. *(Aside.)* Selen.

STUDENT 2. *(To STUDENT 1.)* What's the matter?

STUDENT 1. I'm afraid to go outside.

(Two THIEVES descend the stairs. Four LADIES in evening dresses come rushing from the balcony. The STUDENTS argue.)

LADY 1. Do you think the coaches are still at the door?

LADY 2. This is horrible!

LADY 3. They found the director in the tomb.

LADY 1. What about Romeo?

LADY 4. They were stripping him naked when we left.

BOY 1. The audience wants the author drawn and quartered by the horses.

LADY 1. But why? It was a delightful play, and the mob has no right to desecrate tombs.

LADY 2. The voices were vivacious, as were the costumes. What need was there to lick the skeletons clean?

BOY 1. You're right. The tomb scene was amazing. But I discovered the lie when I saw Juliet's feet. They were so small.

LADY 2. Delightful! You're not going to find fault with that, are you?

BOY 1. Yes. They were too small for a woman's feet. Too perfect and too feminine. They were a man's feet, feet invented by a man.

LADY 2. Ghastly!

(The sound of voices and swords is heard in the theater.)

LADY 3. Are we going to be able to get out?

BOY 1. The mob is on its way to the cathedral. Let's go up the stairs.

(Exit [BOY 1 and LADIES].)

STUDENT 4. The commotion began when they saw that Romeo and Juliet really loved each other.

STUDENT 2. Actually it was just the opposite. The commotion began when they realized that they didn't love each other, that they could never love each other.

STUDENT 4. The audience is wise enough to figure it all out and that's why they protested.

STUDENT 2. Exactly right. The skeletons loved each other and were yellow with flame, but the costumes didn't love each other, and on several occasions the audience glimpsed the train of Juliet's dress covered in disgusting little toads.

STUDENT 4. People forget about costumes in a play, and the mob formed when they found the real Juliet bound and gagged under the chairs and covered in cotton so she wouldn't scream.

STUDENT 1. That's the big mistake everyone makes, and it's the reason theater is dying. The audience isn't meant to cross through the silk and papier-mâché the author dreams up in his bedroom. Romeo could be a bird and Juliet could be a stone. Romeo could be a grain of salt and Juliet could be a map. What does this matter to the audience?

STUDENT 4. It doesn't. But a bird can't be a cat, nor can a stone be an ocean breaker.

STUDENT 2. It's a question of form, of masks. A cat can be a frog, and the winter moon can easily be a cord of firewood covered in frostbitten worms. The audience is meant to be entranced by words and isn't supposed to see through the columns to the bleating sheep and the clouds moving across the sky.

STUDENT 4. That's why the mob formed. The director opened the trapdoors, and the people were able to see how the poison of false veins had caused the real death of so many children. It's not the costumed figures that bring about life but rather the barometer hair that lies behind them.

STUDENT 2. At any rate, do Romeo and Juliet have to be a man and a woman for the tomb scene to feel real and terrifying?

STUDENT 1. Not necessarily, and that's what the director tried to show so ingeniously.

STUDENT 4. *(Annoyed.)* Not necessarily? Then stop the machinery and throw the grains of wheat onto a field of steel.

STUDENT 2. And what would happen? Mushrooms would sprout up, and people's pulses might grow even more intense and passionate. The thing is, we know what nourishes a grain of wheat; we don't know what nourishes a mushroom.

STUDENT 5. *(Entering from the balcony.)* The judge is here, and before executing them, he's going to make them replay the tomb scene.

STUDENT 4. Let's go. You'll see that I'm right.

STUDENT 2. Yes. Let's go watch the last truly feminine Juliet who will ever appear in theater.

(The STUDENTS exit quickly.)

NAKED MAN. Forgive them, Father, for they know not what they do.

MALE NURSE. *(To the THIEVES.)* Why are you here at this hour?

THIEVES. The prompter made a mistake.

MALE NURSE. Did they give you your injections?

THIEVES. Yes.

(They sit at the foot of the bed with lighted votive candles. The scene falls into shadow. Enter the PROMPTER.)

MALE NURSE. You're giving cues at this hour?

PROMPTER. I'm so sorry, but they couldn't find Joseph of Arimathea's beard.

MALE NURSE. Is the operating room ready?

PROMPTER. We're just waiting on the candlesticks, the chalice, and the vials of camphor oil.

MALE NURSE. Make it snappy.

(Exit the PROMPTER.)

NAKED MAN. How much longer?

MALE NURSE. Not much. They just rang the third bell. When the Emperor dresses as Pontius Pilate, it'll be time.

BOY 1. *(Entering with the LADIES.)* Please! Don't allow yourselves to give in to panic.

LADY 1. It's horrible to get lost in the theater and not find the exit.

LADY 2. What scared me the most was the cardboard wolf and the four serpents on the tinfoil pond.

LADY 3. As we were climbing through the ruins we thought we saw the light of dawn, but we tripped over the theater curtains and now my lamé slippers are stained with oil.

LADY 4. *(Peeking through the arches.)* They're playing the tomb scene again. The fire will surely break through the doors now. When I saw it just a second ago, the guards' hands were already scorched and they couldn't contain it.

BOY 1. From the branches of that tree we can reach one of the balconies and call for help from there.

MALE NURSE. *(Loudly.)* When are they going to sound the death knell?

(A bell sounds.)

THIEVES. *(Raising the candles.)* Holy. Holy. Holy.

NAKED MAN. Father, into your hands I commit my spirit.

MALE NURSE. You're two minutes ahead of yourself.

NAKED MAN. But the nightingale already sang.

MALE NURSE. That's true. And the pharmacies are open for the final agony.

NAKED MAN. For the final agony of man alone, on platforms and on trains.

MALE NURSE. *(Checking the clock. Loudly.)* Bring the sheet. Careful that the wind that's about to blow doesn't carry off your wigs. Hurry.

THIEVES. Holy. Holy. Holy.

NAKED MAN. 'Tis finished.

(The bed spins on its axis and the NAKED MAN disappears. On the other side lies MAN 1, still wearing his tuxedo and black beard.)

MAN 1. *(Closing his eyes.)* The agony!

(The light takes on a strong silvery tint, as on a movie screen. The arches and stairways in the background become bathed in a granular blue light. The MALE NURSE and the THIEVES exit with dance steps, without turning their backs to the audience. The STUDENTS enter beneath the arches. They carry small electric lanterns.)

STUDENT 4.   The attitude of the audience was detestable.

STUDENT 1.   Detestable. A spectator should never be part of the play. When people go to the aquarium they don't kill the sea snakes or the water rats or the leprous fish. Instead they glide their eyes over the glass and learn.

STUDENT 4.   Romeo was a thirty-year-old man and Juliet a fifteen-year-old boy. The audience complained vociferously.

STUDENT 2.   The director ingeniously prevented the mass of spectators from discovering that fact, but the horses and the mob destroyed his plans.

STUDENT 4.   What's unforgiveable is that they murdered them.

STUDENT 1.   And that they also murdered the real Juliet, who was groaning beneath the chairs.

STUDENT 4.   Out of pure curiosity, to see what they held on the inside.

STUDENT 3.   And what did they discover? A cluster of wounds and total disarray.

STUDENT 4.   The replay of the scene was marvelous because it was clear that they loved each other incalculably, even if I can't explain it. When the nightingale sang I couldn't suppress my tears.

STUDENT 3.   No one could. But then they raised their knives and staffs because the words were more powerful than they were, and when doctrine lets her hair down she fearlessly tramples the most innocent of truths.

STUDENT 5.   *(Ecstatically.)* Look, I got one of Juliet's shoes. The nuns were embalming her and I stole it.

STUDENT 4.   *(Soberly.)* Which Juliet?

STUDENT 5.   Which one do you think? The one who was on stage, the one with the most beautiful feet in the world.

STUDENT 4.   *(Astonished.)* But don't you realize that the Juliet who was at the tomb was a boy in costume, a special effect of the director, and that the real Juliet was bound and gagged beneath the chairs?

STUDENT 5.   *(Bursting into laughter.)* Well I liked her! I found her very beautiful, and if she was a boy in disguise I don't care one bit. On the other hand, I wouldn't have taken the shoe of that girl covered in dust who was screeching like a cat beneath the chairs.

STUDENT 3. And yet that's why they killed her.

STUDENT 5. Because they're insane. But I climb the mountain two times every day, and when the school day ends I tend an enormous herd of bulls that I have to fight with and beat down every second, so I don't have time to worry whether it's a man or a woman or a child. Just whether it fills me with joyful desire.

STUDENT 1. Perfect! And if I want to fall in love with a crocodile?

STUDENT 5. Go for it.

STUDENT 1. And if I want to fall in love with you?

STUDENT 5. *(Throwing the shoe at him.)* Go for that too. I'll let you, and I'll even carry you on my shoulders over the crags.

STUDENT 1. And we'll destroy everything.

STUDENT 5. The rooftops and the families.

STUDENT 1. And wherever there's talk of love we'll go in with football gear hurling mud onto mirrors.

STUDENT 5. And we'll burn the book from which priests say Mass.

STUDENT 1. Let's do it. Let's do it now!

STUDENT 5. I have four hundred bulls. With the ropes my father made we'll yoke them to the rocks so that they pull them apart and provoke a volcanic eruption.

STUDENT 1. Joy! Joy to boys and girls and frogs and tiny wooden blocks.

PROMPTER. *(Entering.)* Gentlemen! Descriptive geometry class.

MAN 1. The agony.

(The set falls into shadow. The STUDENTS light their lanterns and enter the university.)

PROMPTER. *(Disdainfully.)* Don't make the glass suffer!

STUDENT 5. *(Fleeing through the arches with STUDENT 1.)* Joy! Joy! Joy!

MAN 1. The agony. Solitude of a man in a dream full of elevators and trains where you're traveling at unattainable speeds. Solitude of buildings and corners and beaches that you will never again inhabit.

LADY 1.   (*Entering from the stairway.*) The same set all over again? It's horrible!

BOY 1.   One of these doors must be the right one!

LADY 2.   Please! Don't let go of my hand!

BOY 1.   When day breaks we'll guide ourselves by the skylights.

LADY 3.   I'm getting cold in this dress.

MAN 1.   (*In a weak voice.*) Enrique, Enrique!

LADY 1.   What was that?

BOY 1.   Shhh.

(*The scene is dark. The BOY's lantern illuminates MAN 1's dead face.*)

—CURTAIN—

Soliloquy of the Buffoon Shepherd

(*Blue curtain. At center stage stands a large armoire full of white masks of different expressions. Each mask has a light shining on it. The BUFFOON SHEPHERD enters from the right. Dressed in wild animal skins, he wears a funnel stuffed with feathers and tiny wheels on his head. He cranks the handle of a windup music box and dances to a slow rhythm.*)

SHEPHERD.
  The buffoon shepherd tends the asks-may.
  Asks-may
  of beggars and oets-pay
  who kill the osprey
  that flies over tranquil aters-way.
  Asks-may
  of children who with trifles play
  and beneath toadstools waste away.
  Asks-may
  of eagles with utches-cray.
  Mask of the ask-may
  made of Cretan aster-play
  and dusted in iolet-vay
  for the murder of uliet-Jay.
  Fortune-teller, fortune-peddler, fortune-outer-spay
  in a theater with no front-row eats-say

and a sky full of airs-chay
made from the hollow of an ask-may.
Bleat, bleat, bleat, O asks-may.

(The masks bleat like sheep with intermittent coughing.)

The horses eat the oadstool-tay
and beneath weathervanes waste away.
The eagles with trifles play
and muddy themselves beneath the omet-cay,
and the comet devours the osprey
that clawed at the poet's east-bray.
Bleat, bleat, bleat, O asks-may!
Europe pulls at her its-tay,
Asia is left without an eat-say,
and America is an ocodile-cray
with no need of an ask-may.
Musicky usic-may
of wounded quills and stubby ottles-bay.

(He pushes the armoire, which is mounted on wheels, and exits. The masks bleat.)

Tableau 5

(The same set as in Tableau 1. On the left, a giant horse head sits on the floor. On the right, an enormous eye and a cluster of trees and clouds are leaned against the wall. Enter the DIRECTOR with the CONJUROR. The CONJUROR wears a tuxedo, a white satin cape that reaches to his feet, and a top hat. The DIRECTOR is dressed as he was in Tableau 1.)

DIRECTOR.   A conjuror cannot resolve this matter. Neither can a doctor or an astronomer or anyone else. It's very easy to let lions loose and then rain sulfur on them. You needn't continue talking.

CONJUROR.   It occurs to me that you, a man of the mask, don't remember that we use a dark curtain.

DIRECTOR.   When people are in heaven. But tell me: What curtain can be used in a place where the wind is so violent that it strips people naked and even children carry little knives to slash the velvet?

CONJUROR.   Naturally, the conjuror's curtain presupposes an order behind the obscurity of the illusion, so why did you all select such a well-worn tragedy instead of putting on an original play?

DIRECTOR. To show what happens every day in every big city as well as in the countryside, with a case that occurred only once and that everyone accepts despite its originality. I could have chosen *Oedipus* or *Othello*. In contrast, if I'd raised the curtain with the original truth, the seats would have run with blood from the very first scene.

CONJUROR. If your troupe had employed the love-in-idleness that the anguished Shakespeare used to ironic effect in *A Midsummer Night's Dream*, the performance probably would've been successful. If love is pure chance and Titania, queen of the fairies, can fall in love with an ass, by the same logic Gonzalo should be able to have a drink in the music hall with a kneeling boy dressed in white.

DIRECTOR. Please stop talking, I beg you.

CONJUROR. What you should do is build a proscenium arch of wire, a curtain, and a tree with fresh leaves; then raise and lower the curtain on cue and no one will be surprised that the tree turns into a serpent's egg. What you were trying to do was kill the dove and leave in its place a piece of marble covered in wisps of talking spit.

DIRECTOR. It was impossible to do anything else. My friends and I dug a tunnel beneath the sand without the city residents noticing. We were helped by many workers and students who now deny it despite having their hands covered in scratches. When we got to the tomb we raised the curtain.

CONJUROR. And what kind of theater can emerge from a tomb?

DIRECTOR. All theater comes from confined dampness. All true theater has that deep, rotten-moon stink. When costumes speak, living people become bone buttons on Calvary's wall. I dug the tunnel to take over the costumes and, through them, to show the outlines of a dark force at a point when the audience, full of interest and overcome by the plot, would have no choice but to pay attention.

CONJUROR. It's a simple thing for me to transform an inkwell into a severed hand heavy with ancient rings.

DIRECTOR. *(Annoyed.)* But that's a lie. That's theater! If I spent three days fighting against roots and riptides, it was to destroy the theater.

CONJUROR. I thought so.

DIRECTOR. And to show that if Romeo and Juliet wither and die only to wake up smiling when the curtain falls, my characters, in contrast, burn down the curtain and die for real in the presence of the spectators. The horses, the ocean, the army of weeds prevented it. But some day, when all theaters are burned down, you will find the assembly of our dead—on sofas, behind mirrors, and in goblets of golden cardboard—locked up there by the audience. You have to destroy the theater or live in the theater! It won't do to whistle from the windows. And if the dogs whimper tenderly, then you have to raise the curtain without prejudice. I knew a man who swept his rooftop and dusted the skylights and railings just out of politeness to heaven.

CONJUROR. Take one more step, and man will be nothing to you but a blade of grass.

DIRECTOR. Not a blade of grass. A navigator.

CONJUROR. I can transform a navigator into a sewing needle.

DIRECTOR. That's exactly what happens in the theater. That's why I dared to attempt such a difficult poetic game, hoping that love would rip the costumes to shreds and imbue them with new form.

CONJUROR. When you say love, it astonishes me.

DIRECTOR. What astonishes you about that?

CONJUROR. I see a landscape of sand reflected in a darkened mirror.

DIRECTOR. What else?

CONJUROR. A dawn that never comes.

DIRECTOR. Perhaps.

CONJUROR. *(Disdainfully, tapping the horse head with his fingertips.)* Love.

DIRECTOR. *(Taking a seat at the table.)* When you say love, it astonishes me.

CONJUROR. What astonishes you about that?

DIRECTOR. I see each grain of sand turning into the liveliest of ants.

CONJUROR. What else?

DIRECTOR. A night that falls every five minutes.

CONJUROR. *(Staring at him.)* Perhaps.

(Pause.)

But what can be expected from people who inaugurate a theater beneath the sand? If you opened that door this place would be swarming with mastiffs, with madmen, with falling rain, with monstrous leaves, with sewer rats. Who ever heard of breaking down all doors in a play?

DIRECTOR.   Breaking down all doors is the only way drama can justify itself. That's how it comes to see with its own eyes that the law is a wall that dissolves in the tiniest drop of blood. I'm disgusted by the dying man who draws a door on the wall with his finger and peacefully goes to sleep. True drama is a circus of arches through which the wind and the moon and living creatures come and go, with nowhere to rest. You are walking upon a stage where authentic plays were performed and where a real battle cost the lives of all the actors.

(He breaks into tears.)

SERVANT.   *(Rushing in.)* Sir.

DIRECTOR.   What is it?

(Enter the white HARLEQUIN COSTUME and a MOTHER dressed in black with her face obscured by a thick veil.)

MOTHER.   Where's my son?

DIRECTOR.   What son?

MOTHER.   My son Gonzalo.

DIRECTOR.   *(Annoyed.)* When the performance ended he rushed into the orchestra pit with that boy standing next to you. Later the prompter saw him lying on the king-size bed in the dressing room. Don't ask me where he is. Today all of that is below ground.

HARLEQUIN COSTUME.   *(Crying.)* Enrique.

MOTHER.   Where is my son? This morning the fishermen brought me an enormous moonfish, pale and decomposed, and shouted: Here's your son! An endless trickle of blood spilled from the fish's mouth, and the children laughed and painted the soles of their boots red. When I closed my door I could hear the people from the markets dragging it toward the sea.

HARLEQUIN COSTUME.   Toward the sea.

DIRECTOR.   The performance ended hours ago and I have no responsibility for what happened afterwards.

MOTHER.   I will lodge my complaint and make a public call for justice.

(She begins her exit.)

CONJUROR.   Madam, you can't get out that way.

MOTHER.   Oh, right. The vestibule is in complete darkness.

(She turns to go out the door on the right.)

DIRECTOR.   That way won't work either. You would fall through the skylights.

CONJUROR.   Madam, if you'd be so kind, I will lead you out.

> (*He takes off his cape and covers the MOTHER with it. He waves his hands over the cape two or three times, pulls at it, and the MOTHER disappears. The SERVANT pushes the HARLEQUIN COSTUME out the door on the left. The CONJUROR takes out a gigantic white fan and begins fanning himself as he sings softly.*)

DIRECTOR.   I'm cold.

CONJUROR.   What's that?

DIRECTOR.   I said I'm cold.

CONJUROR.   *(Fanning himself.)* It's a beautiful word, cold.

DIRECTOR.   Thank you for everything.

CONJUROR.   You're welcome. Striking is very easy. The hard part is setting up.

DIRECTOR.   Substituting is much harder.

SERVANT.   *(Entering, after exiting with the HARLEQUIN COSTUME.)* It's a bit cold in here. Do you want me to turn on the heat?

DIRECTOR.   No. We're just going to have to endure it because we've broken down the doors and raised the roof. All that remains are the four walls of the play.

> (*The SERVANT exits through the center door.*)

But it doesn't matter. There are still some soft weeds to sleep on.

CONJUROR.   To sleep on!

DIRECTOR.   Because in the end to sleep is to sow.

SERVANT.   *[Entering.]* Sir! I can't take this cold.

DIRECTOR.   I told you we have no choice. We're not going to give in to a common stage effect. Do your duty.

> (*The DIRECTOR puts on a pair of gloves and raises the collar of his tuxedo with trembling hands. The SERVANT exits.*)

CONJUROR.   *(Fanning himself.)* Is the cold such a bad thing?

DIRECTOR.   *(In a weak voice.)* The cold is a stage effect like any other.

SERVANT.   *(He peeks through the door, trembling, his hands over his chest.)* Sir!

DIRECTOR.   What?

SERVANT. *(Falling to his knees.)* The audience is here.

DIRECTOR. *(Falling back onto the table.)* Show them in!

> *(The CONJUROR, seated near the horse head, whistles and fans himself with great joy. The whole left side of the set splits open, revealing a brightly lit sky with long clouds and a slow rain of white gloves, rigid and intermittent.)*

VOICE. *(Offstage.)* Sir.

VOICE. *(Offstage.)* What.

VOICE. *(Offstage.)* The audience.

VOICE. *(Offstage.)* Show them in.

> *(The CONJUROR shakes his fan vigorously in the air. Snowflakes begin to fall across the set.)*

—SLOW CURTAIN—

Blood Wedding:
Tragedy in Three Acts
and Seven Tableaux

DRAMATIS PERSONAE

Mother [of the Groom]
Bride
Mother-in-Law [of Leonardo]
Leonardo's Wife
Maid
Neighbor Woman
Girls
Leonardo
Groom
Father of the Bride
Moon
Death (as Beggar Woman)
Woodcutters
Young Men

Act 1, Tableau 1

(A yellow room.)

GROOM.   *(Entering.)* Mother.

GROOM'S MOTHER.   Son?

GROOM.   I'm off.

GROOM'S MOTHER.   Where to?

GROOM.   To the vineyard.

(He moves to exit.)

GROOM'S MOTHER.   Wait.

GROOM.   Do you need something?

GROOM'S MOTHER.   Son, your lunch.

GROOM.   Don't worry about it. I'll eat some grapes. Give me the knife.

GROOM'S MOTHER.   What for?

GROOM.   *(Laughing.)* To cut the grapes from the vine.

GROOM'S MOTHER.   *(Muttering as she looks for the knife.)* The knife, the knife . . . Damn them all and the scoundrel who invented them.

GROOM.   Let's change the subject.

GROOM'S MOTHER.   And shotguns and pistols and the tiniest blades, and even hoes and pitchforks.

GROOM.   Enough.

GROOM'S MOTHER.   Anything that can cut a man's body. A beautiful man, tender as a flower, who goes out to the vineyards or to his own olive groves, because they're his by inheritance . . .

GROOM.   *(Lowering his head.)* Stop it.

GROOM'S MOTHER.   . . . and he never returns. Or if he does it's shrouded in palm leaves or sprinkled with rock salt so his body doesn't bloat. I don't know how you dare to go out with a knife on you or how I allow a serpent in our midst.

GROOM.   Are we done?

GROOM'S MOTHER.   I could live a hundred years and never speak of anything else. First your father, who smelled of carnations and gave me barely three years of happiness. Then your brother. By what right does a thing as tiny as a pistol or a knife finish off a bull of a man? I'll never stop talking about it. Months go by and the anguish still stings my eyes and even the tips of my hair.

GROOM. *(Angrily.)* Are you finished?

GROOM'S MOTHER. No. I'm not finished. Can anyone bring your father back to me? Or your brother? And then the jail. What is a jail after all? A place where they eat, smoke, play their instruments! My dead are full of weeds, mute, turning to dust—two men who were a pair of geraniums—and the killers are in jail, bright-eyed, contemplating the mountains . . .

GROOM. Are you saying you want me to kill them?

GROOM'S MOTHER. No . . . If I speak it's because . . . How can I avoid speaking when I see you headed out that door? I don't like you carrying a knife. I would prefer . . . that you not go to the fields!

GROOM. *(Laughing.)* Come now!

GROOM'S MOTHER. I'd like it if you were a woman. You wouldn't be heading toward the stream now and we'd be embroidering lacy hems and little woolen dogs.

GROOM. *(Putting his arm around his MOTHER and laughing.)* Oh, Mother. What if I took you to the fields with me?

GROOM'S MOTHER. What would an old woman do in the vineyards? Would you hide me beneath the grapevines?

GROOM. *(Lifting her in his arms.)* So old you are. Ancient!

GROOM'S MOTHER. Your father used to take me, it's true. Good stock, he was. Red-blooded. Your grandfather left a child on every corner. I like that. Men who are men, wheat that is wheat.

GROOM. And what about me, Mother?

GROOM'S MOTHER. What about you?

GROOM. Do I have to tell you again?

GROOM'S MOTHER. *(Turning serious.)* Oh!

GROOM. Do you have a problem with it?

GROOM'S MOTHER. No.

GROOM. So then . . .

GROOM'S MOTHER. I don't know what to say. When you bring it up so suddenly it catches me by surprise. I know she's a good girl. Isn't she? Decent. Hardworking. Kneads her dough and sews her skirts. Yet when I say her name I feel as though my forehead were being pelted with stones.

GROOM. Don't be silly.

GROOM'S MOTHER. I'm not being silly. It's about being left alone. You're all I have now and it hurts to imagine you leaving.

GROOM. But you'll come with us.

GROOM'S MOTHER. No. I can't leave your father and brother alone here. I have to go to them every morning, and if I go away someone from the Félix clan—that family of murderers!—might die and be buried next to them. I can't allow that! No way. I won't allow it! I'd claw them out of the ground with my fingernails and smash them against the garden wall.

GROOM. *(Angrily.)* Here we go again.

GROOM'S MOTHER. I'm sorry.

(Pause.)

How long have you been courting her?

GROOM. Three years. I finally managed to buy the vineyard.

GROOM'S MOTHER. Three years. She had a fiancé once, didn't she?

GROOM. I don't know. I doubt it. A girl needs to look carefully at the man she marries.

GROOM'S MOTHER. True. I didn't look at anyone. Just your father, and when they murdered him I looked at the wall in front of me. A woman with a man, end of story.

GROOM. You know she's a good girl.

GROOM'S MOTHER. I have no doubt. I just wish I knew what her mother was like.

GROOM. What difference does that make?

GROOM'S MOTHER. *(Studying him.)* Son.

GROOM. What are you thinking?

GROOM'S MOTHER. I'm thinking that it's true, that you're right! When do you wish to ask for her hand?

GROOM. *(Cheerfully.)* What about Sunday?

GROOM'S MOTHER. *(Turning serious.)* I'll bring her my brass earrings, which are antiques, and you can buy her . . .

GROOM. You understand these things better than I . . .

GROOM'S MOTHER. You can buy her a pair of lace stockings, and two suits for yourself. No, three! You're all I've got!

GROOM. I'm going. I'll go see her tomorrow.

GROOM'S MOTHER. Yes, yes, and let's see if you can make me happy with six grandchildren, or as many as you like, given that your father wasn't able to give me any more children.

GROOM. The firstborn will be for you.

GROOM'S MOTHER. Just make sure there are some girls in the mix. I want to embroider and make lace and live in peace.

GROOM. I'm certain you'll love my bride.

GROOM'S MOTHER. Of course I will.

(She goes to kiss him and stops herself.)

Go, you're too big for kisses. You can give them to your wife.

(Pause. Aside.)

When she becomes your wife.

GROOM. I'm going now.

GROOM'S MOTHER. Make sure to tend the area around the mill. You've been neglecting it lately.

GROOM. Remember what I said!

GROOM'S MOTHER. God keep you.

(Exit the GROOM. The GROOM'S MOTHER remains seated, with her back to the door. A NEIGHBOR WOMAN appears in the doorway, dressed in dark colors and a kerchief over her head.)

Come in.

NEIGHBOR WOMAN. How are you?

GROOM'S MOTHER. See for yourself.

NEIGHBOR WOMAN. I came down to the store and decided to stop by. We live so far apart!

GROOM'S MOTHER. It's been twenty years since I've been to the top of the street.

NEIGHBOR WOMAN. You're looking good.

GROOM'S MOTHER. You think?

NEIGHBOR WOMAN. Things happen. Two days ago they brought my neighbor's son back home with his arms cut off by the thresher.

(She sits.)

GROOM'S MOTHER. You mean Rafael?

NEIGHBOR WOMAN. Yes. Just imagine. I often think your son and mine are better off where they are: sleeping, resting, unexposed to such dangers.

GROOM'S MOTHER. Stop it. Those are just words. They bring no comfort.

(The NEIGHBOR WOMAN sighs heavily, followed by the GROOM'S MOTHER. Pause.)

NEIGHBOR WOMAN. *(Sadly.)* So where is your son?

GROOM'S MOTHER. He just left.

NEIGHBOR WOMAN. He finally bought the vineyard!

GROOM'S MOTHER. He's been fortunate.

NEIGHBOR WOMAN. Now it's time for him to marry.

GROOM'S MOTHER. *(As if awakening, she moves her chair closer to the NEIGHBOR WOMAN.)* Listen.

NEIGHBOR WOMAN. *(With an air of confidentiality.)* Yes?

GROOM'S MOTHER. Do you know my son's girl?

NEIGHBOR WOMAN. A fine girl!

GROOM'S MOTHER. Yes, but . . .

NEIGHBOR WOMAN. No one knows her well. She lives alone with her father way out there, miles from the nearest house. But she's a decent girl. Accustomed to solitude.

GROOM'S MOTHER. What was her mother like?

NEIGHBOR WOMAN. I knew her. Beautiful. Her face lit up like a saint's, but I never liked her. She didn't love her husband.

GROOM'S MOTHER. *(Angrily.)* The things you people know!

NEIGHBOR WOMAN. Sorry. I didn't mean to offend you. But it's true. Now, whether or not she was a decent woman, no one says. It's never been spoken of. She considered herself above everyone else.

GROOM'S MOTHER. There you go again!

NEIGHBOR WOMAN. You asked.

GROOM'S MOTHER. I'd prefer that no one knew either of them, living or dead, that they be like a pair of thistles that prick when you try to name them.

NEIGHBOR WOMAN. You're right. Your son deserves the best.

GROOM'S MOTHER. Indeed. That's why I take such care of him. I heard the girl had another fiancé a while back.

NEIGHBOR WOMAN. When she was fifteen or so. He got married a couple of years ago to a cousin of hers. No one remembers their engagement anymore.

GROOM'S MOTHER. But you do?

NEIGHBOR WOMAN. So many questions!

GROOM'S MOTHER. We all have a certain morbid curiosity. Who was the fiancé?

NEIGHBOR WOMAN. Leonardo.

GROOM'S MOTHER. Leonardo who?

NEIGHBOR WOMAN. Leonardo Félix.

GROOM'S MOTHER. *(Standing.)* The Félixes!

NEIGHBOR WOMAN. You're going to blame Leonardo for that? He was eight years old when it happened.

GROOM'S MOTHER. That's true . . . It's just that I hear the word Félix and

   (Muttering.)

my mouth fills with bile

   (She spits.)

and I have to spit, I have to spit to avoid killing someone.

NEIGHBOR WOMAN. Control yourself. What do you gain from thinking that way?

GROOM'S MOTHER. Nothing. But you understand.

NEIGHBOR WOMAN.   Don't get in the way of your son's happiness. Don't say anything to him. You're getting old. Me too. We should just keep quiet.

GROOM'S MOTHER.   I won't say anything.

NEIGHBOR WOMAN.   *(Giving her a kiss.)* Nothing at all.

GROOM'S MOTHER.   *(Composed.)* The things that happen!

NEIGHBOR WOMAN.   I need to go. My people will be returning from the fields soon.

GROOM'S MOTHER.   Can you believe this heat?

NEIGHBOR WOMAN.   The boys that take water to the harvesters are burnt to a crisp. Goodbye.

GROOM'S MOTHER.   Goodbye.

(The GROOM'S MOTHER begins walking toward the door at the left. She stops midway and slowly makes the sign of the cross.)

—CURTAIN—

Act 1, Tableau 2

(A pink room hung with copperware and wreaths of wildflowers. A table with a tablecloth stands in the center. It's morning. LEONARDO'S MOTHER-IN-LAW rocks a child in her arms. LEONARDO'S WIFE knits in another corner.)

LEONARDO'S MOTHER-IN-LAW.
　　To sleep, my baby, to dream:
　　the great horse refused to drink.
　　The water ran dark and deep
　　beneath the tree's leafy limbs.
　　When it reaches the bridge
　　it stops and sings.
　　Who can say, my son,
　　what the water brings
　　with its flowing skirts
　　and its chambers of green?

LEONARDO'S WIFE.   *(Softly.)*
　　To sleep, my little tulip, to sleep,
　　for the horse refuses to drink.

LEONARDO'S MOTHER-IN-LAW.
>   To sleep, my little rose, to sleep,
>   for the horse has begun to weep.
>   With wounded hooves
>   and a frozen mane
>   and in its eyes
>   a silver blade.
>   To the river they went.
>   Oh, what a descent!
>   Where flowing blood
>   outruns the current.

LEONARDO'S WIFE.
>   To sleep, my little tulip, to sleep,
>   for the horse refuses to drink.

LEONARDO'S MOTHER-IN-LAW.
>   To sleep, my little rose, to sleep,
>   for the horse has begun to weep.

LEONARDO'S WIFE.
>   It refused to touch
>   the dewy shore,
>   its muzzle covered
>   in silvery bugs.
>   To the harsh hills
>   did it whinny alone
>   as the lifeless river
>   encircled its throat.
>   Oh, how the great horse
>   refused to drink!
>   Oh, snow-ridden pain,
>   horse of the dawn!

LEONARDO'S MOTHER-IN-LAW.
>   Don't come! Stop,
>   close the shutters
>   with branches of dreams
>   and dreams of branches.

LEONARDO'S WIFE.
>   My baby falls asleep.

LEONARDO'S MOTHER-IN-LAW.
>   My baby falls silent.

LEONARDO'S WIFE.
    Horse, my baby has a pillow.

LEONARDO'S MOTHER-IN-LAW.
    And a crib of steel.

LEONARDO'S WIFE.
    A mattress of finest linen.

LEONARDO'S MOTHER-IN-LAW.
    Rock-a-bye, baby.

LEONARDO'S WIFE.
    Oh, how the great horse
    refused to drink!

LEONARDO'S MOTHER-IN-LAW.
    Don't come, don't!
    Off to the valley of gray,
    off to the mountain
    where the mare awaits.

LEONARDO'S WIFE. *(Observing.)*
    My baby falls asleep.

LEONARDO'S MOTHER-IN-LAW.
    My baby begins to dream.

LEONARDO'S WIFE. *(Softly.)*
    To sleep, my little tulip, to sleep,
    for the horse refuses to drink.

LEONARDO'S MOTHER-IN-LAW. *(Standing and singing very softly.)*
    To sleep, my little rose, to sleep,
    for the horse has begun to weep.

(They take the child away. Enter LEONARDO.)

LEONARDO.   Where's the baby?

LEONARDO'S WIFE.   He fell asleep.

LEONARDO.   Something was wrong with him yesterday, the way he cried all night.

LEONARDO'S WIFE.   *(Cheerfully.)* Today he's like a dahlia. What about you? Did you go see the horseshoer?

LEONARDO.   Just came from there. Would you believe it? I've been putting new shoes on the horse for two months and they keep falling off. Apparently he wears them off on the rocks.

LEONARDO'S WIFE. Could it be you're overworking him?

LEONARDO. No. I almost never work him.

LEONARDO'S WIFE. Yesterday they said they'd seen you near the edge of the plains.

LEONARDO. Who's "they"?

LEONARDO'S WIFE. The women who pick the capers. It sure surprised me. Was it you?

LEONARDO. No. What would I be doing out in the hinterlands?

LEONARDO'S WIFE. That's what I said. But the horse was dripping in sweat.

LEONARDO. You saw him?

LEONARDO'S WIFE. No. My mother did.

LEONARDO. Is she with the baby?

LEONARDO'S WIFE. Yes. Would you like some lemonade?

LEONARDO. Yes, very cold.

LEONARDO'S WIFE. I can't believe you didn't come home for lunch!

LEONARDO. I was with the wheat dealers. They always keep me past time.

LEONARDO'S WIFE. *(Making the lemonade, very tenderly.)* And do they give you a good price?

LEONARDO. Just enough.

LEONARDO'S WIFE. I need a new dress, and the baby could use a bonnet with bows.

LEONARDO. *(Standing.)* I'm going to go peek in on him.

LEONARDO'S WIFE. Careful, he's asleep.

LEONARDO'S MOTHER-IN-LAW. *(Entering.)* Who ran the horse ragged like that? He's out there collapsed on the grass, his eyes bulging as if he'd just returned from the ends of the earth.

LEONARDO. *(Bitterly.)* It was me.

LEONARDO'S MOTHER-IN-LAW. Forgive me. It's your animal.

LEONARDO'S WIFE. *(Timidly.)* He was with the wheat dealers.

LEONARDO'S MOTHER-IN-LAW. Fine. The horse could fall to pieces for all I care.

(She sits. Pause.)

LEONARDO'S WIFE.   Here's your drink. Is it cold enough?

LEONARDO.   Yes.

LEONARDO'S WIFE.   You know they're coming to ask for my cousin's hand?

LEONARDO.   When?

LEONARDO'S WIFE.   Tomorrow. The wedding will be within the month. I hope we'll be invited.

LEONARDO.   *(Turning serious.)* I don't know about that.

LEONARDO'S MOTHER-IN-LAW.   I don't think his mother was very happy with the arrangement.

LEONARDO.   She may be right. That girl is unpredictable.

LEONARDO'S WIFE.   I don't like you two bad-mouthing such a nice girl.

LEONARDO'S MOTHER-IN-LAW.   *(Slyly.)* He speaks from experience. Didn't you know they had a thing for three years?

LEONARDO.   But I left her.

(To his WIFE.)

Are you going to cry now? Come on!

(He pulls her hands from her face.)

Let's go see the baby.

(They exit arm in arm. Enter the GIRL, cheerfully. She comes in running.)

GIRL.   Ma'am.

LEONARDO'S MOTHER-IN-LAW.   What is it?

GIRL.   The groom stopped by the store and bought up the best of everything they had.

LEONARDO'S MOTHER-IN-LAW.   Was he alone?

GIRL.   No, he was with his mother. A tall, serious woman.

(She imitates her.)

But such elegance!

LEONARDO'S MOTHER-IN-LAW.   They have money.

GIRL.   And they bought a pair of lace stockings! So lovely. The dream of all women in stockings! They have a lark here . . .

(She points to her ankle.)

a ship here . . .

(She points to her calf.)

and a rose here.

(She points to her thigh.)

LEONARDO'S MOTHER-IN-LAW. Watch yourself, girl!

GIRL. Stem and all! And all made of silk!

LEONARDO'S MOTHER-IN-LAW. Two fortunes are about to be united.

(Enter LEONARDO and his WIFE.)

GIRL. I came to tell you what they're buying.

LEONARDO. *(Angrily.)* We don't care.

LEONARDO'S WIFE. Don't be rude to the girl.

LEONARDO'S MOTHER-IN-LAW. It's nothing to get angry about.

GIRL. Forgive me, sir.

(She exits in tears.)

LEONARDO'S MOTHER-IN-LAW. Why do you have to act that way with people?

LEONARDO. I didn't ask her for her opinion.

(He sits.)

LEONARDO'S MOTHER-IN-LAW. Fine.

(Pause.)

LEONARDO'S WIFE. *(To LEONARDO.)* What's the matter with you? What's going through that head of yours? Don't leave me hanging like this, without telling me anything.

LEONARDO. Get away from me.

LEONARDO'S WIFE. No. I want you to look at me and tell me.

LEONARDO. Leave me be.

(He stands.)

LEONARDO'S WIFE. Where are you going, darling?

LEONARDO. *(Bitterly.)* Will you be quiet?

LEONARDO'S MOTHER-IN-LAW. *(Vehemently, to her daughter.)* Be quiet!

(Exit LEONARDO.)

Oh, the baby!

(She exits and reappears with the baby in her arms. LEONARDO'S WIFE has remained standing, motionless.)

> With wounded hooves
> and a frozen mane
> and in its eyes
> a silver blade.
> To the river they went.
> Oh, what a descent!
> Where flowing blood
> outruns the current.

LEONARDO'S WIFE. *(Turning slowly, as if in a dream.)*
> To sleep, my little tulip, to sleep,
> for the horse has begun to drink.

LEONARDO'S MOTHER-IN-LAW.
> To sleep, my little rose, to sleep,
> for the horse has begun to weep.

LEONARDO'S WIFE.
> Rock-a-bye, baby.

LEONARDO'S MOTHER-IN-LAW.
> Oh, how the great horse
> refused to drink!

LEONARDO'S WIFE. *(Dramatically.)*
> Don't come in, stop!
> Be off to the mountain.
> Oh, snow-ridden pain,
> horse of the dawn!

LEONARDO'S MOTHER-IN-LAW. *(Crying.)*
> My baby falls asleep.

LEONARDO'S WIFE. *(Crying and approaching slowly.)*
> My baby begins to dream.

LEONARDO'S MOTHER-IN-LAW.
> To sleep, my little tulip, to sleep,
> for the horse refuses to drink.

LEONARDO'S WIFE. *(Crying and steadying herself on the table.)*
  To sleep, my little rose, to sleep,
  for the horse has begun to weep.

—CURTAIN—

Act 1, Tableau 3

(Interior of the cave in which the BRIDE lives. Upstage, a cross of large pink flowers. Arched doors with lace curtains and pink sashes. On the hard white walls hang unfurled handheld fans, blue vases, and tiny mirrors.)

MAID. Come in.

(Fawning, full of false humility. Enter the GROOM and his MOTHER, who is dressed in black satin and a lace mantilla. The GROOM wears black corduroy and a large gold chain.)

Would you like to sit? They'll be right with you.

(Exit the MAID. The GROOM'S MOTHER and the GROOM sit and remain as motionless as statues. Long pause.)

GROOM'S MOTHER. Did you bring your watch?

GROOM. Yes.

(He takes it out and looks at it.)

GROOM'S MOTHER. We need to watch the time. These people live so far away!

GROOM. These are good lands.

GROOM'S MOTHER. Good, but too isolated. Four hours to get here and not a house or tree in sight.

GROOM. That's what the plains are like.

GROOM'S MOTHER. Your father would have covered them in trees.

GROOM. With no water?

GROOM'S MOTHER. He would have found some. In the three years he was married to me, he planted ten cherry trees.

(Struggling to remember.)

Plus three walnut trees by the mill, a whole vineyard, and a plant called Jupiter that makes crimson flowers, which dried up.

(*Pause.*)

GROOM. (*Referring to the BRIDE.*) She must be getting dressed.

(*Enter the BRIDE'S FATHER, elderly with snow-white hair. He holds his head at an angle. The GROOM'S MOTHER and the GROOM rise and shake his hand in silence.*)

BRIDE'S FATHER. Was it a long journey?

GROOM'S MOTHER. Four hours.

(*They sit.*)

BRIDE'S FATHER. You took the longest route.

GROOM'S MOTHER. I'm getting too old to come along that steep river road.

GROOM. She gets queasy.

(*Pause.*)

BRIDE'S FATHER. A good esparto grass harvest this year.

GROOM. I can see that.

BRIDE'S FATHER. In my day, even esparto wouldn't grow in this land. We've had to thrash it and reduce it to tears to produce something worthwhile.

GROOM'S MOTHER. But now it does. Don't complain. I'm not here to ask for any of it.

BRIDE'S FATHER. (*Smiling.*) You're wealthier than I. Vineyards are worth a fortune: each grapevine a silver coin. What bothers me is that my lands are . . . you know . . . separated. I like for everything to be together. It's painful for me to see that little orchard stuck between my lands, but they won't sell it to me for all the gold in the world.

GROOM. That happens a lot.

BRIDE'S FATHER. If only the oxen could drag your vineyards here and place them on the slope, what joy that would bring me!

GROOM'S MOTHER. Why would we do that?

BRIDE'S FATHER. What's mine is hers and what's yours is his. That's why. To see it all together. It'd be lovely!

GROOM. And it'd be less work.

GROOM'S MOTHER. When I die, you can sell off my lands and buy more here.

BRIDE'S FATHER. Sell them off? Bah! You should be buying, dear, buying up everything you can. If I'd had any boys I'd have bought this whole hillside down to the stream. It's not good land, but you can make it so with hard work. And since no one comes out this way, they don't steal your harvest and you can sleep easy at night.

(Pause.)

GROOM'S MOTHER. You know why I'm here.

BRIDE'S FATHER. Yes.

GROOM'S MOTHER. And?

BRIDE'S FATHER. I think it's a fine idea. They've talked it over.

GROOM'S MOTHER. My son is a worthy match.

BRIDE'S FATHER. As is my daughter.

GROOM'S MOTHER. He's a beautiful man. Never known a woman. Honor more spotless than a sheet drying in the sun.

BRIDE'S FATHER. What can I tell you about my daughter? She's up every day at three, making bread by the starlight. She doesn't talk, she's soft as fleece and great at embroidery, and she has a set of teeth that can chew through a rope.

GROOM'S MOTHER. God bless your house.

BRIDE'S FATHER. May God bless it.

(Enter the MAID with two trays, one with wine glasses and another with sweets.)

GROOM'S MOTHER. *(To the GROOM.)* When do you want the wedding to be?

GROOM. Next Thursday.

BRIDE'S FATHER. Her twenty-second birthday to the day.

GROOM'S MOTHER. Twenty-two! That's how old my eldest son would be if he were alive. He'd be just the way he was, hot-blooded and manly . . . if only men had never invented knives.

BRIDE'S FATHER. You can't think that way.

GROOM'S MOTHER. Not a minute goes by that I don't. Think how you'd feel.

BRIDE'S FATHER. Thursday, then, right?

GROOM. Right.

BRIDE'S FATHER. We'll go by coach with the bride and groom to the church, which is very far away, and the guests will go in whatever carts and horses they have.

GROOM'S MOTHER. Agreed.

(The MAID walks by.)

BRIDE'S FATHER. Tell her she can come in.

(To the GROOM'S MOTHER.)

I'll be very happy if she pleases you.

(Enter the BRIDE. She carries her hands modestly at her sides and her head down.)

GROOM'S MOTHER. Come closer. Are you happy?

BRIDE. Yes, ma'am.

BRIDE'S FATHER. Don't be so serious. After all she's going to be your new mother.

BRIDE. I'm happy. When I say yes it's because I mean it.

GROOM'S MOTHER. Of course.

(She places her hand beneath the BRIDE's chin to raise it.)

Look at me.

BRIDE'S FATHER. She looks just like my wife.

GROOM'S MOTHER. Is that right? Such beautiful eyes! You know what it means to get married, child?

BRIDE. *(Solemnly.)* I do.

GROOM'S MOTHER. A man, some children, and a thick wall for everything else.

GROOM. Is there anything else we need to do?

GROOM'S MOTHER. No. Long live the both of you, that's all! Long live the both of you!

BRIDE. I will be a good wife.

GROOM'S MOTHER. Here are some presents for you.

BRIDE. Thank you.

BRIDE'S FATHER. Shall we have something?

GROOM'S MOTHER. Nothing for me.

   (To the GROOM.)

   What about you?

GROOM. I'll have something.

   (He takes a sweet. The BRIDE takes another.)

BRIDE'S FATHER. *(To the GROOM.)* Wine?

GROOM'S MOTHER. He doesn't drink.

BRIDE'S FATHER. Better that way!

   (Pause. All are standing.)

GROOM. *(To the BRIDE.)* I'll stop by tomorrow.

BRIDE. What time?

GROOM. Five.

BRIDE. I'll be here.

GROOM. When I leave your side something comes undone inside me, and I feel a kind of lump in my throat.

BRIDE. When you're my husband that won't happen anymore.

GROOM. That's what I think.

GROOM'S MOTHER. Let's get going. The sun won't wait for us.

   (To the BRIDE'S FATHER.)

   We're agreed on everything, then?

BRIDE'S FATHER. Yes, all agreed.

GROOM'S MOTHER. *(To the MAID.)* Goodbye.

MAID. God keep you.

   (The GROOM'S MOTHER gives the BRIDE a kiss and begins her exit with the GROOM.)

GROOM'S MOTHER. *(From the doorway.)* Goodbye, child.

   (The BRIDE waves.)

BRIDE'S FATHER. I'll walk out with you.

   (Exit the BRIDE'S FATHER, GROOM'S MOTHER, and GROOM.)

MAID.   I'm dying to see your presents.

BRIDE. *(Bitterly.)* Go away.

MAID.   Come on, child, show them to me.

BRIDE. I will not.

MAID.   At least the stockings. They're supposed to be all lace. Just a peek!

BRIDE. I said no!

MAID.   For heaven's sake. Okay. You'd think you weren't happy to be getting married.

(The BRIDE flinches and sighs heavily.)

Child, what's the matter with you? Are you sorry to give up your cushy life? Don't do this to yourself. You have no reason to be bitter. Let's see the presents.

(She grabs the box.)

BRIDE. *(Grabbing the MAID by the wrists.)* Put it down.

MAID.   Really, child!

BRIDE. Put it down I said.

MAID.   You're stronger than a man.

BRIDE. Don't I work like a man? I wish I were one!

MAID.   Don't talk that way!

BRIDE. Enough. Let's change the subject.

(The light begins to disappear from the set. There is a long pause.)

MAID.   Did you hear a horse outside last night?

BRIDE. What time?

MAID.   Around three.

BRIDE. It must have been a horse that broke loose from the herd.

MAID.   No. There was a rider.

BRIDE. How do you know?

MAID.   Because I saw him. He was standing at your window. It really surprised me.

BRIDE. Could it have been my fiancé? He's passed by several times at that hour.

MAID. No.
BRIDE. You saw him?
MAID. Yes.
BRIDE. Who was it?
MAID. It was Leonardo.
BRIDE. *(Angrily.)* That's a lie! A lie! Why would he come around here?
MAID. It was him.
BRIDE. Stop it! Damn that tongue of yours!

(The sound of a horse is heard offstage.)

MAID. *(At the window.)* Come, take a peek. So?
BRIDE. It was him!

—QUICK CURTAIN—

Act 2, Tableau 1

(Front room of the BRIDE's house, with the door to the outside upstage. It's early morning, before dawn. The BRIDE enters wearing a ruffled white petticoat covered in lacework and embroidery, and a white bodice that leaves her arms bare. The MAID is dressed similarly.)

MAID. I'll finish brushing your hair here.
BRIDE. The heat is unbearable.
MAID. In these parts even dawn brings no relief.

(The BRIDE sits in a low chair and looks at herself in a small hand mirror. The MAID brushes her hair.)

BRIDE. My mother came from a land with many trees and rich earth.
MAID. That's why she was always so happy!
BRIDE. But she wasted away here.
MAID. Such was her fate.
BRIDE. As we are all wasting away. The walls breathe fire. Ouch, don't pull so hard!

MAID. I'm trying to fix your bangs so they'll fall just right over your forehead.

(The BRIDE observes herself in the mirror.)

You look so lovely!

(The MAID gives her an affectionate kiss.)

BRIDE. *(Solemnly.)* Keep brushing.

MAID. *(She continues brushing.)* Lucky you to embrace a man, to kiss him, to feel his weight on you!

BRIDE. Stop it.

MAID. And the best part is when you wake up: you'll feel him at your side, caressing your shoulders with his breath, like the feather of a nightingale.

BRIDE. *(Angrily.)* Will you please stop?

MAID. But child, what do you think marriage is about? The sweets? The bouquets of flowers? No. It's about this and nothing more: a bed all aglow with the heat of a man and a woman.

BRIDE. It shouldn't be talked about.

MAID. That's a different issue. But it's pure joy.

BRIDE. Or pure bitterness.

MAID. I'm going to place the orange blossoms where they'll show up best against your hair.

(She places a wreath of orange blossoms on the BRIDE's head, testing different positions.)

BRIDE. *(She looks at herself in the mirror.)* Give it here.

(She grabs the wreath and looks at it, dropping her head in disappointment.)

MAID. What's wrong?

BRIDE. Leave me be.

MAID. This isn't a time to be sad.

(Reassuringly.)

Give it here.

(The BRIDE throws the wreath to the ground.)

Child! You're going to bring a curse on yourself throwing the wreath to the ground like that! Raise that head! Don't you want to get married? Say so. There's still time to change your mind.

(The MAID stands.)

BRIDE. *[She stands.]* I'm just jittery. Who wouldn't be?

MAID. You love your fiancé.

BRIDE. I do.

MAID. Yes, yes, I'm certain of it.

BRIDE. But this is a huge step.

MAID. It must be taken.

BRIDE. I've already given my word.

MAID. I'm going to put the crown back on.

BRIDE. *(She sits.)* Hurry. They'll be arriving soon.

MAID. They've been on the road now for at least two hours.

BRIDE. How far is it from here to the church?

MAID. Five leagues if you follow the creek, twice that far along the road.

(The BRIDE stands. The MAID exults at her appearance.)

> May the bride awaken
> on her wedding morn.
> May the rivers of the world
> deliver her crown!

BRIDE. *(Smiling.)* Let's go.

MAID. *(She gives the BRIDE an excited kiss and dances about.)*
> May she awaken
> to the tender fronds
> of the laurel leaves.
> May she awaken
> beneath the trunk and branch
> of the laurel trees.

(Knocking is heard at the door.)

BRIDE. Get the door! It must be the first guests.

(Exit the BRIDE. The MAID opens the door and expresses surprise.)

MAID. You?

LEONARDO. Yes, me. Good morning.

MAID. You had to be the first?

LEONARDO. Wasn't I invited?

MAID. Yeah.

LEONARDO. So here I am.

MAID. Where's your wife?

LEONARDO. I came on horseback. She's coming in a coach along the road.

MAID. You didn't run into anyone?

LEONARDO. I passed several people on my horse.

MAID. You're going to kill the animal with all that racing.

LEONARDO. If it dies, it dies!

(Pause.)

MAID. Have a seat. No one's up yet.

LEONARDO. *[He sits.]* Where's the bride?

MAID. I'm going to dress her right now.

LEONARDO. The bride! She must be happy!

MAID. *(Changing the subject.)* How's the boy?

LEONARDO. What boy?

MAID. Your son.

LEONARDO. *(As if waking from a dream.)* Oh!

MAID. Are they bringing him?

LEONARDO. No.

(Pause. Voices are heard singing far away.)

VOICES.
> May the bride awaken
> on her wedding morn!

LEONARDO.
> May the bride awaken
> on her wedding morn.

MAID. It's the other guests. They're still a ways off.

LEONARDO. *(Standing.)* The bride must be wearing a large crown of flowers, no? It shouldn't be too big. Something smaller would look nice on her. Did the groom bring the orange blossom she'll be wearing about her breast?

BRIDE. *(Entering, still dressed in her petticoat and with the wreath on her head.)* Yes, he brought it.

MAID. *(Angrily.)* You shouldn't be coming out here like that.

BRIDE. What difference does it make?

(Sternly.)

Why were you asking about the orange blossom? What are you implying?

LEONARDO. Nothing. What would I be trying to imply?

(Drawing near.)

You know me well enough to know that. Tell me: What did I ever mean to you? Be honest and think about it. But a pair of oxen and a crumbling shack aren't much. That's what sticks in your craw.

BRIDE. Why did you come here?

LEONARDO. To see your wedding.

BRIDE. Just like I saw yours!

LEONARDO. You all but performed the ceremony yourself. I can be killed, but I refuse to be spit upon. And even polished silver has been known to spit.

BRIDE. Stop it!

LEONARDO. I'll say no more. I'm a man of honor, and I don't want these hills hearing my shouts.

BRIDE. My shouts would be more shocking.

MAID. This conversation can't continue. No more talk of the past.

(The MAID looks toward the door, full of anxiety.)

BRIDE. She's right. I shouldn't even be talking to you. But it burns me up to see you here looking for me and snooping around my wedding and asking about the orange blossom like that. Go away and wait for your wife outside the door.

LEONARDO. Is there something wrong with you and I exchanging a word or two?

MAID. *(Angrily.)* Yes, there's plenty wrong with it.

LEONARDO. Since my marriage I've thought long and hard about who was to blame, and every time I do I find a new fault that swallows up the old one. There's never a shortage of blame!

BRIDE. A man on his horse will go to no end to wear down a poor girl in the desert. But I have my pride. That's why I'm getting married. And I plan on locking myself away with my husband, who I'm supposed to love above all else.

LEONARDO. Pride will get you nowhere.

(He draws near.)

BRIDE. Stop, don't come any closer!

LEONARDO. To burn in silence is the greatest punishment we can bring upon ourselves. What good did my pride do me? What good did it do me to pry my eyes from you and leave you awake night after night? Nothing! It just engulfed me in fire! You think that time heals all and that walls block out everything, but it's not true. It's not true. When things sink into your core, no one can pull them out!

BRIDE. *(Trembling.)* I can't listen to you. I can't handle your voice. It's like I'm drinking a bottle of anisette and sleeping on a quilt of roses. It drags me down, and I know I'm drowning but I can't turn back.

MAID. *(Grabbing LEONARDO by the lapels.)* You've got to get out of here, right now!

LEONARDO. It's the last time I'm going to speak to her. You have nothing to fear.

BRIDE. And I know I'm crazy and that my breast is wasted from so much waiting, yet here I am, soothed by the lilt of his voice and the sway of his arms.

LEONARDO. I had to get these things off my chest. I got married. Now it's your turn.

MAID. *(To LEONARDO.)* Don't worry, she will!

VOICES. *(Singing closer.)*
>   May the bride awaken
>   on her wedding morn.

BRIDE. May the bride awaken!

(Exit running into her room.)

MAID. The guests are here.

(To LEONARDO.)

Don't come near her again.

LEONARDO. Not to worry.

(Exit to the left. The day begins to brighten.)

GIRL 1. *(Entering.)*
    May the bride awaken
    on her wedding morn;
    may she be serenaded
    with wreaths on every porch.

VOICES.
    May the bride awaken!

MAID. *(Rousing the crowd.)*
    May she awaken
    to the tender fronds
    of flowering love.
    May she awaken
    beneath the trunk and branch
    of the laurel buds!

GIRL 2. *(Entering.)*
    May she awaken
    with flowing hair,
    a snow-white gown,
    patent leather pumps,
    and jasmine at her brow.

MAID.
    Oh, shepherdess,
    how the moon peeks through!

GIRL 1.
    Oh, suitor,
    leave your hat behind you!

YOUNG MAN 1. *(Entering with his hat held high.)*
    May the bride awaken,
    for through the fields
    come the wedding guests
    bearing trays of dahlias
    and heavenly bread.

VOICES.
    May the bride awaken!

GIRL 2.
    The bride dons a crown of white.
    With a golden thread he ties it tight.

MAID.
>	Amid a scent of lemon
>	the bride is restless.

GIRL 3. *(Entering.)*
>	Amid a scent of orange
>	the groom doth beckon.

(Enter three GUESTS.)

YOUNG MAN 1.
>	Awake, sweet dove!
>	The dawn will shake the dark
>	from its golden tresses.

GUEST.
>	The bride, the fair bride:
>	today a maid, tomorrow a wife.

GIRL 1.
>	Come down, brunette beauty,
>	dragging your train of silk.

GUEST.
>	Come down, brunette beauty,
>	and savor the morning dew.

YOUNG MAN 1.
>	Awaken, my lady, awaken,
>	for the air is astir with orange.

MAID.
>	I shall embroider her a tree
>	of garnet ribbons.
>	On each ribbon a kiss
>	flowing with inscriptions.

VOICES.
>	May the bride awaken.

YOUNG MAN 1.
>	The wedding morn is here!

GUEST.
>	On your wedding morn,
>	How beautiful you'll be.
>	You look, O wildflower, like
>	the wife of a captain at sea.

BRIDE'S FATHER. *(Entering.)*
> The wife of a captain at sea
> has caught the groom's eye.
> Goading his oxen he comes for his prize.

GIRL 3.
> The groom is like a flower of gold.
> About his feet swirl petals of rose.

MAID.
> Oh, my fortunate girl!

YOUNG MAN 2.
> May the bride awaken.

MAID.
> Oh, my beauty!

GIRL 1.
> The wedding guests call
> from all about.

GIRL 2.
> Let the bride step out.

GIRL 1.
> Let her step out, out!

MAID.
> Let them ring the bells,
> let them call aloud!

YOUNG MAN 1.
> She's coming! She's stepping out!

MAID.
> How the guests bellow and shout!

(The BRIDE appears. She wears a turn-of-the-century black dress flared at the hip, with a long train trimmed in pleated tulle and heavy lace. A wreath of orange blossoms crowns her head. Guitars begin strumming. The GIRLS greet the BRIDE with kisses.)

GIRL 3.   What fragrance are you wearing?

BRIDE.   *(Giggling.)* None.

GIRL 2.   *(Eying the dress.)* That fabric is a dream.

YOUNG MAN 1.   The groom is here!

GROOM. Cheers!

GIRL 1. *(Placing a flower behind his ear.)*
  The groom is like a flower of gold.

GIRL 2.
  With inner peace, his eyes aglow.

(The GROOM walks toward the BRIDE.)

BRIDE. Why are you wearing those shoes?

GROOM. They're more cheerful than the black ones.

LEONARDO'S WIFE. *(Entering and greeting the bride with a kiss.)* Cheers!

(Everyone talks excitedly.)

LEONARDO. *(Entering with an air of formality.)*
  We crown you on your bridal morn.

WOMAN.
  May the fields sing and croon
  At your tresses ripe with dew.

GROOM'S MOTHER. *(To the BRIDE'S FATHER.)* Why did *they* have to show up?

BRIDE'S FATHER. They're family. Today is a day to forgive!

GROOM'S MOTHER. I'll keep it to myself, but I can't forgive.

GROOM. It's so lovely to see you wearing that crown!

BRIDE. Let's be off to the church!

GROOM. Are you in a rush?

BRIDE. Yes. I'm eager to be your wife and to be alone with you. I don't want to hear any voice but yours.

GROOM. I want the same thing!

BRIDE. And I don't want to see any eyes but yours. And I want you to hold me so tightly that even if my dead mother called my name she wouldn't be able to pry me away.

GROOM. Strength abounds in my arms. I'm going to hold you for forty years straight.

BRIDE. *(Dramatically, grabbing his arm.)* Forever!

BRIDE'S FATHER. Let's go, quickly! To the horses and carts! The sun is already up.

GROOM'S MOTHER. Be careful! We don't need any accidents.

(*The outside door opens. The exit begins.*)

MAID. (*Tearfully.*)
>So far from home, fair maiden,
>from home you stray so far,
>off you go like a rising star.

GIRL 1.
>With chaste body and spotless clothes,
>go forth to your betrothed.

(*They begin leaving.*)

GIRL 2.
>Off you go, from house to temple!

MAID.
>The breeze strews flowers at your ankles!

GIRL 3.
>Oh, my fair maid!

MAID.
>In lacy darkness veiled.

(*EXIT. Guitars, castanets, and tambourines are heard playing. LEONARDO and his WIFE remain alone onstage.*)

LEONARDO'S WIFE. Let's go.

LEONARDO. Where to?

LEONARDO'S WIFE. To the church. But you're not going on horseback. You're coming with me.

LEONARDO. In the cart?

LEONARDO'S WIFE. How else?

LEONARDO. I'm not the kind of man who rides in a cart.

LEONARDO'S WIFE. And I'm not the kind of woman who goes to a wedding without her husband. I've had it!

LEONARDO. So have I!

LEONARDO'S WIFE. Why do you look at me like that? Your eyes pierce me like thorns.

LEONARDO. Let's just go!

LEONARDO'S WIFE.   I don't understand what's happening. I imagine things and have to stop myself. One thing I do know: I've been cast aside. But I have a son. And another on the way. Let's get going. My mother had the same fate. But I'm not leaving here alone.

(Voices are heard outside.)

VOICES.
> Altar-bound maiden,
> off you go like a rising star!

LEONARDO'S WIFE.   *(Tearfully.)*
> Off you go like a rising star!
> That's just how I left home, with the world as my oyster.

LEONARDO.   *(Standing.)* Let's go.

LEONARDO'S WIFE.   Together!

LEONARDO.   Yes.

(Pause.)

Spur the horses!

(Exit.)

VOICES.
> Altar-bound maiden,
> off you go like a rising star.

—SLOW CURTAIN—

Act 2, Tableau 2

(Outside the BRIDE's cave. Shades of grayish white and cold blue. Large prickly pear cactuses. Somber, silvery hues. Wheat-colored panoramas, harsh like the landscapes of folk art.)

MAID.   *(Arranging cups and trays at a table.)*
> Turning, turning went the wheel
> as the water ran through,
> and now the wedding is here
> so let the branches be parted
> and let the moon shine true
> on its veranda so pale.

(*Loudly.*)

Set the table!

(*Emotionally.*)

> Singing, singing went the lovers
> as the water beat the wheel,
> and now the wedding is here
> so let the frost shimmer
> and let the bitter almonds
> with sweetest honey fill.

(*Loudly.*)

Prepare the wine!

(*Emotionally.*)

> My beauty, my pastoral beauty,
> see how the water runs.
> Your wedding is here
> so gather your clothes
> under your husband's wing
> and never leave your home.
> For your groom is a dove
> with his breast afire
> and the hills do await
> the whisper of blood.
> Turning, turning went the wheel
> as the water ran through.
> Your wedding is here,
> may it sparkle like dew!

GROOM'S MOTHER. (*Entering.*) Finally!

BRIDE'S FATHER. Are we the first to arrive?

MAID. No. Leonardo and his wife arrived a while ago. They raced like the devil. His wife was scared to death. They covered the distance as if on horseback.

BRIDE'S FATHER. He's looking for trouble, that one. He doesn't come from good blood.

GROOM'S MOTHER. What do you expect from that family? The evil blood goes back to his great-grandfather, who started the killing, and it continues in the whole sorry clan today. Backstabbers, all of them.

BRIDE'S FATHER. Let's drop it!

MAID.　How do you expect her to drop it?

GROOM'S MOTHER.　Grief runs to the tips of my veins. Face to face with all of them and I see nothing but the hand that killed what was mine. You see the state I'm in? Do I seem crazy to you? It comes from bottling up what deserves to be shouted from the rooftop. There's a voice in my breast that's always about to shout and I just have to push it down and muzzle it. The dead are carted away and you have to keep your mouth shut or people will gossip.

(She takes off her shawl.)

BRIDE'S FATHER.　Today's not the day to think about all that.

GROOM'S MOTHER.　When it comes up, I have to have my say. Today of all days, when my home has been emptied.

BRIDE'S FATHER.　It'll be full again soon enough.

GROOM'S MOTHER.　That's my hope: grandchildren.

(They sit.)

BRIDE'S FATHER.　I want them to have a lot. This land is desperate for skilled hands. It's a constant battle against the weeds, the thistles, the rocks that spring up from who knows where. No more hired hands. Only landowners know how to thrash the earth and dominate it and make it sprout with seed. Many sons are needed.

GROOM'S MOTHER.　And a daughter or two! Men come and go like the wind! They have to carry weapons. Girls never even go outside.

BRIDE'S FATHER.　*(Cheerfully.)* I think they'll have a lot of both.

GROOM'S MOTHER.　My son won't disappoint. He's of fertile stock. His father could have had many children with me.

BRIDE'S FATHER.　What I wish is that it could happen quickly. A couple of grown men in an instant.

GROOM'S MOTHER.　But that's not the way it works. It takes a long time. That's why it's so awful to see your own blood spilt on the soil: a spurt that took years to nourish runs out in a minute. When I found my son he was facedown in the middle of the street. I bathed my hands in his blood and licked it up. Because it was mine. You have no idea. I would save the blood-soaked earth in a monstrance of crystal and topaz if I could.

BRIDE'S FATHER.　It's just a matter of time. My daughter has childbearing hips and your son is a vigorous lad.

GROOM'S MOTHER. That's my hope.

(They stand.)

BRIDE'S FATHER. Get the trays of wheat ready.

MAID. They're ready.

LEONARDO'S WIFE. *(Entering, with LEONARDO.)* My best wishes for all!

GROOM'S MOTHER. Thank you.

LEONARDO. Will there be a reception?

BRIDE'S FATHER. Just a small one. People will need to get going.

MAID. They're here!

(The GUESTS begin entering in merry groups. The BRIDE and GROOM enter arm in arm. Exit LEONARDO.)

GROOM. Never was there a wedding with so many people.

BRIDE. *(Gloomily.)* Never.

BRIDE'S FATHER. It was beautiful.

GROOM'S MOTHER. Whole branches of families turned out.

GROOM. People who aren't used to leaving their houses.

GROOM'S MOTHER. Fruit of all the seed your grandfather sowed.

GROOM. There were cousins of mine I barely recognized.

GROOM'S MOTHER. The whole clan from the coast.

GROOM. *(Cheerfully.)* They were afraid of the horses.

(Background conversation.)

GROOM'S MOTHER. *(To the BRIDE.)* What are you thinking about?

BRIDE. I'm not thinking about anything.

GROOM'S MOTHER. Marriage is a heavy responsibility.

(Guitars play.)

BRIDE. Like lead.

GROOM'S MOTHER. *(Sternly.)* But it doesn't have to feel that way. You should feel as light as a dove.

BRIDE. Are you spending the night here?

GROOM'S MOTHER. No. My house is empty.

BRIDE. You should stay!

BRIDE'S FATHER. *(To the GROOM'S MOTHER.)* Look at the way they're dancing. Must be a fad from the coast.

(Enter LEONARDO, who sits. His WIFE stands stiffly behind him.)

GROOM'S MOTHER. Those are my husband's cousins. They take their dancing seriously.

BRIDE'S FATHER. It makes me happy to watch them. What a nice change for this house!

(Exit.)

GROOM. *(To the BRIDE.)* Do you like the orange blossom?

BRIDE. *(Staring at him.)* Yes.

GROOM. It's all wax. It'll last forever. I would have liked to see you wear it all over your dress.

BRIDE. There's no need for that.

(Exit LEONARDO to the right.)

GIRL 1. Let's go take out your pins.

BRIDE. *(To the GROOM.)* I'll be right back.

(Exit.)

LEONARDO'S WIFE. I hope you'll be happy with my cousin!

GROOM. I'm sure I will.

LEONARDO'S WIFE. Both of you right here. No need to pick up and move elsewhere. I wish I lived this far away!

GROOM. Why don't you buy some land? The countryside is cheap and it's a better place to raise children.

LEONARDO'S WIFE. We haven't the money. Not with the way things are going.

GROOM. Your husband's a hard worker.

LEONARDO'S WIFE. Yes, but he's too flighty. Always moving from one thing to the next. A restless man.

MAID. Aren't you having anything? I'm going to wrap some cookies for your mother. I know she loves them.

GROOM. Give her three dozen.

LEONARDO'S WIFE. No, no. A half dozen will be fine.

GROOM. This is a special occasion.

LEONARDO'S WIFE. *(To the MAID.)* Where's Leonardo?

MAID. Haven't seen him.

GROOM. He must be with the guests.

LEONARDO'S WIFE. I'm going to go check!

(Exit.)

MAID. The dancing is beautiful.

GROOM. You're not going to give it a try?

MAID. No one has asked me.

(Two GIRLS cross upstage, which hums with lively mingling throughout the scene.)

GROOM. *(Cheerfully.)* It's their loss. Lively old women like you dance better than young girls.

MAID. Are you trying to flirt with me, boy? What a family you come from! Macho men, all of you. I saw your grandfather's wedding when I was a girl. What an imposing man. Like a mountain at the altar.

GROOM. I'm not as big.

MAID. But you've got the same sparkle in your eyes. Where's your girl?

GROOM. Getting out of her dress.

MAID. Oh, listen! If you get hungry during the night—since you won't be sleeping—I've made you a ham and poured two tall goblets of nice wine. It's in the bottom of the cupboard. In case you need it.

GROOM. *(Smiling.)* I don't eat in the middle of the night.

MAID. *(Mischievously.)* If not you, then your bride.

(Exit. Enter two YOUNG MEN.)

YOUNG MAN 1. You have to come have a drink with us.

GROOM. I'm waiting for my bride.

YOUNG MAN 2. You'll have her in the wee hours of the morning!

YOUNG MAN 1.   Which is when it feels best!

YOUNG MAN 2.   Just for a minute.

GROOM.   Let's go then.

(Exit. A great commotion is heard. Enter the BRIDE. Opposite her, enter two GIRLS running toward her.)

GIRL 1.   Who did you give the first pin to? Me or this girl?

BRIDE.   I don't remember.

GIRL 1.   You gave it to me, right here.

GIRL 2.   No, you gave it to me at the altar.

BRIDE.   *(Flustered, struggling to remember.)* I don't know.

GIRL 1.   It's just that I'd like—

BRIDE.   *(Interrupting.)* I don't care what you'd like. I've got a lot to think about.

GIRL 2.   Sorry.

(LEONARDO crosses upstage.)

BRIDE.   *(Eying LEONARDO.)* You've caught me at a difficult moment.

GIRL 1.   We wouldn't know about that!

BRIDE.   You will when your time comes. It's a big step.

GIRL 1.   Are you upset with us?

BRIDE.   No. I'm sorry.

GIRL 2.   Sorry for what? Anyway, both pins will bring marriage, right?

BRIDE.   Yes, both of them.

GIRL 1.   But only one of us gets to go first.

BRIDE.   Are you that eager?

GIRL 2.   *(Embarrassed.)* Yes.

BRIDE.   Why?

GIRL 1.   Well . . .

(She hugs the other GIRL, and both run off. Enter the GROOM, who sneaks up behind the BRIDE and embraces her.)

BRIDE.   *(Jumping with fright.)* Don't do that!

GROOM. What, are you afraid of me?
BRIDE. Oh! It's you!
GROOM. Who else would it be?

(*Pause.*)

Either your father or me.

BRIDE. That's true!
GROOM. Though your father would have grabbed you more gently.
BRIDE. *(Gloomily.)* Right.
GROOM. *(Hugging her a bit roughly.)* Because he's an old man.
BRIDE. *(Coldly.)* Take your hands off me.
GROOM. Why?

(*He releases her.*)

BRIDE. Because. People can see us.

(*The MAID crosses upstage, without looking at the BRIDE and GROOM.*)

GROOM. So what? It's sanctified now.
BRIDE. Yes, but just leave me be for now. Later.
GROOM. What's wrong with you? It's like you're terrified.
BRIDE. Nothing's wrong. Don't go.

(*Enter LEONARDO'S WIFE.*)

LEONARDO'S WIFE. I don't mean to interrupt . . .
GROOM. What is it?
LEONARDO'S WIFE. Did my husband come through here?
GROOM. No.
LEONARDO'S WIFE. I can't find him, and the horse isn't in the stable either.
GROOM. *(Cheerfully.)* He must be out riding.

(*Exit LEONARDO'S WIFE, preoccupied. Enter the MAID.*)

MAID. So many well-wishers!
GROOM. I'm about ready for it all to end. The bride is a little tired.
MAID. What's wrong with you, child?

BRIDE. My temples are pounding!

MAID. A bride from these parts should be strong.

   (To the GROOM.)

   You're the only one who can help her because she's yours now.

   (Exit running.)

GROOM. *(Embracing her.)* Let's join the dancing for a bit.

   (He kisses her.)

BRIDE. *(Anxiously.)* No. I'd like to lie down for a while.

GROOM. I'll go with you.

BRIDE. Absolutely not! With all these guests here? What would they think? Just let me rest for a bit.

GROOM. Fine! But I hope you're not like this tonight!

BRIDE. *(In the doorway.)* I'll be better tonight.

GROOM. That's what I like to hear!

   (Enter the GROOM'S MOTHER.)

GROOM'S MOTHER. Son.

GROOM. Where have you been?

GROOM'S MOTHER. Lost in all the commotion. Are you happy?

GROOM. Yes.

GROOM'S MOTHER. What about your wife?

GROOM. She's resting for a bit. Not a good day for brides!

GROOM'S MOTHER. Not a good day? It's the only good day. For me it was like a long-awaited inheritance.

   (The MAID enters and walks toward the BRIDE's bedroom.)

   The plowing of the earth, the planting of new trees.

GROOM. Are you going to go?

GROOM'S MOTHER. Yes. I need to be in my own house.

GROOM. Alone.

GROOM'S MOTHER. No, not alone. My head is full of things: men, fighting . . .

GROOM. There's not much more fighting to speak of.

(*The MAID enters quickly, then exits upstage.*)

GROOM'S MOTHER. As long as one lives, there will be fighting.

GROOM. You know I'll always listen to you.

GROOM'S MOTHER. Try to be affectionate with your wife, and if you find her distracted or standoffish, do something that startles her: a bear hug or a little nibble, followed by a soft kiss. Not enough to upset her, but enough so she understands who's the man, the boss, the one who calls the shots. That's what I learned from your father. And since you don't have him around, it's up to me to teach you these tricks.

GROOM. I'll always follow your advice.

BRIDE'S FATHER. (*Entering.*) Where's my daughter?

GROOM. In her room.

[*Exit the BRIDE'S FATHER.*]

GIRL 1. Come forth, bride and groom. We're going to dance the Wheel.

YOUNG MAN 1. (*To the GROOM.*) You'll lead.

BRIDE'S FATHER. (*Entering.*) She's not there!

GROOM. No?

BRIDE'S FATHER. She must have gone up to the balcony.

GROOM. I'll go see!

(*Exit the GROOM. Guitars are heard amid a commotion.*)

GIRL 1. They've already started dancing!

(*Exit.*)

GROOM. (*Entering.*) She's not there either.

GROOM'S MOTHER. (*Anxiously.*) No?

BRIDE'S FATHER. Where could she have gone?

MAID. (*Entering.*) Where's the girl?

GROOM'S MOTHER. (*Gravely.*) We don't know.

(*Exit the GROOM. Enter three GUESTS.*)

BRIDE'S FATHER. (*Alarmed.*) Maybe she's dancing?

MAID. No.

BRIDE'S FATHER. *(Beside himself.)* There's a lot of people dancing. Look carefully!

MAID. I did!

BRIDE'S FATHER. *(Crestfallen.)* Well where is she then?

GROOM. *(Entering.)* Gone. She's nowhere.

GROOM'S MOTHER. *(To the BRIDE'S FATHER.)* What's the meaning of this? Where's your daughter?

(Enter LEONARDO'S WIFE.)

LEONARDO'S WIFE. They've run off together! They've run off! She and Leonardo! On the horse like a bolt of lightning, clinging to each another.

BRIDE'S FATHER. That can't be! Not my daughter!

GROOM'S MOTHER. Yes, your daughter! Evil just like her mother. Him too. But she's the wife of my son now!

GROOM. Let's go after them! Who's got a horse?

GROOM'S MOTHER. Yes, a horse, who has a horse? Now! I'll give him anything I have: my eyes, my tongue . . .

VOICE. We have one here.

GROOM'S MOTHER. *(To the GROOM.)* Go! After them!

(Exit the GROOM with two YOUNG MEN.)

No! Don't go! Those people know how to kill . . . but yes, go, and I'll be right behind you!

BRIDE'S FATHER. This isn't like her. Maybe she threw herself into the cistern.

GROOM'S MOTHER. Drowning is for honorable women, for clean women: not that one! But she's the wife of my son now. Two sides. There are two sides here.

(Enter ALL.)

My family and yours. Go, all of you. Shake the dust from your shoes. Let's go help my son.

(People separate into two groups.)

Because he's got people behind him: cousins from the coast plus all the ones from inland. Go! Spread out and start tracking them! The time for blood has come again. Two sides. You and yours, me and mine. After them, after them!

—CURTAIN—

Act 3, Tableau 1

(A woods a night. Thick, dew-covered tree trunks. Darkness. Violins are playing. Enter three WOODCUTTERS.)

WOODCUTTER 1. So did they find them?

WOODCUTTER 2. No, but they're searching everywhere.

WOODCUTTER 3. It's just a matter of time.

WOODCUTTER 2. Shhh!

WOODCUTTER 3. What?

WOODCUTTER 2. I hear footsteps all around.

WOODCUTTER 1. When the moon comes out they'll find them.

WOODCUTTER 2. They should just leave them alone.

WOODCUTTER 1. It's a big world. Enough space for everybody.

WOODCUTTER 3. They're going to kill them.

WOODCUTTER 2. You've got to follow your instincts. They were right to flee.

WOODCUTTER 1. They were fooling each other and in the end their blood won out.

WOODCUTTER 3. Blood!

WOODCUTTER 1. You have to follow where blood leads.

WOODCUTTER 2. But blood that sees the light gets drunk up by the earth.

WOODCUTTER 1. So what? Better to bleed to death than to live with stagnant veins.

WOODCUTTER 3. Quiet.

WOODCUTTER 1. What, do you hear something?

WOODCUTTER 3. I hear crickets, frogs, the advance of the night.

WOODCUTTER 1. But not the horse.

WOODCUTTER 3. No.

WOODCUTTER 1. He must have his hands all over her right now.

WOODCUTTER 2. Their bodies were meant for each other.

WOODCUTTER 3. They'll find them and they'll kill them.

WOODCUTTER 1.   But they've probably already coupled their blood. At this point they're like an empty pitcher, a dry stream.

WOODCUTTER 2.   It's very cloudy. The moon may not come out.

WOODCUTTER 3.   The groom will find them with or without the moon. I saw him racing out like a lunatic comet, all ash colored, glowing with the destiny of his clan.

WOODCUTTER 1.   His clan: stone dead and facedown in the street.

WOODCUTTER 2.   Exactly!

WOODCUTTER 3.   Do you think they'll manage to break past the search party?

WOODCUTTER 2.   It won't be easy. The forest is teeming with knives and shotguns.

WOODCUTTER 3.   He's got a good horse.

WOODCUTTER 2.   But he's got a woman too.

WOODCUTTER 1.   Here's our tree.

WOODCUTTER 2.   A forty-brancher. We'll have it down in no time.

WOODCUTTER 3.   The moon's coming out now. Let's hurry.

(A brightening appears to the left.)

WOODCUTTER 1.
    Oh, emergent moon!
    Large-leafed moon!

WOODCUTTER 2.
    Blood with jasmine strewn.

WOODCUTTER 1.
    Oh, lonesome moon!
    Green-leafed moon!

WOODCUTTER 2.
    The silver-faced bride doth swoon.

WOODCUTTER 3.
    Oh, evil moon!
    The dark branch of love is hewn.

WOODCUTTER 1.
    Oh, melancholy moon!
    The dark branch of love is hewn.

(Exit WOODCUTTERS. In the brightening at the left, the MOON appears, a young woodcutter with a white face. The scene is bathed in blue light.)

MOON.
>A plump swan in the river,
>an eye in the cathedral,
>a fraudulent dawn in the foliage
>am I: they shall not escape!
>Who's that hiding? Who sobs
>in the thicket of the valley?
>The moon leaves a dagger
>freely exposed to the air,
>a stalking blade of lead
>that desires the pain of blood.
>Let me in! My flesh freezes
>outside walls and windows!
>Open a roof or bare breast
>where I might warm myself.
>So cold I am! My ashes
>of sleep-weary metal
>search for a crest of fire
>along mountains and alleys.
>But the snow bears me
>on its shoulders of jasper,
>and I drown in the pools,
>rough and cold, of stagnant valleys.
>But tonight my cheeks
>shall glow red with blood,
>and the reeds shall cluster
>at the wide foot of the breeze.
>Let there be no shadowy ambush
>from which they escape!
>For I need a bare breast
>for refuge and warmth.
>A heart of my own,
>beating hot, that spills
>down the hills of my chest!
>Let me in, oh, and let me rest!

(To the branches.)

>I want no shadows. My glow
>must reach every corner,

so that your dark trunks
may rustle with soft light,
so that my cold cheeks
may run with sweet blood,
so that the reeds may cluster
at the wide foot of the breeze.
Who hides there! Out I say!
No, they shall not escape!
I will bathe their horse in light,
a feverish diamond in the night.

(The MOON disappears among the tree trunks, and the scene returns to normal dark lighting. An OLD BEGGAR WOMAN enters, covered from head to foot in threadbare, greenish-black rags. She walks barefoot, her face barely visible through the rags. This character does not appear in the Dramatis Personae.)

BEGGAR WOMAN.
The moon retreats and they draw closer.
They won't pass this point. The roar of the river,
joined to the rustle of the trees, will drown out
the bloodcurdled rush of their screams.
This is where it happens, and soon. I am weary.
Linen chests open and white sheets,
spread out on bedroom floors,
await heavy bodies with slashed throats.
Not a bird shall stir, and the breeze,
gathering up their groans in its skirt,
shall flee with them through the darkened trees
or bury them in the gentle dirt.

(Impatiently.)

That moon, that moon!

(The MOON reappears, and the blue light returns.)

MOON. They're getting close: through the ravine and along the river. I'm going to shine some light on the rocks. What do you need?

BEGGAR WOMAN. Nothing.

MOON. The wind is picking up. It has a double edge.

BEGGAR WOMAN. Shine some light on his vest and make the buttons glow. The knives will find their way.

MOON.
> May their death be slow.
> May their blood whistle softly on my fingers.
> See how my valleys of ash awaken
> before this spurting fount that lingers.

BEGGAR WOMAN. We mustn't let them cross the stream. Silence!

MOON. Here they come!

(Exit. The set goes dark.)

BEGGAR WOMAN. Hurry. Pour on the light! Do you hear me? They can't escape!

(Enter the GROOM and YOUNG MAN 1. The BEGGAR WOMAN sits and covers herself with her shawl.)

GROOM. This way.

YOUNG MAN 1. You'll never find them.

GROOM. *(Bristling.)* The hell I won't!

YOUNG MAN 1. I think they followed a different trail.

GROOM. No. I heard a gallop just a second ago.

YOUNG MAN 1. It must've been a different horse.

GROOM. *(Dramatically.)* Listen to me. There's only one horse in the world, and it's this one. Do you understand? If you insist on coming with me, keep your mouth shut.

YOUNG MAN 1. I just—

GROOM. Quiet. I'm certain I'll find them here. Do you see this arm? Well it's not my arm. It's the arm of my brother and of my father and of my whole dead family. And it's strong enough to pull this tree up by the roots. Let's do this thing quickly, for I feel the teeth of my clan gnawing at me and I can't breathe.

BEGGAR WOMAN. *(In a whining voice.)* Oh!

YOUNG MAN 1. Did you hear that?

GROOM. Go that way and circle back.

YOUNG MAN 1. This is a real hunt.

GROOM. Yes, a hunt. The greatest of all.

(*Exit YOUNG MAN 1. The GROOM moves quickly to the left and runs into the BEGGAR WOMAN, who is Death.*)

BEGGAR WOMAN. Oh!

GROOM. What do you want?

BEGGAR WOMAN. I'm cold.

GROOM. Where are you going?

BEGGAR WOMAN. (*Continuing to whine like a beggar.*) Far away . . .

GROOM. Where are you coming from?

BEGGAR WOMAN. From over there . . . from far away.

GROOM. Did you see a man and a woman galloping away on horseback?

BEGGAR WOMAN. (*Perking up.*) Just a moment . . .

> (*She looks at him.*)
>
> You're a handsome young man.
>
> (*She stands.*)
>
> But you'd be much more handsome if you were asleep.

GROOM. Answer me: Did you see them?

BEGGAR WOMAN. Just a moment . . . What a broad back you have! You should be lying on it instead of walking around on those tiny feet.

GROOM. (*Grabbing and shaking her.*) I'm asking you if you saw them! Did they come through here?

BEGGAR WOMAN. (*Vehemently.*) No, they didn't, but they're coming down the hill now. Don't you hear them?

GROOM. No.

BEGGAR WOMAN. You don't know the trail?

GROOM. I'll get there regardless.

BEGGAR WOMAN. I'll go with you. I know these parts.

GROOM. (*Impatiently.*) Let's go then! Which way?

BEGGAR WOMAN. (*Dramatically.*) That way!

> (*The GROOM and BEGGAR WOMAN exit quickly. In the distance violins play a theme that represents the woods. The WOODCUTTERS return, their axes slung over their shoulders. They move slowly among the tree trunks.*)

WOODCUTTER 1.
> Oh, emergent death!
> Large-leafed death.

WOODCUTTER 2.
> Don't open the bloody spigot, death!

WOODCUTTER 1.
> Oh, lonesome death!
> Dry-leafed death.

WOODCUTTER 3.
> The wedding of flowers bereft!

WOODCUTTER 2.
> Oh, melancholy death!
> May the green branch for love be left.

WOODCUTTER 1.
> Oh, evil death!
> May the green branch for love be left.

(They begin exiting as they speak. Enter LEONARDO and the BRIDE.)

LEONARDO.
> Quiet, my love!

BRIDE.
> I'll go on alone from here.
> Flee! I want you to return.

LEONARDO.
> Quiet, I said!

BRIDE.
> With your teeth,
> with your hands, however you wish,
> strip from my honorable neck
> the metal of this chain
> and leave me in a corner
> back in my earthen hut.
> And if you won't kill me
> like a poisonous snake,
> then place in my betrothed hands
> the barrel of the gun.
> Oh, what grief, what fever
> swirls up to my head!
> What shards of glass perforate my tongue!

LEONARDO.
    We can't undo our steps. Quiet!
    For they're drawing closer
    and I aim to take you with me.

BRIDE.
    It'll have to be by force!

LEONARDO.
    By force? Who was the one
    who first came down the stairs?

BRIDE.
    It was I.

LEONARDO.
        And who put
    a new bridle on the horse?

BRIDE.
    I did. It's true.

LEONARDO.
          Whose hands
    strapped spurs to my boots?

BRIDE.
    Mine, which are also yours,
    but in your presence they long
    to plumb the blue branches
    and the soft murmur of your veins.
    I love you! I love you! Away with you!
    If I could kill you,
    I'd cover you in a shroud
    embroidered with violets.
    Oh, what grief, what fever
    swirls up to my head!

LEONARDO.
    What shards of glass perforate my tongue!
    For I tried to forget you,
    and I raised a stone wall
    between your house and mine.
    It's true. Do you not recall?
    And when I saw you from afar
    I hurled sand in my own eyes.

>   But when I mounted my horse
>   it would take me to your door.
>   The silver pins of your gown
>   turned my red blood black,
>   and sleep choked my flesh
>   with the bitterest of weeds.
>   The fault is not my own,
>   for it lies with the earth
>   and with the fragrance
>   that spills from your breasts.

BRIDE.
>   Oh, what madness! I wish not
>   to share your bed or table,
>   yet there's not a minute of the day
>   I don't desire your company,
>   for you drag me and I go,
>   you tell me to turn around
>   and I follow you on the wind
>   like a delicate blade of grass.
>   I left a strong, decent man
>   and his entire family
>   abandoned at the altar,
>   wedding crown on my head.
>   You will be the one punished
>   and I cannot have that.
>   Leave me! Go, please, flee!
>   You have no one on your side.

LEONARDO.
>   The birds of dawn
>   are stirring in the trees.
>   The night is expiring
>   beneath a blade of stone.
>   Let's be off to a dark corner
>   where I can love you forever,
>   for I care not for anyone
>   or the venom they will spew.

(He embraces her vigorously.)

BRIDE.
>   And I will sleep at your feet
>   and watch over your dreams.
>   Naked, gazing out at the land

(Dramatically.)
>like a bitch in heat,
>for that's what I am!
>Scorched by your beauty.

LEONARDO.
>Fire begets fire.
>A tiny flame
>kills two ears of wheat.
>Let's be off!

(He drags her forward.)

BRIDE.
>Where are you taking me?

LEONARDO.
>Where we can't be found
>by these men who hunt us.
>Where I can look at you!

BRIDE. *(Sarcastically.)*
>Bring me to the county fair
>where proper women can frown
>and everyone can see me
>with my wedding sheets
>waving like banners in the breeze.

LEONARDO.
>I, too, would abandon you
>if I thought the way others do.
>But I go where you go.
>Just try to take a step without me.
>We're clamped together by the moon,
>my loins to yours.

(This entire scene carries a hint of violence and great sensuality.)

BRIDE.
>Did you hear that?

LEONARDO.
>>They're coming.

BRIDE.
>>>Run!
>It's right for me to die here

> with my feet in the water
> and thorns upon my head.
> To be mourned by the leaves,
> a ruined woman and a virgin.

LEONARDO.
> Shh! They're almost here.

BRIDE.
> Run!

LEONARDO.
> Silence or they'll hear us.
> You first. Go, I say!

(The BRIDE hesitates.)

BRIDE.
> Arm in arm.

LEONARDO. *(Embracing her.)*
> As you wish!
> They will have to pry you
> from my lifeless grip.

BRIDE.
> And you from my stiffened limbs.

(Exit, arm in arm. The MOON appears slowly, and an intense blue light bathes the scene. The violins play. Two bloodcurdling screams are heard, and the violins stop. After the second scream the BEGGAR WOMAN appears and stands with her back to the audience. She spreads her shawl at center stage like a great bird with enormous wings. The MOON freezes. The curtain drops in absolute silence.)

—CURTAIN—

Act 3, Tableau 2

White room with arches and thick walls. White stairs to the right and left. Upstage, a large arch and a wall of the same color. The floor, too, is a brilliant white. The simple room has the historic feeling of a church. There are no grays, no shadows, not even enough to give perspective. Two GIRLS dressed in dark blue are unwinding a skein of red yarn while a little girl watches.)

GIRL 1.
> Ball of yarn, ball of yarn,
> what do you spin?

GIRL 2.
> A jasmine dress,
> a paper window.
> Born at four,
> dead by ten.
> A thread of wool,
> a chain at your feet,
> a knot that ties
> the bitter leaf.

LITTLE GIRL. *(Humming.)*
> Were you two at the wedding?

GIRL 1.
> No.

LITTLE GIRL.
> Neither was I!
> What could have happened
> among the stalks of the vineyard?
> What could have happened
> among the leaves of the olive grove?
> How can it be that
> no one has returned?
> Did you go to the wedding?

GIRL 2.
> We told you no.

LITTLE GIRL. *(Moving to exit.)*
> Neither did I!

GIRL 2.
> Ball of yarn, ball of yarn,
> what do you sing?

GIRL 1.
> Wounds of wax,
> pain of myrtle.
> Asleep in the morning,
> awake all night.

LITTLE GIRL. *(In the doorway.)*

>   The yarn gets caught
>   on the hardened flint.
>   The blue mountains
>   let it pass right through.
>   It runs and runs
>   and finally comes
>   to brandish a knife
>   and steal the buns.

GIRL 2.
>   Ball of yarn, ball of yarn,
>   what do you say?

GIRL 1.
>   A speechless lover.
>   A crimson groom.
>   Along the river
>   I saw them swoon.

(She pauses, staring at the skein.)

LITTLE GIRL. *(Peeking through the door.)*
>   It runs and runs,
>   the thread runs to here.
>   Covered in mud,
>   I hear them near.
>   Splayed bodies,
>   ivory fear.

(Exit the LITTLE GIRL. Enter LEONARDO'S WIFE and his MOTHER-IN-LAW, full of anguish.)

GIRL 1.
>   Are they coming now?

LEONARDO'S MOTHER-IN-LAW. *(Bitterly.)*
>   We don't know.

GIRL 2.
>   So how was the wedding?

GIRL 1.
>   Tell us.

LEONARDO'S MOTHER-IN-LAW. *(Coldly.)*
>   No.

LEONARDO'S WIFE.
>	I want to return to see what happened.

LEONARDO'S MOTHER-IN-LAW.   *(Vehemently.)*
>	What you need is to go home.
>	Brave and alone in your house,
>	weeping as you grow old,
>	and on your door a bolt.
>	No guests, dead or alive, no.
>	We'll nail your windows closed.
>	May rain and darkness
>	with your bitter herbs be sown.

LEONARDO'S WIFE.
>	But what could've happened?

LEONARDO'S MOTHER-IN-LAW.
>	It matters not.
>	Draw a veil across your face.
>	Your children are all you've got.
>	Place a cross of ashes on your bed
>	where his pillow used to rest.

(Exit LEONARDO'S WIFE and MOTHER-IN-LAW.)

BEGGAR WOMAN.   *(At the door.)*
>	Can you spare a piece of bread, girls?

LITTLE GIRL.
>	Go away!

(The three GIRLS cluster together.)

BEGGAR WOMAN.
>	 But why?

LITTLE GIRL.
>	 Because you whine.

GIRL 1.
>	Such harsh words, little girl!

BEGGAR WOMAN.
>	I could have asked for your eyes!
>	A cloud of birds chases me. Want one?

LITTLE GIRL.
>	 I want out of here!

GIRL 2.   *(To the BEGGAR WOMAN.)*
      Don't pay her any mind.

GIRL 1.
      Did you come by way of the stream?

BEGGAR WOMAN.
      Yes, that's how I came!

GIRL 1.   *(Timidly.)*
      May I ask?

BEGGAR WOMAN.
      They'll be here soon: two torrents,
      finally at peace among the boulders,
      two men at the foot of a horse.
      Killed in the beauty of darkness.

  (Savoring.)
      Killed, yes, killed.

GIRL 1.
      Shut up, you old crone!

BEGGAR WOMAN.
      I saw them. Their eyes ruptured flowers,
      their teeth fistfuls of hardened snow.
      Both of them fallen low,
      the bride's skirt caked in their blood.
      Covered by a pair of blankets they come,
      by tall shoulders and strong hands borne.
      That's how it was, and it was just.
      Filthy sand atop the flower of gold.

(Exit the BEGGAR WOMAN. The older GIRLS tilt their heads and begin leaving rhythmically.)

GIRL 1.
      Filthy sand.

GIRL 2.
      Atop the flower of gold.

LITTLE GIRL.
      Atop the flower of gold
      they bring those killed by the brook.
      Olive-skinned the one,
      and the second one too.

> The nightingale flies somber
> over the flower of gold!

(Exit. The scene is deserted. Enter the GROOM'S MOTHER with a tearful NEIGHBOR WOMAN.)

GROOM'S MOTHER. Stop it.

NEIGHBOR WOMAN. I can't.

GROOM'S MOTHER. Stop it, I say.

(In the doorway.)

Is there no one here?

(She wipes her brow.)

My son should be answering me. But my son is now an armful of dried flowers. My son is now a dark voice behind the mountains.

(Angrily.)

Will you please stop? I want no crying in this house. Your tears come only from your eyes, but mine will come when I'm alone: from the bottom of my feet, from my roots, hotter than blood.

NEIGHBOR WOMAN. Come to my house. Don't stay here by yourself.

GROOM'S MOTHER. This is where I want to be. At peace. They're all dead now. I'll sleep through the night, I'll sleep soundly without fear of the shotgun or the knife. Other mothers will lean out the window in the pouring rain to see the faces of their sons. Not me. I'll carve a cold ivory dove from my sleep, which will bear camellias of frost over the graveyard. Wait, not a graveyard: a bed of earth, a bed that will shelter them and rock them in the sky.

(Enter a WOMAN in black who turns to the right and kneels. The GROOM'S MOTHER continues to address the NEIGHBOR WOMAN.)

Take your hands from your face. We're in for some terrible days. I don't want to see anyone. Just me and the land. Me and my tears. And these four walls. Oh! Oh!

(She sits, overcome.)

NEIGHBOR WOMAN. Have some mercy on yourself.

GROOM'S MOTHER. *(Smoothing her hair.)* I'll be fine. Because the neighbor women will come and I don't want them to see me so bereft. So bereft! A woman who doesn't even have a son she can press her lips to.

(Enter the BRIDE, without her crown of orange blossoms. She wears a black shawl.)

NEIGHBOR WOMAN. *(Eying the BRIDE. Wrathfully.)* Where do you think you're going?

BRIDE. Here: I'm coming here.

GROOM'S MOTHER. *(To the NEIGHBOR WOMAN.)* Who is it?

NEIGHBOR WOMAN. Don't you recognize her?

GROOM'S MOTHER. That's why I'm asking you who it is. Because I have to avoid recognizing her, or I'll sink my teeth into her neck. Serpent!

(She rushes toward the BRIDE with a threatening gesture, then stops herself, continuing to address the NEIGHBOR WOMAN.)

Can you believe this? There she is, crying, and I stand here without gouging her eyes out. I don't understand myself. Did I not love my son? And what of his honor? Where is his honor now?

(She slaps the BRIDE, who falls to the floor.)

NEIGHBOR WOMAN. For God's sake!

(She tries to separate them.)

BRIDE. Don't stop her. I came here so she could kill me and I could be dragged away with the other bodies.

(To the GROOM'S MOTHER.)

But not with your hands. With a pair of meat hooks or a sickle, and with all your might, until the metal hits my bones. Let her! I just want her to know that I'm pure. I may be mad, but I will go to the grave unsullied: not a single man has known the whiteness of my breasts.

GROOM'S MOTHER. Shut your mouth. What difference does that make to me?

BRIDE. Because I ran off with the other one, I did!

(With anguish.)

You would have done the same. I was a parched woman, covered in blisters inside and out, and your son was a little trickle of water that was supposed to give me children, land, well-being. But the other man was a dark river swirling with leaves who would come near me with his rustling reeds and his soothing song. And I'd run to your son and he was like a little boy with a sip of cool water, while the other would send me flocks of birds that would block my way and leave my wounds poulticed in frost: the wounds of a miserable, scorched woman, of a little girl licked by fire. I didn't want to do it—hear me out!—I did not want to. Your son was my only purpose and I didn't cheat on him, but the other man's arm swept me away like an ocean breaker, like the pull of a mule, and it would have swept me along forever and ever, even when I got to be an old woman and your son's sons tried to pull me away by the hair!

(Enter another NEIGHBOR WOMAN.)

GROOM'S MOTHER. Of course: she's not to blame. Nor am I!

(Sarcastically.)

Who's to blame, then? Only a loose, weak, indecent woman throws away her wedding crown to go in search of a bed warmed by another man's wife!

BRIDE. Enough! Just take your vengeance: that's why I'm here! My neck is softer than the dahlias you pluck from your garden. But I won't listen to you impugn my honor. I'm purer than a newborn. And brave enough to prove it. Light the fire and we'll stick our hands in: you for your son and me for my body. I guarantee you you'll pull yours out first.

(Enter another NEIGHBOR WOMAN.)

GROOM'S MOTHER. What does your honor matter to me? Or your death? What does anything matter to me? Blessed be the wheat, for my sons lie beneath it. Blessed be the rain, for it moistens the faces of the dead. Blessed be the Lord, for he lays us all together to rest.

(Enter another NEIGHBOR WOMAN.)

BRIDE. Let me weep with you.

GROOM'S MOTHER. Weep then. But in the doorway.

(Enter the LITTLE GIRL. The BRIDE stands in the doorway, the GROOM'S MOTHER center stage. LEONARDO'S WIFE enters and walks to the left.)

LEONARDO'S WIFE.
  Once a beautiful horseman,
  now a mound of snow.
  He visited fairs and hillsides
  and the arms of women.
  Now the moss of night
  adorns his forehead.

GROOM'S MOTHER.
  My child, my sunflower,

mirror of the earth.
May your breast
with bitter oleander be crossed
and covered in a sheet
of shimmering silk;
may the water weep
between your motionless hands.

LEONARDO'S WIFE.
Oh, I see four young men
who arrive with weary shoulders!

BRIDE. Oh, I see four handsome youth
who bring death upon the wind!

GROOM'S MOTHER.
Neighbors—

LITTLE GIRL. *(In the doorway.)*
They're bringing them now.

GROOM'S MOTHER.
It doesn't matter.
The Cross, the Cross.

WOMEN.
Sweet the nails,
sweet the Cross,
sweet the name
of Christ our Lord.

BRIDE.
May the Cross provide shelter
to the living and the dead.

GROOM'S MOTHER.
Neighbors: with a knife,
with a tiny knife,
on a fateful day between two and three,
two men killed each other for love.
With a knife,
with a tiny knife
that barely fills the hand
but slices delicately
through terrified flesh
and comes to a halt where
the dark root of the scream

sits in a quivering coil.
This from a knife,
a tiny knife
that barely fills the hand:
a monstrous thing
like a fish without scales,
all so that on a fateful day
between two and three,
this knife could turn two men stiff
and turn their lips yellow.
And it barely fills the hand
yet it slices coldly
through terrified flesh
and comes to a halt where
the dark root of the scream
sits in a quivering coil.

(The NEIGHBOR WOMEN kneel on the floor and weep.)

—CURTAIN—

Yerma:
Tragic Poem in Three Acts and Six Tableaux

DRAMATIS PERSONAE

Yerma
María
Old Pagan Woman
Dolores
Washerwoman 1
Washerwoman 2
Washerwoman 3
Washerwoman 4
Washerwoman 5
Washerwoman 6
Girl 1
Girl 2
Female Mask
Yerma's Sister-in-Law 1
Yerma's Sister-in-Law 2
Woman 1
Woman 2
Boys
Juan
Víctor
Male Mask
Man 1
Man 2
Man 3

Act 1, Tableau 1

(When the curtain rises YERMA is asleep with a sewing basket at her feet. The scene has a strange dreamy light. A SHEPHERD enters on tiptoe, staring at YERMA. He walks hand in hand with a little BOY dressed in white. The clock strikes. When the SHEPHERD exits, the light becomes cheerful like that of a spring morning. YERMA wakes up.)

SONG. *(Offstage.)*
    Rock-a-bye, baby, rock-a-bye,
    let's be off to the countryside.
    We'll build a hut there, baby,
    and lock ourselves inside.

YERMA.   Juan? Are you there? Juan.

JUAN.   *[Entering.]* I'm here.

YERMA.   It's time.

JUAN.   Did the plows go by?

YERMA.   All of them.

JUAN.   I'm off.

(He begins to exit.)

YERMA.   Why don't you have a glass of milk?

JUAN.   What for?

YERMA.   You work very hard and don't have the kind of body that will hold up.

JUAN.   When men grow lean they get strong, like steel.

YERMA.   But not you. When we got married you were a different person. Now your face is so pale it's as if the sun never touched it. I'd like to see you go to the river and swim and go up to the rooftop when the rain soaks our house. We've been married for two years and you keep getting sadder, leaner, as if you were growing in reverse.

JUAN.   Are you finished?

YERMA.   *(Standing up.)* Don't take it the wrong way. If I were sick I'd like you to care for me. "My wife is sick: I'm going to slaughter this lamb to make her a nice stew. My wife is sick: I'm going to set aside this chicken fat to rub on her chest. I'm going to bring her this sheepskin to keep her feet warm." That's the way I am. That's why I take care of you.

JUAN. And I'm grateful.

YERMA. But you don't let yourself be cared for.

JUAN. Because there's nothing wrong with me. It's all in your head. I work hard. I'm getting older with each year.

YERMA. With each year . . . You and I will be here, year after year.

JUAN. *(Smiling.)* Of course. And we'll be comfortable. Work is plentiful, and we have no children to eat up our money.

YERMA. No children . . . Juan!

JUAN. What?

YERMA. Do I not love you?

JUAN. You do.

YERMA. I know girls who trembled and cried before getting into bed with their husbands. Did I cry the first time? Didn't I sing as I turned back the linens? Didn't I say to you: "How sweet these sheets smell, like apple!"

JUAN. You did!

YERMA. My mother cried because I wasn't sad to leave her. And it was true! No one was happier to get married. And yet . . .

JUAN. Stop it.

YERMA. And yet . . .

JUAN. Stop it. I work too hard to be always listening to—

YERMA. Stop, don't repeat what they say. I can see with my own eyes that it's not happening . . . With just a bit of rain the rocks grow tender and give rise to wild mustard, which people say is worthless. But I see its yellow flowers swaying in the breeze.

JUAN. Patience!

YERMA. Yes, and love!

(She boldly embraces and kisses her husband.)

JUAN. If you need anything let me know and I'll bring it. You know I don't like you going out.

YERMA. I never go out.

JUAN. You're better off here.

YERMA. Right.

JUAN.   Outside is for idlers.

YERMA.   *(Gloomily.)* Of course.

(JUAN exits and YERMA walks toward the sewing area. She runs her hand over her abdomen, stretches her arms with a sleepy yawn, and sits down to sew.)

> Where do you come from, my child?
> "From the summit cold and wild."

(She threads a needle.)

> What do you need, my love?
> "The warm fabric of your glove."
> Let the branches shake in the sun
> and the brooks babble and run!

(As if talking to a child.)

> The dog barks at the breeze,
> the wind sings in the trees.
> The oxen bray at the plow,
> the moon caresses my brow.
> What, faraway child, do you request?

(Pause.)

> "The white hills that rise in your breast."
> Let the branches shake in the sun
> and the brooks babble and run!

(Sewing.)

> I will say, my child, yes to you.
> For you I'm broken and split in two.
> How my womb weighs like lead
> where you'll make your tiny bed!
> When, my child, will you make me well?

(Pause.)

> "When your flesh of jasmine smells."
> Let the branches shake in the sun
> and the brooks babble and run!

(YERMA continues to sing. MARÍA enters with a bundle of clothes.)

YERMA.   Where have you been?

MARÍA.   The store.

YERMA.   At this hour?

MARÍA.   I'd have stood in line forever. Guess what I bought!

YERMA.   Coffee, sugar, and bread for breakfast.

MARÍA.   No. I bought lace, three spools of thread, ribbons, and colored wool to make tassels. My husband gave me the money himself.

YERMA.   You must be making a fancy blouse for yourself.

MARÍA.   No, it's because . . . can't you guess?

YERMA.   What?

MARÍA.   It's finally here!

(She lowers her head in modesty. YERMA stands and stares at her in amazement.)

YERMA.   After only five months!

MARÍA.   Yes.

YERMA.   Did you know right away?

MARÍA.   Of course.

YERMA.   *(With curiosity.)* What does it feel like?

MARÍA.   I don't know.

(Pause.)

I feel anxious.

YERMA.   Anxious.

(Moving very close to MARÍA.)

So when did it happen, tell me. I'll bet you weren't even thinking about it.

MARÍA.   Not at all . . .

YERMA.   I'll bet you were singing, right? I sing. Do you? . . . Tell me.

MARÍA.   Don't ask such things. Have you ever held a live bird in your hand?

YERMA.   Yes.

MARÍA.   Well it's like that . . . but in your blood.

YERMA.   How lovely!

(She gazes at MARÍA in rapture.)

MARÍA.   I'm still in a daze. I don't know anything.

YERMA.   About what?

MARÍA.   About what I'm supposed to do. I'll have to ask my mother.

YERMA.   I wouldn't bother her. She's getting old and won't remember. Just don't move about a lot, and when you breathe do it softly, as if holding a rose between your teeth.

MARÍA.   They say later on you can feel it kicking with its little legs.

YERMA.   That's when you'll really start to love it, when you can finally say "My child"!

MARÍA.   Mixed in with everything else I feel shame.

YERMA.   What does your husband say?

MARÍA.   Nothing.

YERMA.   Does he love you a lot?

MARÍA.   He doesn't say so, but he when gets close to me his eyes quiver like a pair of tender green leaves.

YERMA.   Did he guess that you were . . . ?

MARÍA.   Yes.

YERMA.   How?

MARÍA.   I don't know. But on our wedding night he kept talking about it with his lips pressed against my cheek. So now I think of this child as a glowing dove that he slipped into me through my ear.

YERMA.   You're so lucky!

MARÍA.   But you know a lot more about all this than me.

YERMA.   For all the good it does me.

MARÍA.   It's true! What could the reason be? Of all the new wives you're the only one who still . . .

YERMA.   So it is. Of course there's still time. Elena took three years, and some older women, from my mother's generation, took even longer. But two years and twenty days is already too long for me. It feels unfair to waste away like this. Often I go out to the patio barefoot just to feel the earth beneath my feet, I don't know why. If I keep on like this I'll end up going crazy.

MARÍA.   Oh, poor darling, come here! You speak as if you were an old woman. Don't pay any attention to me! There's no predicting these things. One of my mother's sisters took fourteen years, and you should have seen what a beautiful little boy she had!

YERMA. *(Anxiously.)* What was he like?

MARÍA. He would cry like a little bull, like a thousand cicadas singing in unison, and he'd pee on us and pull at our braids, and at four months he filled our faces with scratches.

YERMA. *(Laughing.)* But those things don't hurt.

MARÍA. I'll tell you—

YERMA. Come on! I've watched my sister suckle her baby with her breast full of scratch marks. Very painful, but a good pain, nice and healthy.

MARÍA. They say children cause much suffering.

YERMA. Nonsense. That's what the weakling mothers say, the complainers. Why do they go and have children in the first place? A child is not a bed of roses. We must suffer to see them grow. I think we must give them about half our blood. But that's a good thing, wholesome and beautiful. Every woman has blood for four or five children, and when they don't bear any the blood turns to venom, which is what's going to happen to me.

MARÍA. I don't know what's wrong with me.

YERMA. I've always heard that those who conceive early are skittish.

MARÍA. *(Timidly.)* We'll see. Anyway, since you sew so well . . .

YERMA. *(Reaching for the bundle.)* Sure, I'll make the clothes for you. What are these for?

MARÍA. For the diapers.

YERMA. Okay.

(She sits.)

MARÍA. Okay then . . . I'll see you.

(She draws near, and YERMA runs her hand affectionately across her abdomen.)

YERMA. Don't go running across the cobblestones.

MARÍA. Bye.

(She gives her a peck on the cheek and exits.)

YERMA. Come back soon!

(YERMA adopts the same attitude as at the beginning. She takes the scissors and begins cutting. Enter VÍCTOR.)

Víctor!

VÍCTOR. *(Intense and serious.)* Where's Juan?

YERMA. In the field.

VÍCTOR. What are you sewing?

YERMA. I'm making some diapers.

VÍCTOR. *(Smiling.)* You don't say!

YERMA. *(She laughs.)* I'm going to line them with lace.

VÍCTOR. If it's a girl you can give her your name.

YERMA. *(Startled.)* What . . . ?

VÍCTOR. I'm happy for you.

YERMA. *(Stumbling for words.)* No . . . they're not for me. They're for María's child.

VÍCTOR. Well, let's see if you can follow her example. This house needs a child.

YERMA. *(Anxiously.)* Yes it does.

VÍCTOR. Well then. Tell your husband to stop thinking so much about work. He wants to save money and he will, but who will he leave it all to when he dies? Anyway, tell him I've got the sheep. He can come by for the two he bought from me. As for the other matter, tell him to . . . concentrate!

(He exits smiling.)

YERMA. *(Exuberantly.)* Exactly, concentrate!

(YERMA stands pensively and walks to where VÍCTOR was standing. She breathes in deeply as if taking in fresh mountain air, then goes to the other side of the room as if looking for something. She sits again and reaches anew for the sewing materials. She begins to sew, staring at a fixed point.)

> I will say, my child, yes to you.
> For you I'm broken and split in two.
> How my womb weighs like lead
> where you'll make your tiny bed!
> When, my child, will you make me well?
> "When your flesh of jasmine smells."

—CURTAIN—

Act 1, Tableau 2

(A field in the countryside. Enter YERMA, carrying a basket, and an OLD WOMAN.)

YERMA.   Good afternoon.

OLD WOMAN.   Good afternoon to the pretty girl. Where are you off to?

YERMA.   I just took lunch to my husband, who's working in the olive groves.

OLD WOMAN.   Have you been married long?

YERMA.   Three years.

OLD WOMAN.   Any children?

YERMA.   No.

OLD WOMAN.   Don't worry. They'll come!

YERMA.   *(Anxiously.)* You really think so?

OLD WOMAN.   Why wouldn't they?

(She sits.)

I also just brought lunch to my husband. He's old, but he still works the fields. I have nine children bright as the sun, but since none of them are women, here I am still doing all the chores.

YERMA.   You live on the other side of the river.

OLD WOMAN.   Yes. Near the mill. What family do you come from?

YERMA.   I'm the daughter of Enrique the shepherd.

OLD WOMAN.   Oh, Enrique the shepherd! I knew him. A good man. Rose with the sun, sweated in the fields, ate his bread, and died. No fun and games, no nothing. Not a man for the county fair. He came from a silent bunch. I could have married one of your uncles. But please! I've always been a woman with my skirt in the air. I go straight for the ripest piece of the melon, for the party, for the pastry piled with sugar. Many times I've gotten up early and gone to the door thinking I'd heard banjo music coming and going in the distance, but it was just the wind.

(She laughs.)

You're going to laugh at me. I've had two husbands and fourteen children, six of whom died, yet I'm not the least bit sad. I'd like to go on living for much longer. It's like I always say: fig trees, they last forever; houses, they last forever; it's just us bedeviled women who break down for no good reason.

YERMA. I'd like to ask you a question.

OLD WOMAN. Go ahead.

(She looks at her.)

Though I know what you're going to ask. One of those things that can't be spoken.

(She stands.)

YERMA. *(Stopping her.)* Can't be spoken why? You seem so wise, and I've been wishing to talk to a woman of your age for a while now. I have questions I think you could answer . . .

OLD WOMAN. What questions?

YERMA. *(Lowering her voice.)* You know. Why I'm . . . childless. Am I just supposed to turn my back on the prime of my life and start raising pigeons or hanging curtains? No. You will tell me what I have to do, and I'll do whatever it is, even jabbing needles in my eyes.

OLD WOMAN. Me? I know nothing. I just laid on my back and started singing. The children came like water. Don't let anyone tell you this isn't a beautiful body you have! You just have to take a step and the horse down the street will neigh. Oh, you'd better leave me, girl! Don't get me started talking. There are too many things I shouldn't say.

YERMA. Why not? This is all I talk about with my husband!

OLD WOMAN. Do you fancy your husband?

YERMA. What do you mean?

OLD WOMAN. Do you fancy him? Do you desire to be with him?

YERMA. I don't know.

YERMA. Do you tremble when he comes near? Do you feel dizzy when he draws his lips close? Answer me.

YERMA. No, I've never felt anything like that.

OLD WOMAN. Never? Not even when you dance?

YERMA. *(Struggling to remember.)* Maybe once . . . with Víctor . . .

OLD WOMAN. Go on.

YERMA. He grabbed me by the waist and I couldn't say anything because I couldn't speak. Another time, when I was fourteen, this same Víctor—he was just a boy—he took me in his arms to jump over a ditch, and I caught such a shiver that my teeth chattered. But normally I'm very modest.

OLD WOMAN. What about with your husband?

YERMA. My husband is another story. My father arranged it all and I accepted. Happily. That's the honest truth. And as soon as we got engaged I started thinking about children. I'd observe myself in his eyes, yes, but it was to see myself in miniature, as if I were my own child.

OLD WOMAN. Nothing like me. Maybe that's why you haven't conceived. Men are there to give us pleasure, girl. They're supposed to unbraid our hair and bring us water to drink in their own mouths. That's the way of the world.

YERMA. Your world, not mine. I think about things, many things that I'm certain are meant for my child to act upon. I gave myself to my husband for this reason, and I continue giving myself to him to see if a child will result from it, but I never do it for pleasure.

OLD WOMAN. And you're surprised your womb is empty!

YERMA. No, not empty, for it's filling with hate. Tell me, am I really to blame? Are you supposed to look for the man in the man, nothing more? What about when he turns from you in bed, leaves you staring glumly at the ceiling, and falls asleep? Am I supposed to keep thinking about him or about the glowing life that might arise from my body? I don't know, but please tell me, for pity's sake.

(She kneels.)

OLD WOMAN. Oh, what a rosebud you are, such a lovely creature! Leave me, please. Don't make me talk any further. I can't tell you anything else. These are private matters and it's not my place to get involved. You understand. All I'll say is that you should be less innocent.

YERMA. *(Sadly.)* All doors are closed to country girls like me. Everything's a whisper, a half gesture, for they say these things can't be spoken. And you're no better. You turn away and keep all your wisdom to yourself, denying it to she who dies of thirst.

OLD WOMAN. I would share it with a calmer woman, but not with you. Trust me: I know what I'm talking about.

YERMA. God help me then.

OLD WOMAN. Not likely. I've never been fond of God. When are people going to realize he doesn't exist? It's men to whom you should turn for help.

YERMA. Why are you telling me this? Why?

OLD WOMAN. *(Moving toward the exit.)* There should be a god, though, even a tiny one, to strike down those men of rotten seed who dampen the happiness of the countryside.

YERMA. I don't understand your words.

OLD WOMAN. No matter, I understand them. Don't get lost in sadness. Be strong. You're still very young. What do you want from me?

(Exit OLD WOMAN. Enter two GIRLS.)

GIRL 1. We keep running into people everywhere.

YERMA. Of course. Someone has to deliver food to the men in the olive groves. The houses are empty except for the elderly.

GIRL 2. Are you headed back to the village?

YERMA. I am.

GIRL 1. I'm in a hurry. My little boy is taking a nap and there's no one at home.

YERMA. Well get moving, girl! You can't leave children alone like that. Do you have hogs at your house?

GIRL 1. No, but you're right. I need to hurry.

YERMA. Hurry then. This is how things happen. Surely you closed all the doors?

GIRL 1. Of course.

YERMA. Good, but you never know what could happen. A small child can be done in by the most harmless of things. A needle, a sip of water.

GIRL 1. You're right, I don't know where my head is. I'm off.

YERMA. Go!

[Exit GIRL 1.]

GIRL 2. If you had four or five of them, you wouldn't be talking that way.

YERMA. What! Even forty wouldn't change my mind.

GIRL 2. At any rate, you and I live calmer lives without children.

YERMA. Not me.

GIRL 2. Well I do. They're nothing but trouble! My mother keeps giving me herbal potions to help me conceive and in October we're going to the shrine. They say it grants fertility to anyone who prays to it with conviction. My mother will pray, not me.

YERMA. Why did you get married?

GIRL 2. Because it was arranged. All the girls are getting married. At this rate the only single women left will be eight-year-olds. And anyway . . . a girl gets married long before arriving at the altar. But the elders insist on these things. I'm nineteen years old and I don't like to cook or clean. So all day long I'm doing things I don't like. And for what purpose? Why does my husband have to be my husband? We did the same things we do now before we tied the knot. It's all a bunch of nonsense peddled by the old-timers.

YERMA. Shush, don't say such things.

GIRL 2. Go ahead and call me crazy like everyone else. "Here comes that crazy girl!"

(She laughs.)

I'll tell you the only thing I've learned in life: everyone is stuck at home doing things they don't like. It's so much better outside. You can go to the stream, you can climb the bell tower, you can order a cool drink with a drop of anisette.

YERMA. You're just a child.

GIRL 2. Okay, but I'm not a crazy one.

(She laughs.)

YERMA. Your mother lives at the top of the village, doesn't she?

GIRL 2. Yes.

YERMA. In the last house?

GIRL 2. Yes.

YERMA. What's her name?

GIRL 2. Dolores. Why do you ask?

YERMA. No reason.

GIRL 2. You must have asked for a reason.

YERMA. I don't know . . . it's nothing . . .

GIRL 2. If you say so. Anyway, I have to go make lunch for my husband.

(She laughs.)

That's the way things are. What a shame I can't call him my boyfriend! Know what I mean?

(She starts to exit, laughing happily.)

Bye.

VOICE OF VÍCTOR. (Singing. YERMA listens.)
   Why, shepherd, do you sleep alone?
   To my woolen quilt you are better prone.
   Why, shepherd, do you sleep alone?
   To my woolen quilt you are better prone.
   Shepherd: your quilt of dark stone
   and your shirt of cool frost
   and the gray reeds of winter
   fill the night you have sown.
   Shepherd: the oak trees put quills
   beneath your softest pillow,
   and if you hear the song of the daughter,
   it'll be the cracked voice of the water.
   Shepherd, shepherd:
   what does the hillside want of you?
   Hillside of bitter bristle:
   who is the child that kills you?
   The thorn of the thistle!

(She goes to exit and runs into VÍCTOR as he enters.)

VÍCTOR. (Cheerfully.) Where goes such beauty?

YERMA. Was that you singing?

VÍCTOR. It was.

YERMA. Beautiful! I'd never heard you sing before.

VÍCTOR. No?

YERMA. Such a powerful voice, like a torrent of water that fills your mouth.

VÍCTOR. I'm a cheerful person.

YERMA. That's true.

VÍCTOR. As you're a sad one.

YERMA. Not always. I'm just going through a sad phase.

VÍCTOR.   And your husband is even sadder.

YERMA.   With him it's true. It's in his character.

VÍCTOR.   He was always that way.

> *(Pause. YERMA sits.)*

You came to bring him lunch?

YERMA.   Yes.

> *(She looks at VÍCTOR. Pause.)*

What have you got there?

> *(She points at his face.)*

VÍCTOR.   Where?

YERMA.   *(She stands and approaches VÍCTOR.)* Here, on your cheek. It looks burned.

VÍCTOR.   It's nothing.

YERMA.   I thought I saw something.

> *(Pause.)*

VÍCTOR.   Must be the sun . . .

YERMA.   I guess so . . .

> *(Pause. The silence grows and a subtle tension builds between the two characters. YERMA trembles.)*

Do you hear that?

VÍCTOR.   What?

YERMA.   You don't hear that crying?

VÍCTOR.   *(Listening.)* No.

YERMA.   I thought I heard a child crying.

VÍCTOR.   Really?

YERMA.   It sounded close. Deep drowning sobs.

VÍCTOR.   Kids are always coming around here to steal fruit.

YERMA.   No, it's the voice of a small child.

> *(Pause.)*

VÍCTOR. I don't hear a thing.

YERMA. Must be my imagination.

   (*She stares at him. VÍCTOR stares back, then looks away slowly, as if frightened. Enter JUAN.*)

JUAN. Why are you still here?

YERMA. I was talking.

VÍCTOR. Good day.

   (*Exit.*)

JUAN. You should be inside.

YERMA. I got distracted.

JUAN. What could possibly distract you out here?

YERMA. I heard the birds singing.

JUAN. Perfect. More gossip for the neighbors.

YERMA. (*Angrily.*) Juan, what do you take me for?

JUAN. It's not about you. It's about what people will say.

YERMA. To hell with people!

JUAN. Don't curse. It's unseemly in a woman.

YERMA. If only I were a woman.

JUAN. Don't start. Go home.

   (*Pause.*)

YERMA. Okay. Shall I wait up for you?

JUAN. No, I'll be watering all night. With so little rain, I have to defend what's mine from the thieves until the sun comes up. I'll expect you to get in bed and go to sleep.

YERMA. (*Dramatically.*) Fine, I'll go to sleep!

   (*Exit.*)

—CURTAIN—

Act 2, Tableau 1

(Stream in which the village women are washing clothes, seated at various angles. They sing as the curtain rises.)

SONG.
>In the frigid stream
>I wash your sash.
>Like glowing jasmine
>responds your laugh.

WASHERWOMAN 1. I don't like to gossip.

WASHERWOMAN 3. Well gossip is what you'll get here.

WASHERWOMAN 4. And there's nothing wrong with it.

WASHERWOMAN 5. She who wants respect must earn it.

WASHERWOMAN 4.
>I planted some thyme
>and watched it grow.
>If you want respect
>then behave just so.

(They laugh.)

WASHERWOMAN 5. That sounds about right.

WASHERWOMAN 1. But there's never any news.

WASHERWOMAN 4. What I know is that her husband brought his two sisters to live with them.

WASHERWOMAN 5. The unmarried ones?

WASHERWOMAN 4. Yes. They were in charge of looking after the church and now they'll be looking after their sister-in-law. There's no way I could live with them.

WASHERWOMAN 1. Why not?

WASHERWOMAN 4. Because they're frightening. They're like those vines that spring up on tombstones. Smeared with wax and twisted in on themselves. I bet they cook their food with lamp oil.

WASHERWOMAN 3. So they're already in the house?

WASHERWOMAN 4. As of yesterday. The husband has to return to working his land.

WASHERWOMAN 1. Can I ask what happened?

WASHERWOMAN 5. She spent the whole night before last on the doorstep, despite the chill.

WASHERWOMAN 1. Why?

WASHERWOMAN 4. She can't keep herself inside.

WASHERWOMAN 5. That's the way of these barren macho women. When they could be making lace or apple preserves, they prefer to climb up to the rooftop or wade barefoot through the river.

WASHERWOMAN 1. Who are you to say such things? She's childless through no fault of her own.

WASHERWOMAN 4. She who wants children will have them. But these spoiled, sugarcoated weaklings aren't cut out for stretch marks.

(*They laugh.*)

WASHERWOMAN 3. And they paint up their faces and pin sprigs of oleander to their breast, all in search of men who aren't their husbands.

WASHERWOMAN 5. You said it!

WASHERWOMAN 1. Have any of you seen her with another man?

WASHERWOMAN 4. Not us, but people have.

WASHERWOMAN 1. People, always people!

WASHERWOMAN 5. Supposedly they saw her twice.

WASHERWOMAN 2. And what were they doing?

WASHERWOMAN 4. Talking.

WASHERWOMAN 1. Talking isn't a sin.

WASHERWOMAN 4. It's about a certain way of looking. My mother used to say so. A woman looking at a rose isn't the same as a woman looking at a man's thighs. She *looks* at him.

WASHERWOMAN 1. At who?

WASHERWOMAN 4. At him, okay? Go figure it out for yourself. You want me to say it louder?

(*Laughter.*)

And when she's not looking at him, because she's by herself and can't see him, she carries his image in her eyes.

WASHERWOMAN 1. That's ridiculous!

(Muffled excitement.)

WASHERWOMAN 5. What about the husband?

WASHERWOMAN 3. The husband is as oblivious as a lizard lying in the sun.

(Laughter.)

WASHERWOMAN 1. All this would turn out fine if they could just have some children.

WASHERWOMAN 2. The issue here is people who can't accept their fate.

WASHERWOMAN 4. Every hour that goes by just intensifies the hell in that house. Imagine her and her sisters-in-law, never speaking, spending all day whitewashing the walls, scrubbing the pots, cleaning the windows, polishing the floors. And the more the house sparkles on the outside, the more it burns on the inside.

WASHERWOMAN 1. It's his fault. Him. When a man can't have children he should spend time taking care of his wife.

WASHERWOMAN 4. No, she's the one at fault. And that razor-like tongue of hers.

WASHERWOMAN 1. What demon possesses your brain to make you speak that way?

WASHERWOMAN 4. Who gave your mouth permission to offer me advice?

WASHERWOMAN 5. Enough!

(Laughter.)

WASHERWOMAN 1. I'd like to stitch all your gossipy tongues together with a knitting needle.

WASHERWOMAN 5. Stop it!

WASHERWOMAN 4. And I the hearts of the self-righteous.

WASHERWOMAN 5. Silence. Don't you see who's coming?

(Excited whispers. Enter YERMA's two SISTERS-IN-LAW, dressed in mourning. They begin washing amid silence. Cowbells are heard in the distance.)

WASHERWOMAN 1. Are the shepherds finishing up?

WASHERWOMAN 3. Yes, all the flocks are heading out.

WASHERWOMAN 4.   *(Breathing in.)* I like the smell of sheep.

WASHERWOMAN 3.   Really?

WASHERWOMAN 4.   Sure. It's the smell of what belongs to us. Like the smell of the red silt the river brings in winter.

WASHERWOMAN 3.   Those are silly whims.

WASHERWOMAN 5.   *(Observing.)* All the flocks are crowding together.

WASHERWOMAN 4.   It's a flood of wool. They sweep away everything in their path. If the wheat stalks had eyes, they'd tremble to see what's on the way.

WASHERWOMAN 3.   Look how they run! Like a pack of bandits!

WASHERWOMAN 1.   That's it, they're all gone.

WASHERWOMAN 4.   No, wait: there's one left.

WASHERWOMAN 5.   Where?

WASHERWOMAN 4.   Over there. It's Víctor's.
(The SISTERS-IN-LAW raise their heads to look.)
>In the frigid stream
>I wash your sash.
>Like glowing jasmine
>responds your laugh.
>Please let me in
>to your snowy jasmine.

WASHERWOMAN 1.
>Woe unto the barren bride!
>Woe unto her breasts so dry!

WASHERWOMAN 5.
>Tell us if your husband
>is stocked with seed
>and let the water
>sing your need.

WASHERWOMAN 4.
>Behold your clothing,
>a ship of silver wind
>in water flowing.

WASHERWOMAN 3.
>I come to wash
>my little boy's clothes

so the water may cleanse
wherever it flows.

WASHERWOMAN 2.
    Through the hills comes
    my husband for stew.
    He brings me a rose
    and I give him two.

WASHERWOMAN 5.
    Through the fields comes
    my husband to eat.
    The fury he brings
    with myrtle I meet.

WASHERWOMAN 4.
    Through the air comes
    my husband to rest.
    A red flower is he,
    a red flower my breast.

WASHERWOMAN 3.
    Bud shall mingle with bud
    when summer heats the farmer's blood.

WASHERWOMAN 4.
    The womb shall open to dreamless birds
    when winter calls with trembling words.

WASHERWOMAN 1.
    One must seek pleasure in bed!

WASHERWOMAN 4.
    One must sing without dread!

WASHERWOMAN 5.
    It's our man keeps us fed.

WASHERWOMAN 4.
    For our arms do interlace.

WASHERWOMAN 5.
    And the light strikes our face.

WASHERWOMAN 4.
    And the supple boughs embrace.

WASHERWOMAN 5.
    And wind to the mountain gives chase.

WASHERWOMAN 6. *(Entering near the top of the stream.)*
    So a child may to the dawn bring grace.

WASHERWOMAN 4.
    So our bodies may bear the coral's trace.

WASHERWOMAN 5.
    So oarsmen on the sea may take their place.

WASHERWOMAN 1.
    A child, a small child do I see.

WASHERWOMAN 2.
    The doves spread their wings and beaks.

WASHERWOMAN 3.
    A child cries out from somewhere near.

WASHERWOMAN 4.
    The men advance like wounded deer.

WASHERWOMAN 5.
    Joy, joy, joy at the belly so round.

WASHERWOMAN 2.
    Joy, joy, joy at the navel profound.

WASHERWOMAN 1.
    But woe unto the barren bride!
    Woe unto her breasts so dry!

WASHERWOMAN 4.
    May she shimmer!

WASHERWOMAN 5.
    May she run!

WASHERWOMAN 4.
    May she shimmer some more!

WASHERWOMAN 3.
    May she sing!

WASHERWOMAN 2.
    May she hide!

WASHERWOMAN 3.
    May she sing some more!

WASHERWOMAN 6.
    Sing of the dawn my baby brings.

WASHERWOMEN 1–6. *(In unison.)*
    In the frigid stream
    I wash your sash.
    Like glowing jasmine
    responds your laugh.
    Ha, ha, ha!

(They wash rhythmically, pounding the clothes against stones in the stream.)

—CURTAIN—

Act 2, Tableau 2

(Yerma's house at dusk. JUAN is seated. The two SISTERS-IN-LAW are standing.)

JUAN. You say she just left?

(The older SISTER-IN-LAW nods.)

She must have gone to the spring. But you know I don't like her going out alone.

(Pause.)

Go ahead and set the table.

(The younger SISTER-IN-LAW exits.)

Some life this is I lead.

(To the SISTER-IN-LAW.)

Yesterday was tough. I was pruning the apple trees, and when afternoon came around I started wondering why I should put such effort into the chore if I can never eat an apple. I've had it.

(He rubs his face with his hand. Pause.)

She's not coming back, that one . . . One of you is going to have to go with her whenever she leaves. That's why you're here, eating at my table and drinking my wine. My life is in the fields, but my honor is here. And my honor is your honor.

(The SISTER-IN-LAW bows her head.)

Don't take it the wrong way.

(*Enter YERMA with two water jugs. She stands in the doorway.*)

Did you go to the spring?

YERMA.   It's nice to have fresh water at dinner.

(*Exit the SISTER-IN-LAW.*)

How's the work coming?

JUAN.   I spent yesterday pruning.

(*YERMA sets the jugs down. Pause.*)

YERMA.   Are you staying?

JUAN.   I have to tend to the livestock. That's what being a landowner means.

YERMA.   I know that. No need to keep repeating it.

JUAN.   Every man has his life.

YERMA.   And every woman hers. I'm not asking you to stay. I have everything I need here. Your sisters keep a good watch over me. I've got fresh bread and cheese and roast lamb, and your livestock have the dewy grass of the hillside. I think you should be able to live in peace.

JUAN.   To live in peace one needs a sense of calm.

YERMA.   Which you don't have?

JUAN.   I don't.

YERMA.   Well don't look at me.

JUAN.   You know what I like. Sheep in the fold and women in the house. You go out too often. Haven't you heard me say so?

YERMA.   Of course. Women in the house. When the house isn't a tomb. When the sheets and furniture show signs of use. But that's not the case here. Every night, when I get into bed, I find the mattress new and fresh, as if it'd just been brought from the city.

JUAN.   You know I'm right to protest. I have good reason to be vigilant!

YERMA.   Vigilant about what? I do nothing to offend you. I live by your will, and whatever I suffer I keep to myself. Every day that goes by will be worse. So let's stop talking. I'll bear my cross as best I can, but don't ask me anything. If I could suddenly turn into an old woman with a mouth like a withered flower, I might smile at you and live happily at your side. Now leave me with my crown of thorns.

JUAN. You speak in a manner I don't understand. I don't deprive you of anything. I order things you like from neighboring towns. I have my faults, but I want peace and harmony between us. I want to sleep outside and know that you're sleeping too.

YERMA. But I don't sleep. I can't sleep.

JUAN. Is there something you lack? Tell me.

(Pause.)

Speak!

YERMA. *(Purposefully, staring at JUAN.)* Yes, there's something I lack.

(Pause.)

JUAN. Here we go again. It's been more than five years. I've almost forgotten about it.

YERMA. But I'm not you. Men have their own lives: livestock, trees, conversations. Women have no lives apart from their children.

JUAN. Not everyone is the same. Why don't you adopt one of your brother's children? I'm not opposed to the idea.

YERMA. I don't want to raise someone else's children. I fear my arms would freeze upon holding them.

JUAN. This fixation of yours is driving you mad. You don't think as you should, and you insist on beating your head against a rock.

YERMA. A rock that should be a basket of dewy flowers. It's intolerable.

JUAN. Those around you feel nothing but anxiety, uncertainty. When things don't work out, you need to resign yourself to them.

YERMA. I didn't come to these four walls to resign myself. When my head is tied tight with a shroud to keep my mouth shut, when my arms are locked inside a coffin, only then will I have resigned myself.

JUAN. So what is it you intend to do?

YERMA. I want a drink of water and there's neither glass nor water. I want to climb the hillside and I have no feet. I want to embroider my nightgown and I've lost the thread.

JUAN. The problem is you're not a true woman, and you seek a man's ruin against his will.

YERMA. I don't know who I am. Give me my space. I've done you no wrong.

JUAN.   I don't like people pointing at me. Which is why I want that door closed and everyone inside.

>   *(The first SISTER-IN-LAW enters slowly and approaches a cupboard.)*

YERMA.   Talking to people isn't a sin.

JUAN.   But it can appear to be one.

>   *(The second SISTER-IN-LAW enters and goes to the water jugs, filling a pitcher. JUAN lowers his voice.)*

I don't have the strength for this. When a conversation arises, shut your mouth and remember that you're a married woman.

YERMA.   *(Astonished.)* Married!

JUAN.   And that families have honor, and honor is a burden shared by all.

>   *(The SISTER-IN-LAW with the pitcher exits slowly.)*

But it flows dark and weak in the channels of the blood.

>   *(The other SISTER-IN-LAW exits with a platter, almost ceremonially. Pause.)*

I'm sorry.

>   *(YERMA stares at her husband. He raises his head and meets her gaze.)*

Though the way you look at me makes me wonder why I'm saying sorry. I should be forcing you into submission, locking you up. I'm the husband after all.

>   *(The two SISTERS-IN-LAW appear in the doorway.)*

YERMA.   I beg you, say no more. Let the matter rest.

>   *(Pause.)*

JUAN.   It's time to eat.

>   *(The SISTERS-IN-LAW exit. Pause.)*

Did you hear me?

YERMA.   *(Tenderly.)* You go eat with your sisters. I'm not hungry yet.

JUAN.   As you wish.

>   *(Exit.)*

YERMA.   *(As if in a dream.)*
>   Oh, what a meadow of bile!
>   Oh, how beauty is reduced,

for when I ask to bear a child
I get dahlias of a drowsy moon!
These twin fonts of tepid milk
buried in the thickness of my flesh
are the throbbing veins of a steed,
a clumsy bosom beneath my dress.
Oh, what gray and sightless doves!
Oh, how the channels of my anguish pulse!
Oh, what pain comes from stagnant blood,
like hornet stings at the base of my skull!
But you will come, my child, my love,
because water yields salt, the earth mud,
and our womb will bear a lovely son
just as clouds deliver gentle floods.

(She looks toward the door.)

María! Why are you rushing away?

MARÍA. *(Entering with a CHILD in her arms.)* I try to avoid you whenever I have my little boy with me. It always makes you so sad!

YERMA. It's true.

(She takes the CHILD and sits.)

MARÍA. It makes me sad to see you envious of me.

(She sits.)

YERMA. I'm not envious; I'm bereft.

MARÍA. Better not to complain.

YERMA. How can I not complain when I see you and the other women blooming on the inside? I feel useless in the midst of such beauty!

MARÍA. But you have other things. If you listened to me, you could be happy.

YERMA. A field-worker's wife who doesn't have children is as worthless as a fistful of thistles, even poisonous! I am part and parcel of this godforsaken wasteland.

(MARÍA makes a gesture as if reaching for the child.)

Go ahead; he's happier with you. My hands must not be motherly enough.

MARÍA. Why do you say such things?

YERMA. *(She stands.)* Because I've had it. I'm sick of having hands and nothing to hold. I'm disgusted. Disgusted and humiliated to the core. All around me I watch the wheat ripening, the streams swelling with water, the sheep spilling out lambs and the bitches puppies. It's as if all of nature were rising up to show me its tender, drowsy offspring. And at my breast, instead of the mouth of a child, I feel the pounding of a hammer.

MARÍA. I don't like what you're saying.

YERMA. You women with children can't imagine what it's like for those of us without. You remain happily ignorant, just as the one who swims in an oasis has no concept of thirst.

MARÍA. I don't want to repeat what I always tell you.

YERMA. Each day I have more wants and fewer hopes.

MARÍA. Not a good thing.

YERMA. I'm going to end up thinking I'm my own son. Many nights I go out to feed the oxen, which I never did before because no woman does, and when I pass through the dark part of the shed my footsteps sound to me like those of a man.

MARÍA. Every creature has its purpose.

YERMA. No matter what, don't stop loving me. You see what my life is like!

MARÍA. What's going on with your sisters-in-law?

YERMA. I'd rather be buried without a shroud than speak a word to them.

MARÍA. And your husband?

YERM. It's the three of them against me.

MARÍA. What do they say?

YERMA. Nonsense. Things that could come only from a guilty conscience. They think I might like another man and they don't understand that, even if I did, my caste holds honor above all else. They are stones in my path, and they don't understand that I could sweep them all away like a rushing torrent.

(A SISTER-IN-LAW enters and exits with a loaf of bread.)

MARÍA. At any rate I think your husband still loves you.

YERMA. My husband gives me bread and a roof over my head.

MARÍA. What a trial this must be for you, what hardship, but just remember how our Lord suffered!

(They reach the front door.)

YERMA. *(Looking at the child.)* He's awake.

MARÍA. In a little bit he'll start to coo.

YERMA. He's got your eyes, you know. Have you noticed that?

(Tearing up.)

He's got your eyes!

(YERMA gives an affectionate nudge to MARÍA, who exits silently. YERMA moves toward the doorway through which her husband exited.)

GIRL 2. Pssst!

YERMA. *(Whirling around.)* What?

GIRL 2. I waited until she left. My mother is expecting you.

YERMA. Is she alone?

GIRL 2. She's with two neighbor women.

YERMA. Ask her if they can wait a bit.

GIRL 2. So you're coming? You're not afraid?

YERMA. I'll be there.

GIRL 2. Your choice!

YERMA. Tell them to wait for me no matter how late!

(Enter VÍCTOR.)

VÍCTOR. Is Juan here?

YERMA. Yes.

GIRL 2. *(Dissimulating.)* Okay, I'll bring you that blouse.

YERMA. Whenever you like.

(The GIRL exits.)

Have a seat.

VÍCTOR. I'm fine standing.

YERMA. *(Calling her husband.)* Juan!

VÍCTOR. I'm here to say goodbye.

YERMA. *(She flinches slightly but recovers her calm.)* You're going away with your brothers?

VÍCTOR.   That's how my father wants it.

YERMA.   He must be getting old.

VÍCTOR.   Yes, he's getting up there.

(Pause.)

YERMA.   It's good you're changing fields.

VÍCTOR.   All fields are the same.

YERMA.   Not true. If it were me I'd go very far away.

VÍCTOR.   It's all the same. The same sheep have the same wool.

YERMA.   For men that's true, but women are different. I've never heard a man comment over dinner: "These apples are so delicious!" You go about your tasks without noticing details. All I can tell you is that I've always hated the water of these wells.

VÍCTOR.   You may be right.

(The scene has fallen into soft shadow. Pause.)

YERMA.   Víctor.

VÍCTOR.   Yes?

YERMA.   Why are you leaving? People here love you.

VÍCTOR.   I always behaved myself.

(Pause.)

YERMA.   You did. Once when you were a boy you carried me in your arms, remember? You never know how things are going to turn out.

VÍCTOR.   Everything changes.

YERMA.   Some things don't. There are things locked up behind walls that can't change because no one hears them.

VÍCTOR.   True.

(The second SISTER-IN-LAW enters and walks slowly toward the door, where she remains standing, illuminated by the last of the evening light.)

YERMA.   But if they ever escaped, their screams would fill the world.

VÍCTOR.   It wouldn't do any good. The ditch would still be a ditch, the flock would still be in its fold, the moon in the sky, and the farmer here with his plow.

YERMA. What a pity we can't learn from the teachings of our elders!

> *(In the distance is heard the long and melancholy call of a shepherd's conch shell.)*

VÍCTOR. The flocks.

JUAN. *(Entering.)* Are you on your way?

VÍCTOR. I want to be past the port by dawn.

JUAN. Do we have any accounts unsettled?

VÍCTOR. No. You always paid very punctually.

JUAN. *(To YERMA.)* I bought his flocks.

YERMA. Oh?

VÍCTOR. *(To YERMA.)* They're yours now.

YERMA. I had no idea.

JUAN. *(Satisfied.)* It's true.

VÍCTOR. Your husband's lands will soon be overflowing.

YERMA. The fruit of the harvest comes to the farmer who works for it.

> *(The SISTER-IN-LAW standing at the doorway exits to another room in the house.)*

JUAN. We barely have room for so many sheep.

YERMA. *(Gloomily.)* The earth is a big place.

> *(Pause.)*

JUAN. *[To VÍCTOR.]* I'll go with you as far as the stream.

VÍCTOR. I desire the greatest happiness for this house.

> *(He offers YERMA his hand.)*

YERMA. May God hear you! Best wishes to you.

VÍCTOR. *(He begins to exit and, upon a slight movement from YERMA, turns around.)* Did you say something?

YERMA. *(Dramatically.)* I said best wishes.

VÍCTOR. Thank you.

> *(Exit VÍCTOR and JUAN. YERMA stands anxiously, looking at the hand with which she shook Víctor's. She turns quickly to the left and picks up a veil.)*

GIRL 2.   *(Silently placing the veil over YERMA's face.)* It's time.

YERMA.   Let's go then.

> *(They exit silently. The set is almost completely dark. One SISTER-IN-LAW enters with a candle, which adds almost no light to the set. She walks to the edge of the stage looking for YERMA. The shepherds' conch shells sound in the distance.)*

SISTER-IN-LAW 1.   *(Whispering.)* Yerma!

> *(Enter the second SISTER-IN-LAW. The two look at each other and walk toward the door.)*

SISTER-IN-LAW 2.   *(Louder.)* Yerma!

(Exit.)

SISTER-IN-LAW 1.   *(Walking toward the door, in a raspy voice.)* Yerma!

> *(Exit. The conch shells and horns of the shepherds sound in the distance. The set is pitch black.)*

—CURTAIN—

Act 3, Tableau 1

(House of the folk healer DOLORES. Dawn is breaking. Enter YERMA with DOLORES and two OLD WOMEN.)

DOLORES.   You were brave tonight.

OLD WOMAN 1.   There's no force on earth like desire.

OLD WOMAN 2.   But the cemetery was too dark.

DOLORES.   Many times I've recited these prayers in the cemetery with women who wanted children, and all of them got frightened. All of them but you.

YERMA.   I came for results. And I don't think you're out to swindle me.

DOLORES.   I'm not. May ants swarm over my tongue as in the mouths of the dead if ever I've lied. My last prayer was for a beggar woman who was childless longer than you, and her womb ripened so beautifully that she had two children down by the river's edge because she didn't have time to make it back to town. She brought them here in a bundle for me to tend to.

YERMA. She walked all the way here from the river?

DOLORES. She did. With her shoes and underclothes soaked in blood . . . but her face radiant.

YERMA. And she was okay?

DOLORES. Of course she was okay. God is God.

YERMA. Right. All she had to do was grab them and clean them up in the river. Animals lick their young, don't they? Giving birth doesn't disgust me. New mothers strike me as all aglow on the inside as their infants sleep atop them for hours and hours, listening to that rush of warm milk that fills the maternal breast, suckling and cooing until their heart's content and their head becomes heavy—"Just a little more, my child . . ."—with the baby's face and the mother's breast all splattered in white.

DOLORES. You will bear a child now. I can assure you.

YERMA. I will because I have to, or I don't understand the world. Sometimes, when I'm certain that it will never, ever happen . . . I get this wave of heat that sweeps up my body from my feet and everything goes blank, and the men walking through the street, the bulls in the pasture, the rocks on the ground, all seem like balls of cotton. And I ask myself: Why are they there?

OLD WOMAN 1. It's fine for a married woman to want children, but if it doesn't happen, why all the anguish? What's important in this world is to let the years carry us forward. I'm not criticizing you. You saw how I helped with the prayers. But what do you hope to give your child: land? happiness? a golden high chair?

YERMA. I don't think about tomorrow; I think about today. You're old and you see everything as a book that's already been read. What matters to me is that I'm thirsty and have no freedom. I want to hold my child in my arms so I will sleep secure. Listen to me and don't be shocked by what I'm going to say: even if I knew that my child would eventually torment me and hate me and drag me through the street by the hair, I would welcome his birth with joy, for it's far better to cry over a living man who betrays us than over this ghost that sits year after year upon my heart.

OLD WOMAN 1. You're too young to take advice. But as long as you trust in God's grace, you must seek refuge in your husband's love.

YERMA. Oh! You poke your finger in the deepest wound of my flesh.

DOLORES. Your husband is a good man.

YERMA. *(She stands.)* A good man! A good man! So what? Would that he were evil. But no. Instead he wanders with his sheep through the hills and counts his money at night. When he mounts me he fulfills his responsibility, but I feel a coldness about his waist as if his body were dead. I've always been disgusted by hot-blooded women, but in those moments I would like to become a mountain of fire.

DOLORES. Yerma!

YERMA. I'm not an indecent wife, but I know that children are born of a man and a woman. Oh, if only I could have one by myself!

DOLORES. You must know your husband suffers as well.

YERMA. He doesn't suffer. Because he doesn't yearn for children.

OLD WOMAN 1. Don't say that!

YERMA. I can see it in his eyes, and because he doesn't yearn for them, he doesn't produce any. I don't love him, I don't, yet he's my one salvation. For a good name, a family. My one salvation.

OLD WOMAN 1. *(Anxiously.)* Day will be breaking soon. You should go home.

DOLORES. The shepherds will be up in no time. They shouldn't see you by yourself.

YERMA. I had to get this off my chest. How many times do I say the prayers?

DOLORES. Say the laurel prayer twice and the Santa Ana at midday. When you know you're pregnant, bring me the bushel of wheat you promised.

OLD WOMAN 1. Light is breaking over the mountains. Go.

DOLORES. People will be opening their front gates. Take the back way, along the ditch.

YERMA. *(With disappointment.)* I don't know why I came!

DOLORES. Are you having second thoughts?

YERMA. No!

DOLORES. *(Concerned.)* If you're afraid, I'll go with you to the corner.

YERMA. No!

OLD WOMAN 1. *(Anxiously.)* It's going to be broad daylight by the time you reach your door.

(Voices are heard offstage.)

DOLORES. Shhhhh!

(*They listen.*)

OLD WOMAN 1. It's nothing. God be with you.

(*YERMA walks toward the door, and at this moment her name is called. The three WOMEN remain standing.*)

DOLORES. Who's there?

VOICE. It's me.

YERMA. Open it.

(*DOLORES hesitates.*)

Are you going to open it or not?

(*Grumbling voices are heard. JUAN enters with the two SISTERS-IN-LAW.*)

SISTER-IN-LAW 2. Here she is.

YERMA. Here I am!

JUAN. What on earth are you doing in this place? If I had my way, I'd shout and summon the entire village to see what has become of my good name. But I'll stifle it and keep it all in because you're my wife.

YERMA. If I had my way I'd shout so loud that even the dead would attest to my innocence.

JUAN. Stop it! I can take anything but your deceitful, conniving tongue. I'm a simple farmer. I can't keep up with your cunning.

DOLORES. Juan!

JUAN. Not a word from any of you!

DOLORES. (*Angrily.*) Your wife hasn't done anything wrong.

JUAN. She's done everything wrong since the day of our wedding. Needling me with her gaze, lying awake all night next to me, sighing into the pillows.

YERMA. Shut up!

JUAN. I can't go on like this. You have to be made of bronze to suffer a wife who wants to eat your heart out, who leaves the house at all hours of the night: in search of what? Tell me: in search of what! The streets are full of men, not flowers for picking.

YERMA. Stop right there. Not another word. You think you and your people are the only ones who care about their name? My clan has never had anything to hide. Go ahead. Bury your nose in my dress—do it!—and see if you can find a single smell that isn't yours, that doesn't come from your body. Strip me naked in the middle of the square and spit on me. Do with me what you will, for I'm your wife, but don't go looking for other men's fingerprints on my breasts.

JUAN. I don't have to look for them. Your behavior confirms they're there, and people are beginning to say so. They're saying so quite clearly. When I approach a crowd, everyone grows quiet; when I go to weigh the flour, everyone grows quiet; even at night in the fields, when I wake up, it's as if the branches on the trees grow quiet.

YERMA. Why does the evil wind insist on uprooting the wheat when the wheat is golden?

JUAN. And why does a wife spend all hours of the night away from her house? What is she looking for?

YERMA. *(Embracing her husband in a fit of emotion.)* I'm looking for you. For you. It's you I search for night and day. It's your blood and the shelter of your arms that I desire.

JUAN. Get away from me.

YERMA. Don't push me away. Love me back.

JUAN. Off!

YERMA. Look how alone I am. A moon searching for itself in the sky. Look at me!

(She looks at him.)

JUAN. *(He looks at her and pushes her away.)* Get off me I said!

DOLORES. Juan!

(YERMA falls to the floor.)

YERMA. *(Loudly.)* When I was going out to pick carnations I tripped against the wall. Oh! That's the wall I should bash my skull against.

JUAN. Stop it. Let's go.

DOLORES. My God!

YERMA. *(Shouting.)* Curse my father who left me his fertile blood, the blood of a hundred children. Curse my blood, which beats against walls in search of them.

JUAN.   Stop it I said!

DOLORES.   People are coming! Lower your voice.

YERMA.   I don't care. Let me speak freely now that I'm entering the darkest depths of the well.

(She stands.)

Let this one beautiful thing issue from my body and fill the air.

(Voices are heard approaching.)

DOLORES.   They're coming.

JUAN.   Silence.

YERMA.   Of course, of course. Silence. Not to worry.

JUAN.   Let's go, now!

YERMA.   Fine! Fine! It's no use wringing my hands. One thing is to want something with the head—

JUAN.   Stop it.

YERMA.   *(Lowering her voice.)* One thing is to want something with the head and another is when the body—damn the body!—fails to deliver. It's settled. I'm not going to fight against the tide. So be it. Let my mouth be sealed shut!

(Exit.)

—CURTAIN—

Act 3, Tableau 2

(A rustic shrine in the midst of the mountains. Downstage, the wheels of a cart and a few blankets form YERMA's primitive tent. Enter the PILGRIM WOMEN, barefoot, with offerings for the shrine. The cheerful OLD WOMAN from the first act watches. A song is sung as the curtain rises.)

SONG.
>   I couldn't find you
>   when you were free,
>   but as a wife
>   you'll not escape me.

> I couldn't find you
> when you were free.
> I'll strip you bare,
> O married pilgrim,
> and in the darkness
> you'll have no prayer.

OLD WOMAN.   *(Mocking.)* Have you drunk the holy water yet?

WOMAN 1.   Yes.

OLD WOMAN.   And now the saint works his magic?

WOMAN 2.   You'll see.

OLD WOMAN.   You come to the saint to pray for children and every year more single men show up for this pilgrimage. How odd.

   (She laughs.)

WOMAN 1.   Why did you come if you don't believe?

OLD WOMAN.   To observe. Because I'm dying to see what goes on here. And because I want to look out for my son. Last year two men killed each other over one of these childless wives, so it's good to keep an eye on things. But mainly I'm just curious.

WOMAN 1.   May God forgive you.

   (Exit.)

OLD WOMAN.   *(Sarcastically.)* And you.

   (Exit. Enter MARÍA with GIRL 1.)

GIRL 1.   So did she come?

MARÍA.   That's their cart. It took some effort to convince them to come. She hasn't gotten out of her chair in a month. She scares me. She's latched on to some idea, I don't know what, but I'm certain it's no good.

GIRL 1.   I came with my sister. She's been coming for eight years with no result.

MARÍA.   She who is meant to have children will have them.

GIRL 1.   That's what I say.

   (Voices are heard offstage.)

MARÍA.   I never liked this pilgrimage. Let's go to the threshing floor. That's where everyone is.

GIRL 1.   Last year, when it got dark, someone groped my sister's breasts.

MARÍA. These parts are full of terrible stories.

GIRL 1. I saw about forty barrels of wine back behind the shrine.

MARÍA. A river of single men winds down those hills.

(Voices are heard. Enter YERMA with six WOMEN on the way to the shrine. They are barefoot and carry showy votive candles. It is dusk.)

[WOMAN 1].
    Lord, let the rose flower.
    Leave it not in shadow.

WOMAN 2.
    Upon her stale flesh
    may a yellow rose flower.

MARÍA.
    And in the faithful womb,
    let earth's dark fire smolder.

CHORUS.
    Lord, let the rose flower.
    Leave it not in shadow.

(YERMA and the WOMEN kneel.)

YERMA.
    Heaven's garden glows
    with flowers of joy:
    deep in the gardens
    sits a marvelous rose.
    A bolt of dawn it seems,
    by an angel shielded,
    his wings like storms
    and his eyes like embers.
    All through the greenery
    run streams of milky warmth
    that sprinkle the veneers
    of the benevolent stars.
    Lord, open your flower
    upon my stale flesh.

(She stands.)

WOMAN 2.
    Lord, soothe with your touch
    the flush of her face.

YERMA.
> Listen to this penitent
> of your holy pilgrimage.
> Open your rose on my flesh
> despite its thousand nettles.

CHORUS.
> Lord, let the rose flower,
> leave it not in shadow.

YERMA.
> Upon my stale flesh,
> a marvelous rose.

(Exit [YERMA and the WOMEN]. Enter at left four GIRLS running with long ribbons in their hands, who then exit. Enter at right three more GIRLS, with long ribbons and looking behind their backs; they also exit. There is a rising wave of voices mixed with cowbells and harness bells. Upstage left the seven GIRLS reappear, shaking their ribbons. The noise grows and two mimes enter, one a MALE and the other a FEMALE, wearing large folk masks. The MALE grips a bull's horn in his hand. The figures are not at all grotesque but profoundly beautiful, conveying a sense of pure nature. The FEMALE shakes a harness of cowbells.)

CHILDREN. The Devil and his wife! The Devil and his wife!

(Upstage fills with people who shout and comment on the dance. The sky has grown very dark.)

FEMALE MASK.
> In a high mountain pool
> bathed the sorrowful wife.
> All about her slithered
> snails from the river.
> The sand on the shore
> and the dew in the air
> sparked her to laughter
> and caused her to shiver.
> Oh, how naked the wife
> as she bathed in the river!

BOY.
> Oh, how she lamented!

MAN 1.
> Oh, how bereft of affection!

BOY.
>Amid the wind and the water!

MAN 2.
>Let her say whom she awaits!

MAN 1.
>Let her say whom she expects!

MAN 2.
>Oh, how dry her womb,
>how feeble her hue!

FEMALE MASK.
>When night comes I will talk.
>When the clear night descends.
>When darkness enfolds the pilgrims
>I will slit the folds of my frock.

BOY.
>And night came at once.
>Oh, how the night did come!
>Look how dark the waters
>of the mountain river run.

(Guitars begin to play.)

MALE MASK. *(Standing and shaking his horn.)*
>Oh, so pale the woeful wife!
>Oh, how she laments in the shade!
>Poppy and carnation will you be
>when the Male unfurls his cape.

(He draws near.)

>If you come as a pilgrim
>so that your womb may ripen,
>cast off the veil of mourning
>and dress your limbs in satin.
>Then go alone behind the walls
>where the fig trees grow thickest,
>and bear the earth of my body
>until the dawn's faintest flicker.
>Oh, how the wife glows!
>Oh, how she used to glow!
>Oh, how she sways and bows!

FEMALE MASK.
>   Oh, how love bedecks her
>   in garlands and crowns!
>   Oh, how lances of gold
>   pierce the folds of her gown!

MALE MASK.
>   Seven times she lamented,
>   nine times she arose.
>   Fifteen times were coupled
>   jasmine and gold.

MAN 1.
>   Strike her now with the horn!

MAN 2.
>   With the rose and the thorn.

MAN 1.
>   Oh, how the wife sways and bows!

MALE MASK.
>   In this pilgrimage
>   husbands are bulls,
>   virility is the rule,
>   and women are roses
>   waiting to be chosen.

BOY.
>   Strike her now with the wind.

MAN 2.
>   Strike her now with the whip.

MALE MASK.
>   Come see how she glows
>   fresh from the river's flow!

MAN 1.
>   Like a gentle reed she tilts.

BOY.
>   Like a frail flower she wilts.

MEN.
>   Young girls, shield your eyes!

MALE MASK.
>May the dance be like fire
>to the glowing body
>of the immaculate wife!
>
>*(Exit dancing to the sound of clapping and singing.)*
>
>Heaven's garden glows
>with flowers of joy:
>deep in the gardens
>sits a marvelous rose.
>
>*(Two GIRLS run by shouting. Enter the cheerful OLD WOMAN.)*

OLD WOMAN. Will we ever get any sleep around here? Unlikely.

>*(Enter YERMA.)*
>
>You?
>
>*(YERMA appears demoralized and doesn't speak.)*
>
>Tell me: What have you come here for?
>
>*(YERMA shows signs of fatigue, of a woman worn out by her own obsession.)*

YERMA. I don't know.

OLD WOMAN. How can you not know? Where's your husband?

YERMA. Over there.

OLD WOMAN. What's he doing?

YERMA. Drinking.

>*(Pause. She raises her hands to her forehead and sighs heavily.)*
>
>Oh!

OLD WOMAN. Oh, oh! Less sighing and more feeling. I didn't want to tell you this before, but I'm going to now.

YERMA. What can you tell me that I don't already know!

OLD WOMAN. What can no longer be kept secret. What's plain for all to see. Your husband is the one to blame, you hear me? Cut off my hands if I lie. Neither his father nor his grandfather nor his great-grandfather were men of good stock. They had to move mountains to bear children. They're held together with spit. That's not the case with your people. You've got brothers and sisters and cousins for a hundred miles around. What a curse has taken root in your beautiful flesh!

YERMA. A curse. A pool of poison over a bed of thorns.

OLD WOMAN. But you still have your feet. They can get you out.

YERMA. Get me out?

OLD WOMAN. When I saw you in the pilgrimage my heart leapt in my breast. Women come here to meet new men, and the saint performs the miracle. My son is sitting behind the shrine, waiting for you. My house needs a woman. Go to him and we'll live together, the three of us. My son comes from good blood. As do I. If you enter my house you might still notice the smell of the crib. The ashes of your bed will become bread and salt for your children. Go. Don't worry what people will say. And as for your husband, in my house we have the will and the means to keep him from even crossing the street.

YERMA. Stop it. You misunderstand me! I would never do such a thing. I won't go fishing for a man. You think I want to meet someone new? What do you take me for? A river doesn't reverse its course, nor does the full moon come out at midday. Be gone with you. I'll continue along the path I'm on. You really thought I would bend to another man's will? That I would beg him like a slave for what's owed me? You don't know me or you would never say such a thing. I'm not looking for a man.

OLD WOMAN. When one is thirsty, one is grateful for water.

YERMA. I'm like a dry field wide enough for a thousand teams of oxen to plow, and what you're offering me is a tiny cup of well water. Mine is a pain beyond the flesh.

OLD WOMAN. *(Angrily.)* Continue on this path then. That's your choice. Like thistles in dry soil: prickly, barren.

YERMA. *(Angrily.)* Yes, barren! As if I didn't know! Barren! You don't have to rub it in my face, amusing yourself like a little boy torturing an animal. That word has been swirling in my head since I got married, but now's the first time I've actually heard it, the first time anyone has said it to my face. The first time I understand it's true.

OLD WOMAN. I have no pity for you, none. I'll find another wife for my son.

(Exit. In the distance a chorus of PILGRIMS is heard singing. YERMA moves toward the cart, from behind which JUAN appears.)

YERMA. You've been standing there all along?

JUAN. I have.

YERMA. Stalking me?

JUAN. Stalking you.

YERMA. You overheard what I said?

JUAN. I did.

YERMA. Fine. Go off and sing with the others.

   (She sits on the blankets.)

JUAN. It's time for me to speak.

YERMA. Speak!

JUAN. And to air my complaints.

YERMA. What complaints?

JUAN. There is a bitterness in my mouth.

YERMA. As in my bones.

JUAN. The time has come to stop this obsessive pining over things that are so obscure, so lifeless, so inconsequential.

YERMA. *(Beside herself.)* Lifeless he says! Inconsequential he says!

JUAN. Things that have never happened and that neither of us control.

YERMA. *(Hysterically.)* Go on! Go on!

JUAN. Things I don't care about. You hear me? Things I don't care about. It's time I said so. What I care about is what I hold in my hands. What I see with my eyes.

YERMA. *(Sitting up on her knees in a wounded manner.)* That's it. That's it. That's what I've been wanting to hear from your lips. A woman doesn't feel the truth when it's buried deep inside her, but how big and noisy it becomes when it escapes and waves its arms! He doesn't care! He says so himself!

JUAN. *(Drawing close.)* Consider that this may be how things were meant to happen. Listen to me.

   (He embraces her to hold her steady.)

   Many women would be happy to lead your life. It's easier without children. I'm fine not having any. And it's not our fault at all.

YERMA. So what do you want from me?

JUAN. I want you.

YERMA. *(Agitated.)* Of course! A house, a bit of peace and quiet, a wife. Nothing more. Is that it?

JUAN. That's it. What all men want.

YERMA. Nothing else? What about a child?

JUAN. *(Angrily.)* Didn't you hear what I just said? I don't care! Stop asking me about it! Do I have to shout it into your ear so you'll understand and drop this obsession once and for all?

YERMA. So you never even thought about it when you saw me wanting it?

JUAN. Never.

(They are both on the ground now.)

YERMA. And it's not something I can ever expect?

JUAN. No.

YERMA. Nor you?

JUAN. Nor I. Accept it!

YERMA. Barren!

JUAN We'll live in peace. You and I: in tenderness, in comfort. Come here!

(He embraces her.)

YERMA. What do you want?

JUAN. I want you. You look lovely in the moonlight.

YERMA. You want me the way you want a pigeon when you're hungry.

JUAN. Kiss me . . . like this.

YERMA. No, never. Never!

(YERMA screams and grips her husband's throat. He falls backward, and she strangles him to death. A CHORUS of pilgrims begins to chant.)

Barren, yes, but certain. Now I know for sure. All alone.

(She stands. A crowd begins to form around her.)

Now I can rest without waking up in a panic to see if my blood has announced a new life. My body will be dry forever. What do you want? Don't come closer, for I have murdered my child. I have murdered my child with my own hands!

(People cluster in the background. The CHORUS continues its chant.)

—CURTAIN—

The House of Bernarda Alba: Drama about Women in the Villages of Spain

DRAMATIS PERSONAE

Bernarda, age 60
María Josefa, Bernarda's mother, age 80
Bernarda's daughters:
    Angustias, age 39
    Magdalena, age 30
    Amelia, age 27
    Martirio, age 24
    Adela, age 20
Maid, age 50
Poncia, head domestic, age 60
Prudencia, age 50
Beggar Woman
Women in mourning
Woman 1
Woman 2
Woman 3
Woman 4
Girl

> *The author wishes to communicate that these three acts bear the intent of a photographic documentary.*

Act 1

(*A dazzling white room in Bernarda's house. Thick walls. Arched doorways with jute curtains lined with tassels and ruffles. Wicker chairs. Paintings with whimsical landscapes of nymphs or legendary kings. It is summer. A thick silence extends over the set. When the curtain rises the stage is empty. The tolling of bells is heard in the background. Enter the MAID.*)

MAID. The tolling of those bells is like a knife jabbing at my temples.

PONCIA. (*She enters eating bread and sausage.*) They've been at that Latin gibberish for two hours now. Priests have come from villages all around. The church looks beautiful. During the first prayer for the deceased, Magdalena fainted.

MAID. She's the one who most feels the loss.

PONCIA. The only one the father loved. Oh, thank goodness we're alone for a bit! I just needed a little bite.

MAID. If Bernarda were to catch you!

PONCIA. We're all supposed to die of hunger because she wants to fast! Bossy old tyrant! I've had it. I broke into her stash of chorizo.

MAID. (*Pitifully.*) Can you give me some for my little girl, Poncia?

PONCIA. Go in and grab some, and take a handful of garbanzos too. She won't notice today!

VOICE. (*Offstage.*) Bernarda!

PONCIA. The old lady. Is she locked up tight?

MAID. With two turns of the key.

PONCIA. You've got to put the bar down as well. She can pick locks with those spindly fingers of hers.

VOICE. [*Offstage.*] Bernarda!

PONCIA. (*Shouting back.*) She's on her way!

(*To the MAID.*)

Polish everything up spic and span. If Bernarda finds a spot anywhere she'll tear out the few hairs I've got left.

MAID. What a piece of work!

PONCIA. A terror to everyone around her. She'll stomp on your heart and watch you die with that icy smile of hers. Polish those glasses!

MAID. My hands are already raw from scrubbing.

PONCIA. That's life in the house of the tidiest, the purest, the proudest. At least her husband can finally rest!

(The bells cease tolling.)

MAID. Did all the relatives show up?

PONCIA. Hers did. His people hate her. They came to see his body and make the sign of the cross, that's it.

MAID. Are there enough chairs?

PONCIA. More than enough. Let them sit on the floor if necessary. Ever since Bernarda's father died, no one has set foot beneath this roof. She's afraid to be seen with her mask down. To hell with her!

MAID. She's been good to you.

PONCIA. Thirty years washing her sheets, thirty years eating her leftovers, entire nights caring for her when she's ill, whole days peeking through cracks to spy on the neighbors and fill her in on the gossip. A lifetime with no secrets between us, yet damn if I wouldn't like to see her eyes poked out with nails!

MAID. My God!

PONCIA. Don't worry, I'm a good bitch: I bark when I'm told and I bite the heels of the beggars she sics me on. My children work her fields and are married off now, but one day I'll reach my limit.

MAID. And then?

PONCIA. And then I'll lock myself in a room with her and spit in her face until my heart's content. "Take this, Bernarda, and this, and this," until she's like a skink squashed by a child, which is all she and her kind are worth. Of course I don't envy her life and the five grown women she's stuck with. Five ugly daughters. Angustias has money from the first husband, but the rest of them don't stand to get much more than crumbs for inheritance. Some nice embroidery and cotton sheets, that's it.

MAID. I wouldn't mind having what they have!

PONCIA. What we've got is our hands and a stake planted firmly in the ground of truth.

MAID. Which is the only ground the likes of us will ever own.

PONCIA. *(Inspecting the cupboard.)* This crystal has spots.

MAID. They don't come off no matter how much I soap and scrub.

(The bells toll.)

PONCIA. That's the final prayer. I'm going to go listen. I love hearing the parish priest sing. In the Our Father his voice rose, rose, rose like a clay pitcher filling slowly with water. Of course it cracked at the end, but it's still glorious to hear him. Though there's no one like the old sacristan Tronchapinos. He sang at my mother's funeral, God rest her soul. The walls shook with his voice, and when he got to Amen it was as if a wolf had entered the church.

(She imitates him.)

Ameeen!

(She coughs.)

MAID. You're going to ruin your voice.

PONCIA. I'd like to ruin something else.

(Exit laughing. The MAID continues cleaning. The bells toll.)

MAID. *(Humming to the tune.)* Dee dee dum, dee dee dum. May God forgive him.

BEGGAR WOMAN. *(With a little GIRL.)* Praise be to God!

MAID. Dee dee dum. May it be many years before we join him! Dee dee dum.

BEGGAR WOMAN. *(Louder and with a certain irritation.)* Praise be to God!

MAID. *(Annoyed.)* Always and evermore!

BEGGAR WOMAN. I'm here for your leftovers.

(The bells cease.)

MAID. Don't let the door hit you on the way out. Today's leftovers are for me.

BEGGAR WOMAN. You've got a steady job, Miss. My little girl and I are all alone.

MAID. Dogs live alone and do just fine.

BEGGAR WOMAN. They always give me the scraps here.

MAID. Out! Who gave you permission to come in here? You're tracking in dirt.

(Exit [BEGGAR WOMAN and GIRL]. The MAID cleans.)

Varnished floors, cupboards, pedestals, and steel beds. And the rest of us in our mud huts, grinning and bearing it with nothing to our name but a bowl and a spoon. Let's hope we won't live long enough to tell about it.

(The bells toll again.)

Yes, bring on the clanging. Bring on the casket with its gold trim and silk gloves for the pallbearers. It's all dust in the end, you and I both. Look at you now, Antonio María Benavides: a stiff corpse in a fancy suit and shiny boots. Serves you right! No longer will you be running your hand up my skirts behind the stable door!

(Upstage, two by two, the WOMEN IN MOURNING begin their entrance, dressed all in black: kerchiefs, skirts, and handheld fans. They enter slowly until they've filled the stage. The MAID begins to wail.)

Oh, Antonio María Benavides, no longer will you look upon these walls or eat bread beneath this roof! Of all your servants I loved you the most!

(Pulling her hair.)

How will I go on without you! How!

(The two hundred WOMEN IN MOURNING complete their entrance, followed by BERNARDA and her five DAUGHTERS. BERNARDA supports herself with a staff.)

BERNARDA.   *(To the MAID.)* Silence!

MAID.   *(Whimpering.)* Bernarda!

BERNARDA.   Less screeching and more working! You should have been making sure things were clean enough to receive the mourners. Go. You have no place here.

(The MAID exits in tears.)

The poor are like animals. It's as if they were made of a different substance.

WOMAN 1.   The poor also have their afflictions.

BERNARDA.   But they forget them before a bowl of garbanzos.

GIRL 1.   *(Timidly.)* You have to eat to live.

BERNARDA.   Children your age shouldn't be talking back to grown-ups.

WOMAN 1.   Hush, child.

BERNARDA.   I won't be lectured to by anyone. Be seated.

(They sit. There is a tense pause.)

Magdalena, stop your whimpering! If you want to cry, go crawl under a bed. Do you hear me?

WOMAN 2. *(To BERNARDA.)* Have you started the threshing yet?

BERNARDA. Yesterday.

WOMAN 3. The sun beats down like lead.

WOMAN 1. I can't remember heat like this for years.

(Pause. The women fan themselves.)

BERNARDA. Is the lemonade ready?

PONCIA. Yes, Bernarda.

(She enters with a large tray of white ceramic cups, which she passes around.)

BERNARDA. Serve the men too.

PONCIA. They're already drinking on the patio.

BERNARDA. Make sure they go out the way they came. I don't want them traipsing through here.

GIRL. *(To ANGUSTIAS.)* Pepe el Romano was with the men at the funeral.

ANGUSTIAS. So he was.

BERNARDA. His mother was there. That's who she saw. Neither she nor I saw Pepe himself.

GIRL. But I thought—

BERNARDA. You might be thinking of the widower from Darajalí. He was right next to his aunt. We all saw him.

WOMAN 2. *(Aside, whispering.)* She's a sly one!

WOMAN 3. *(Aside, whispering.)* Tongue like a scalpel!

BERNARDA. Women in church mustn't look upon any man but the priest, and in that case only because he wears a dress. A craning neck is a sign of indecency.

WOMAN 1. *(Whispering.)* Dried up old lizard!

PONCIA. *(Under her breath.)* Hypocrite.

BERNARDA. *(Knocking the floor with her staff.)* Praise be to God.

ALL. *(Making the sign of the cross.)* Forever blessed and praised.

BERNARDA.
> Rest in peace, in the hallowed
> company of angels.

ALL. Rest in peace!

BERNARDA.
> With Saint Michael the Archangel
> and his sword of deliverance.

ALL. Rest in peace!

BERNARDA.
> With the key that opens it all
> and the hand that closes it all.

ALL. Rest in peace!

BERNARDA.
> With the blessed
> and the lights of the earth.

ALL. Rest in peace!

BERNARDA.
> With our holy charity
> and the souls of land and sea.

ALL. Rest in peace!

BERNARDA. Grant rest to your servant, Antonio María Benavides, and crown him in your saintly glory.

ALL. Amen.

BERNARDA. *(Standing and singing.)* Requiem aeternam dona eis, Domine.

ALL. *(Standing and singing in Gregorian fashion.)* Et lux perpetua luceat eis.

(They make the sign of the cross.)

WOMAN 1. May you have the strength to pray for his soul.

(The visitors begin their exit.)

WOMAN 3. May you never go without a loaf of warm bread.

WOMAN 2. Nor a roof over your daughters' heads.

(The WOMEN cross in front of Bernarda on their way out. ANGUSTIAS exits through a different door, one that leads to the patio.)

WOMAN 4. May you continue to enjoy the comforts of your union.

PONCIA. *(Entering with a coin pouch.)* The men send this money for prayers in the name of the deceased.

BERNARDA. Give them my thanks and pour them a cup of brandy.

GIRL. *(To MAGDALENA.)* Magdalena.

BERNARDA. *(To MAGDALENA, who begins to cry.)* Shhh!

(The WOMEN finish their exit. BERNARDA pounds the floor with her staff, addressing them after they've left.)

Back to your caves to gossip about everything you've seen! May many years pass before you ever cross that doorway again.

PONCIA. You can't have any complaints. The whole village turned out.

BERNARDA. Yes, and filled my house with their stink and their venomous tongues!

AMELIA. Mother, don't talk that way!

BERNARDA. That's the reality in this damned riverless village where one lives in fear of drinking from a poisoned well.

PONCIA. Look what they've done to the floor!

BERNARDA. Worse than a herd of goats!

(PONCIA begins cleaning the floor.)

Bring me a fan, child.

ADELA. Here you are.

(She gives BERNARDA a decorative fan with red and green flowers.)

BERNARDA. *(Hurling the fan to the floor.)* Does this look like a fan for a widow? Give me a black one and learn to respect the memory of your father.

MARTIRIO. Take mine.

BERNARDA. What about you?

MARTIRIO. I'm not hot.

BERNARDA. Well, you'd better look for another one. You'll need it soon enough. We'll have no breeze from the street during our eight years of mourning, just as if we'd bricked over all the doors and windows. That's how it was with my father and grandfather. You can work on your trousseaus to pass the time. In my sewing basket you'll find material to start the sheets and spreads. Magdalena can do the embroidery.

MAGDALENA. Whatever you say.

ADELA. *(Resentfully.)* If you don't want to do ours, we'll just keep them plain. That way yours will look special.

MAGDALENA. I'm not doing yours or mine. I already know I'm never getting married. I'd prefer to break my back at the mill. Anything to avoid rotting away day after day in this dark room.

BERNARDA. That's what it means to be a woman.

MAGDALENA. Damn us all.

BERNARDA. In this house you'll do as I say. No more running to your father behind my back. Needles and thread for the women, whips and mules for the men. That's the way of all decent people.

(Exit ADELA.)

VOICE. Bernarda! Let me out!

BERNARDA. *(Raising her voice.)* Let her out!

(Enter the MAID.)

MAID. It took all my strength to subdue her. Despite her eighty years, your mother's as strong as an oak.

BERNARDA. She gets it from my grandmother.

MAID. During the funeral I had to gag her several times with a gunny sack. She wanted to call out for mop water and dog meat, which is what she says you give her.

MARTIRIO. She's up to no good!

BERNARDA. *(To the MAID.)* Let her loose in the patio so she can get some air.

MAID. She took out her rings and amethyst earrings from her jewelry box. She put everything on and said she wants to get married.

(The DAUGHTERS laugh.)

BERNARDA. Go with her and keep her away from the well.

MAID. Don't worry. She's not going to throw herself in.

BERNARDA. That's not my concern. The point is, if she gets near the well the neighbors can see her from their windows.

(Exit the MAID.)

MARTIRIO. We're going to go change clothes.

BERNARDA. Very well, but keep your kerchiefs on.

(Enter ADELA.)

Where's Angustias?

ADELA. *(Slyly.)* I saw her leaning through the bars of the front gate. The men just left.

BERNARDA. And what were you doing at the front gate?

ADELA. I went to see if the hens had laid eggs.

BERNARDA. But the men should have left long ago!

ADELA. *(Slyly.)* There was a group of them still standing around outside.

BERNARDA. *(Furiously.)* Angustias! Angustias!

ANGUSTIAS. *(Entering.)* Mother?

BERNARDA. What were you looking at? And whom?

ANGUSTIAS. No one.

BERNARDA. Do you think it proper for a woman of your class to go sniffing around a man the day of her father's funeral? Answer me! Whom were you looking at?

(Pause.)

ANGUSTIAS. I was just . . .

BERNARDA. Just *what*?

ANGUSTIAS. Nothing!

BERNARDA. *(Drawing near with the staff.)* You indecent little tramp!

(She strikes her.)

PONCIA. *(Rushing over.)* Easy, Bernarda!

(ANGUSTIAS breaks into tears.)

BERNARDA. Out, all of you!

(Exit the DAUGHTERS.)

PONCIA. I can't believe how sly she was about it. I wondered why she went scurrying toward the patio! Then she hid behind a window and listened to all the vile things the men were saying.

BERNARDA. That's their only reason for coming to funerals.

(*With curiosity.*)

What were they saying?

PONCIA. They were talking about Paca la Roseta. Last night they tied her husband to a manger, slung her over a horse, and took her out to the top of the olive grove.

BERNARDA. What did she do?

PONCIA. She went along with it. They say her breasts were hanging out and Maximiliano was strumming her like a guitar. Appalling!

BERNARDA. So what happened?

PONCIA. What do you think? It was almost daylight when they got back. Paca la Roseta had her hair down and a crown of flowers on her head.

BERNARDA. She's the only evil woman we have in the village.

PONCIA. Because she's not from here. She's from far away. And the men who went with her are also the sons of outsiders. The local men aren't capable of such things.

BERNARDA. No, but they like to see it and talk about it, and they lick their chops when it happens.

PONCIA. They said a lot of other things as well.

BERNARDA. (*Looking around apprehensively.*) Like what?

PONCIA. They're too shameful to repeat.

BERNARDA. And my daughter heard them?

PONCIA. Of course!

BERNARDA. She takes after her aunts, that one. They were soft and pliable and melted at the words of any little weasel who paid them a compliment. This just goes to show how one must struggle to uphold common decency and keep instinct at bay!

PONCIA. The thing is, your daughters are all of marrying age. They're not that badly behaved all things considered. Angustias must be well over thirty.

BERNARDA. Thirty-nine exactly.

PONCIA. Imagine. And she's never had a boy—

BERNARDA. (*Furiously.*) No, none of them have, nor do they need one! They can get along just fine without.

PONCIA. I didn't mean to offend you.

BERNARDA. No one for miles around can hold a candle to them. The men of this village are not of their class. Would you have me give them away to a common peasant?

PONCIA. You should have moved to another town.

BERNARDA. Right. And put them up for sale!

PONCIA. No, Bernarda, I meant to give them a fresh start. Of course in other places they would be considered poor!

BERNARDA. Shut that hateful trap of yours!

PONCIA. You're impossible. Can we speak frankly to each other or not?

BERNARDA. No, we cannot. You work for me and I pay you. That's it!

MAID. *(Entering.)* Don Arturo is here for the reading of the will.

BERNARDA. Let's go.

(To the MAID.)

Get busy whitewashing the patio.

(To PONCIA.)

And you, open the chest and start putting away the clothes of the deceased.

PONCIA. We could give some of them away.

BERNARDA. No, not a single button! Not even the veil that covered his face.

(She exits slowly, supporting herself on her staff and turning to watch the MAID and PONCIA, who exit behind her. Enter AMELIA and MARTIRIO.)

AMELIA. Did you take your medicine?

MARTIRIO. For all the good it'll do me!

AMELIA. But you took it.

MARTIRO. I do things with little faith but like clockwork.

AMELIA. Ever since the doctor came you seem more cheerful.

MARTIRIO. I feel the same.

AMELIA. Did you notice? Adelaida wasn't at the funeral.

MARTIRIO. I knew she wouldn't come. Her fiancé forbids her to leave her house. She used to be happy. Now she doesn't even wear makeup.

AMELIA. It's hard to know if getting engaged is even worth it anymore.

MARTIRIO. It's all the same in the end.

AMELIA. It's all the fault of this gossip we're smothered by. Adelaida must have felt terrible.

MARTIRIO. She's afraid of our mother: the only one who knows the story of her father and the origin of his land. Whenever Adelaida comes over, Mother rubs it in her face. Her father killed his first wife's husband in Cuba so he could marry her himself. Then he dumped her and ran off with another woman who had a grown daughter, then had an affair with the daughter, who became Adelaida's mother. He married her when the second wife went mad and died.

AMELIA. And why isn't this pig in jail?

MARTIRIO. Because men cover these things up for one another, and none of them is willing to squeal.

AMELIA. But none of this is Adelaida's fault.

MARTIRIO. No, but history repeats itself. I see it all as a terrible cycle. Adelaida is marked by the fate of her mother and grandmother: both wives to the man who fathered her.

AMELIA. What a disgusting story.

MARTIRIO. It's preferable never to look at a man. I've been afraid of them ever since I was a girl. I'd see them yoking oxen in the yard and grunting and stomping as they carried bushels of wheat from the fields, and I was always afraid of growing up for fear of finding myself locked in their embrace. But God made me weak and ugly and has kept them away from me forever.

AMELIA. Don't say that! Enrique Humanes was interested in you.

MARTIRIO. Those were just rumors! Once I waited all night by the window in a camisole because he told the daughter of one of his workers that he was coming to see me. He never came. It was all gossip. Then he married a woman who's richer than me.

AMELIA. And uglier than a devil.

MARTIRIO. What do they care about ugliness? All they want is land, livestock, and a submissive bitch to bring them dinner.

AMELIA. Martirio!

(Enter MAGDALENA.)

MAGDALENA. What are you two doing?

MARTIRIO. Just sitting.

AMELIA. What about you?

MAGDALENA. I've been walking around the house. Just to stretch my legs. I was looking at our grandmother's needlepoint pieces. There's that shaggy little dog and then that black man wrestling with the lion: remember how much we all used to love it when we were girls? Those were happier times. Weddings lasted ten days and no one gossiped. Today everything's more refined: brides dress in white veils like in the cities and people drink wine from bottles, but we kill ourselves over what the neighbors say.

MARTIRIO. God only knows what really went on back then!

AMELIA. (*To MAGDALENA.*) One of your shoelaces is untied.

MAGDALENA. What does it matter!

AMELIA. You're going to trip and fall.

MAGDALENA. One less mouth to feed!

MARTIRIO. Where's Adela?

MAGDALENA. Oh! She put on that green dress I made for her birthday, went into the yard, and started shouting: "Little hens, little hens, look at me!" I had to laugh.

AMELIA. Imagine if Mother had seen her!

MAGDALENA. Poor thing! She's the youngest of us and still has hope. What I'd give to see her happy.

(*Pause. ANGUSTIAS crosses the stage carrying towels.*)

ANGUSTIAS. What time is it?

MARTIRIO. It must be close to noon.

ANGUSTIAS. Already?

AMELIA. Any minute now.

(*Exit ANGUSTIAS.*)

MAGDALENA. (*Slyly.*) You know what's going on, don't you?

(*Gesturing toward ANGUSTIAS.*)

AMELIA. No.

MAGDELENA. Come on!

MARTIRIO. I don't know what you're talking about!

MAGDALENA. You know good and well, both of you. You're like two little sheep nestled together and bleating away to each other, but you fall silent the minute anyone comes near. Pepe el Romano!

MARTIRIO. Oh!

MAGDALENA. *(Mocking her.)* Oh! It's the talk of the town. Pepe el Romano is coming to ask for Angustias' hand in marriage. Last night he staked out the house, and any moment I expect he'll send a messenger.

MARTIRIO. I'm happy for her. He's a good man.

AMELIA. Me too. Angustias deserves him.

MAGDALENA. Liars. Neither of you is happy for her.

MARTIRIO. Magdalena! What's gotten into you!

MAGDALENA. If he were coming for Angustias herself, for Angustias the woman, I'd be happy. But he's coming for the money. Angustias is our sister, so let's be frank: she's old, she sickly, and she's always been the least desirable of the five of us. At twenty she was a flimsy beanpole, and now she's forty!

MARTIRIO. Don't talk that way. Good fortune comes when you're least expecting it.

AMELIA. But she's right! Angustias has her father's money. She's the only wealthy one among us. So now that our father's dead and the will is being settled, the men are lining up for her!

MAGDALENA. Pepe el Romano is twenty-five years old and the best catch for miles around. The logical thing would be for him to court you, Amelia, or Adela, who's twenty, but not to come in search of the most paltry prize this house has to offer, a woman who talks through her nose just like her father.

MARTIRIO. Maybe he likes her!

MAGDALENA. I've never been able to stomach your hypocrisy.

MARTIRIO. Give me strength, God!

(Enter ADELA.)

MAGDALENA. So, did you get the hens' attention?

ADELA. What else was I supposed to do?

AMELIA. If Mother sees you, she'll drag you off by the hair!

ADELA. I was really looking forward to that dress. I was going to wear it the day we were planning to eat watermelon at the mill. Can't you picture it?

MARTIRIO. It's a lovely dress!

ADELA. And it fits me so well. It's Magdalena's finest work.

MAGDALENA. So what did the hens think?

ADELA. They sicced their fleas on me.

(*They laugh.*)

MARTIRIO. What you could do is dye the dress black.

MAGDALENA. Or give it to Angustias for her wedding with Pepe el Romano!

ADELA. (*Containing her surprise.*) Pepe el Romano?

AMELIA. Haven't you heard?

ADELA. No.

MAGDALENA. Well now you have!

ADELA. But it makes no sense!

MAGDALENA. It does when money's involved!

ADELA. So that's why she ran out after the funeral and was staring through the gate?

(*Pause.*)

And that man, can he really . . .

MAGDALENA. He can do whatever he wants.

(*Pause.*)

MARTIRO. What are you thinking, Adela?

ADELA. I'm thinking that this period of mourning comes at the worst possible time in my life.

MAGDALENA. You'll get used to it.

ADELA. (*Breaking into angry tears.*) Never! I won't live in a cage. I don't want my flesh withering away as it has on the rest of you. I don't want my youth wasting away in these dark rooms. Tomorrow I'm putting on my green dress and walking through the streets. I want out!

(*Enter the MAID.*)

MAGDALENA. (*Forcefully.*) Adela!

MAID. Poor thing, how she misses her father!

(Exit.)

MARTIRIO. Shhh!

AMELIA. What happens to one of us will happen to all of us.

(ADELA quiets down.)

MAGDALENA. The maid almost heard you!

(The MAID reappears.)

MAID. Pepe el Romano is coming over the top of the street.

(AMELIA, MARTIRIO, and MAGDALENA jump from their seats.)

MAGDALENA. Let's go see!

(Exit running [AMELIA, MARTIRIO, and MAGDALENA].)

MAID. *(To ADELA.)* You're not going?

ADELA. It makes no difference to me.

MAID. When he turns the corner you'll be able to see him from your bedroom window.

(Exit the MAID. ADELA remains on stage, hesitating, before running off to her room. Enter BERNARDA and PONCIA.)

BERNARDA. I despise wills!

PONCIA. So much money for Angustias!

BERNARDA. Yes.

PONCIA. And so little for the others!

BERNARDA. You said that three times and I refrained from responding. Yes, they got much less. Now stop repeating it.

(Enter ANGUSTIAS with heavy makeup on her face.)

BERNARDA. Angustias!

ANGUSTIAS. Mother.

BERNARDA. You have the gall to powder your nose? To wash your face the day of your father's funeral?

ANGUSTIAS. He wasn't my father. My father died long ago. Or don't you remember?

BERNARDA. You owe as much to this man, your sisters' father, as to your own. Thanks to him your inheritance has doubled.

ANGUSTIAS. I'll believe that when I see it.

BERNARDA. Anyone with common decency would refrain from going around that way! Show some respect.

ANGUSTIAS. Mother, let me pass.

BERNARDA. Let you pass? Only after you've removed that makeup! You're a pathetic little hussy just like your aunts!

(She grabs her daughter roughly and wipes the makeup off with a handkerchief.)
Now go!

PONCIA. Bernarda, don't be so hard on her!

BERNARDA. My mother may be crazy, but I have all my wits about me and I know exactly what I'm doing.

(Enter the remaining DAUGHTERS.)

MAGDALENA. What's going on?

BERNARDA. Nothing.

MAGDALENA. *(To ANGUSTIAS.)* If you're arguing about the inheritance, you can keep it all, rich girl.

ANGUSTIAS. Shut that dirty trap of yours!

BERNARDA. *(Pounding the floor with the staff.)* Enough, all of you! Until I leave this house feet first, I'm the only one who gives orders around here!

(Arguing is heard offstage. Enter MARÍA JOSEFA, a withered old woman with flowers in her hair and around her neck.)

MARÍA JOSEFA. Bernarda, where's my mantilla? Don't think any of you are getting anything of mine. Not my rings, not my fancy black outfit. Because none of you is ever getting married. None of you! Bernarda, give me my pearl necklace.

BERNARDA. *(To the MAID.)* Why did you let her out?

MAID. *(Apprehensively.)* She slipped away from me.

MARÍA JOSEFA. I escaped because I want to get married. I want to marry a beautiful man by the seashore. Not like here, where the men flee from the women.

BERNARDA. Simmer down, Mother!

MARÍA JOSEFA. I will not. I can't bear watching these grown women chafing at the bit to marry, wasting away at the core. I want to go home to my village. Bernarda, I want to marry a beautiful man and live happily ever after!

BERNARDA. Lock her up!

MARÍA JOSEFA. No, Bernarda, let me go free!

(*The MAID seizes MARÍA JOSEFA.*)

BERNARDA. *[To her DAUGHTERS.]* Don't just stand there, help her!

(*They all begin dragging the old woman away.*)

MARÍA JOSEFA. I want out of here, Bernarda! I want to get married by the seashore. The seashore.

—QUICK CURTAIN—

Act 2

(*A white room in Bernarda's house. Doors at the left lead to the bedrooms. Bernarda's DAUGHTERS sit on low-rise chairs, sewing. MAGDALENA embroiders. PONCIA is seated with them.*)

ANGUSTIAS. I've started the third sheet.

MARTIRIO. That one's Amelia's.

MAGDALENA. Angustias, shall I embroider Pepe's initials as well?

ANGUSTIAS. *(Coldly.)* No.

MAGDALENA. *(Shouting.)* Adela, aren't you coming?

AMELIA. She must be lying down.

PONCIA. Something's wrong with that one. She's been so restless lately, jumpy and frightened as if a lizard had slithered down her blouse.

MARTIRIO. Nothing's wrong with her that isn't wrong with all of us.

MAGDALENA. All of us except Angustias.

ANGUSTIAS. Yes, I'm doing just fine, and whoever has a problem with that can go shove it.

MAGDALENA. You've always been as tactful as you are beautiful.

ANGUSTIAS. Fortunately I'll soon be leaving this hell.

MAGDALENA. Maybe not!

MARTIRIO. Let's change the subject!

ANGUSTIAS. And anyway a few gold coins in the purse are worth more than a pair of beautiful eyes in the face.

MAGDALENA. If you say so.

AMELIA. *(To PONCIA.)* Why don't you open the patio door and see if we can get a cross breeze.

(PONCIA opens the door.)

MARTIRIO. Last night I couldn't get to sleep for the heat.

AMELIA. Same here!

MAGDALENA. I got up for some fresh air. There was an enormous black cloud and a few drops of rain fell.

LA PONCIA. At one in the morning a wave of fire was rising from the earth. I got up too. Angustias was still talking to Pepe at the window.

MAGDALENA. *(Slyly.)* So late? What time did he leave?

ANGUSTIAS. Magdalena, why do you ask if you saw for yourself?

AMELIA. It must have been around one thirty.

ANGUSTIAS. Oh? And how would you know?

AMELIA. I heard his coughs and the clop-clop of his horse.

PONCIA. But I heard him leave around four!

ANGUSTIAS. That couldn't have been him.

PONCIA. I'm certain it was!

AMELIA. I thought I heard him at that hour as well.

MAGDALENA. How strange!

(Pause.)

PONCIA. Angustias, what did he say the first time he came to your window?

ANGUSTIAS. Nothing much. What was he supposed to say? Just small talk.

MARTIRIO. How odd that two people who've never known each other meet once at a window, and suddenly they're engaged.

ANGUSTIAS. Well it doesn't seem odd to me.

AMELIA. I'd be so embarrassed.

ANGUSTIAS. No, because by the time a man approaches a girl's window he already knows from all his proxies that she's going to say yes.

MARTIRIO. Right, but he still has to propose.

ANGUSTIAS. Of course!

AMELIA. *(With curiosity.)* And how did he put it?

ANGUSTIAS. I don't know, something like, "You know I've had my eye on you. I need a good, decent wife, and I'd like it to be you if you agree."

AMELIA. I'd be cringing from shame!

ANGUSTIAS. I was, but it's one of those things you have to do.

PONCIA. Did he say anything else?

ANGUSTIAS. Yes, he did all the talking.

MARTIRIO. What about you?

ANGUSTIAS. I couldn't speak. My heart was beating in my throat. It was the first time I was alone at night with a man.

MAGDALENA. And such a handsome one.

ANGUSTIAS. He's not bad!

PONCIA. These things come more naturally to those with a little more wisdom, with some experience in the world. . . . The first time my husband, Evaristo the Birdman, came to my window . . . ha, ha!

AMELIA. What happened?

PONCIA. It was very dark. I watched him approach, and when he got to the window he said, "Good evening." "Good evening," I replied, and we fell silent for more than half an hour. I was sweating all over. Finally he came close, really close, as if he were trying to slip through the bars, and he said with a whisper: "Come here so I can feel you!"

(They all laugh. AMELIA jumps up and peeks through a crack in the door.)

AMELIA. I thought I heard Mother!

MAGDALENA. Imagine if she heard us talking about this!

(*More laughter.*)

AMELIA. Shhh, or she will hear!

PONCIA. After that he behaved. He got into breeding finches, and that kept him occupied till the day he died. And since you girls are all single, I'll let you in on something: within two weeks of the wedding a man leaves the bed for the dinner table and the dinner table for the tavern, and you can either accept it or waste away crying in a corner.

AMELIA. You accepted it.

PONCIA. I had my say!

MARTIRIO. Is it true you hit him a few times?

PONCIA. Yes, almost left him cross-eyed.

MAGDALENA. All women should be like that!

PONCIA. I have your mother's training. One day he said something I didn't like and I took a pestle to his finches and killed them all.

(*They laugh.*)

MAGDALENA. Adela, girl, you're missing all the fun!

AMELIA. Adela?

(*Pause.*)

MAGDALENA. I'll go check on her.

(*Exit.*)

PONCIA. Something's really wrong with that girl.

MARTIRIO. Not surprising. She hardly sleeps.

PONCIA. What does she do?

MARTIRIO. How should I know what she does!

PONCIA. You'd know better than I. Your bed's on the other side of the wall from hers.

ANGUSTIAS. She's eaten alive with envy.

AMELIA. Don't exaggerate.

ANGUSTIAS. I can see it in her eyes. She's beginning to get that look, like a madwoman.

MARTIRIO. Don't speak of madness. It's not appropriate in this house.

(MAGDALENA returns with ADELA.)

MAGDALENA. So you weren't asleep?

ADELA. I just don't feel well.

MARTIRIO. *(Slyly.)* Didn't you sleep well last night?

ADELA. I slept fine.

MARTIRIO. So what's the problem?

ADELA. *(Angrily.)* Enough already! Whether I sleep or stay up all night, it's none of your business! I'll do with my body as I please!

MARTIRIO. I'm just concerned about you.

ADELA. You have the concern of an inquisitor! Weren't you all sewing? Then get on with it. What I'd give to be invisible and walk around without having to answer to any of you!

MAID. *(Entering.)* Bernarda's calling. The man with the lace is here.

(Exit [ANGUSTIAS, MAGDALENA, and AMELIA]. As MARTIRIO exits, she stares at ADELA.)

ADELA. Stop looking at me! If you want my eyes, take them. Take my back, too, and use it to replace that hideous hump of yours. But turn your head the other way when I pass by!

PONCIA. Adela, that's your sister you're talking to! And the one who loves you the most!

ADELA. She follows me around everywhere. Sometimes she peeks into my bedroom to see if I'm asleep. She doesn't let me breathe. And it's always: "Oh, what a waste. Such a pretty face, such a fetching figure, and no one to claim them!" And it's not true! Someone will!

PONCIA. *(Whispering slyly.)* You mean Pepe el Romano?

ADELA. *(Taken aback.)* What are you talking about!

PONCIA. You know.

ADELA. Stop it!

PONCIA. *(In a normal tone.)* You think I haven't noticed?

ADELA. Lower your voice!

PONCIA. You have to quash those thoughts!

ADELA. What do you know?

PONCIA. Old ladies like me can see through walls. Where do you go when you get up at night?

ADELA. You deserve to be blinded!

PONCIA. I'm all eyes when it comes to this sort of thing. For the life of me, I can't figure out what you think you're doing. Why did you stand practically naked, with a lighted candle and the window open, the second time Pepe came to see your sister?

ADELA. That's not true!

PONCIA. Don't be a child, Adela! Let your sister have what's hers, and if you're attracted to Pepe el Romano, show some self-control.

(ADELA begins to cry.)

And anyway, who says you can't marry him? Angustias is not a healthy specimen. She won't survive her first labor. She's old, her body's weak, and from what I know I'm telling you: she won't last. And then Pepe will do what all widowers around here do: he'll marry the youngest and the most beautiful, and that's you. So nourish your hope or forget it, whatever you prefer, but don't go against God's law.

ADELA. Stop it!

PONCIA. I will not!

ADELA. Mind your own business, you nosy old traitor!

PONCIA. I will be your shadow!

ADELA. Instead of cleaning house and going to bed and praying for the dead, you sniff around like a filthy old pig in search for juicy tidbits to drool over!

PONCIA. I look after the honor of this house! So people don't spit at our doorway when they walk by.

ADELA. Why are you so concerned about my sister all of a sudden?

PONCIA. I have no obligation to any of you. I simply want to live in decency. I don't want my name dragged through the mud in my old age!

ADELA. I have no use for your opinion. It's too late. You'll never stop me. You're just a servant. Even my mother can't stop me from quenching the fire that burns from my legs to my throat. What can you prove? That I lock myself in my room and don't open the door? That I don't sleep? I'm too clever for you. You'll never catch the hare with your clumsy hands.

PONCIA. Don't test me, Adela. Do not test me! I know how to shout, how to shine a light, how to sound an alarm.

ADELA. Bring a million flares and set them up on the fences around the yard. Nothing will stop nature from taking its course.

PONCIA. This is madness!

ADELA. You have no idea! I look in his eyes and feel as though I'm slowly drinking in his blood.

PONCIA. I can't listen to this.

ADELA. Well you're going to hear it! I used to be afraid of you. But I'm stronger than you now!

(Enter ANGUSTIAS.)

ANGUSTIAS. Always arguing!

PONCIA. What do you expect? She insists I go to the store for her in this heat.

ANGUSTIAS. Did you buy the bottle of perfume I asked for?

PONCIA. The most expensive one they had. And the makeup. I put it all on the table in your room.

(Exit ANGUSTIAS.)

ADELA. Keep that mouth shut.

PONCIA. We'll see about that!

(Enter MARTIRIO, AMELIA, and MAGDALENA.)

MAGDALENA. *(To ADELA.)* Have you seen the lace?

AMELIA. The patterns Angustias chose for her bridal sheets are lovely.

ADELA. *(To MARTIRIO, who holds a bundle of lace.)* So what's that for?

MARTIRIO. It's for me. For a nightgown I'm making.

ADELA. *(Sardonically.)* You've got to be kidding!

MARTIRIO. *(Slyly.)* It's for my eyes only. I don't need to show off in front of anyone.

PONCIA. Nightgowns are not for showing off in.

MARTIRIO. *(Slyly, staring at Adela.)* For some they are. Me, I just happen to love lingerie. If I were wealthy I'd have a whole collection of the finest. It's one of the few pleasures left to me.

PONCIA. This lace is perfect for baby bonnets and christening gowns. I never had any for my own children, but maybe Angustias will want some for hers. Once she starts spilling out babies, you'll all be sewing night and day.

MAGDALENA. I don't plan on sewing a single stitch.

AMELIA. Much less look after someone else's kids. Look at the girls across the alley, worn out by four snotty brats.

PONCIA. They're better off than any of you. At least you hear laughter and signs of life from their house!

MARTIRIO. So go work for them.

PONCIA. No. Fate has bound me to this nunnery!

(The sound of bells is heard in the distance, as if across thick walls.)

MAGDALENA. It's the men returning to the fields.

PONCIA. Yes, it just turned three o'clock.

MARTIRIO. Imagine working in this heat!

ADELA. *(Sitting.)* What I'd give to wander freely through the fields!

MAGDALENA. *(Sitting.)* But we're all bound by our station in life.

MARTIRIO. *(Sitting.)* So we are.

AMELIA. *(Sitting.)* Ay!

PONCIA. There's nothing like the joy of the fields in this season. The harvesters arrived yesterday morning. Forty or fifty strapping young men.

MAGDALENA. Where are they from this year?

PONCIA. From very far away. Somewhere in the mountains. Merry souls they are, dark like well-seasoned trees, always looking for mischief! Last night a woman arrived in town, dressed in sequins and dancing to an accordion, and fifteen of them paid to whisk her off to the olive grove. I saw them from a distance. The one who did the dealing was a green-eyed lad, wound up tight like an ear of wheat.

AMELIA. Is that true?

ADELA. Sounds about right!

PONCIA. A few years ago one of these women came through town, and I gave my elder son money to have his way with her. Men need these things.

ADELA. They get away with anything.

AMELIA. Being born a woman is the greatest punishment.

MAGDALENA Not even our eyes belong to us.

(Singing is heard in the distance, gradually drawing closer.)

PONCIA. It's them. They have some lovely tunes.

AMELIA. They're headed out to reap.

CHORUS.
>They work the wheat
>in the month of June,
>and as they reap
>the maidens swoon.

(Tambourines and other rustic instruments can be heard. Pause. The women listen in stuffy silence.)

AMELIA. To think the heat doesn't bother them!

MARTIRIO. They're used to it.

ADELA. I'd like to be a harvester, just to be able to come and go. And to forget all my worries.

MARTIRIO. What do you have that needs forgetting?

ADELA. We all have something.

MARTIRIO. *(Pensively.)* No doubt!

PONCIA. Shhh, shhh!

CHORUS. *(Very far off.)*
>Open doors and windows
>you girls who live in town.
>The reaper requests a rose
>to pin upon his gown.

PONCIA. What a charming song.

MARTIRIO. *(Wistfully.)*
>Open doors and windows
>you girls who live in town . . .

ADELA. *(Passionately.)*
>The reaper requests a rose
>to pin upon his gown.

(The singing fades into the distance.)

PONCIA. They're turning the corner now.

ADELA. Let's go watch them from my bedroom window.

PONCIA. Be careful not to open it too much. They'll push through to see who's watching.

> *(Exit ADELA, MAGDALENA, and PONCIA. MARTIRIO remains seated with her head in her hands. AMELIA draws near.)*

AMELIA. What's the matter?

MARTIRIO. This heat is getting to me.

AMELIA. Is that all?

MARTIRIO. I want it to be November already. Rain, frost: anything but this interminable summer.

AMELIA. It'll pass soon enough. And then it'll be back.

MARTIRIO. As always!

> *(Pause.)*

What time did you get to sleep last night?

AMELIA. I don't know. I sleep like a log. Why?

MARTIRIO. Nothing important. I thought I heard voices in the yard.

AMELIA. Really?

MARTIRIO. Very late.

AMELIA. And you weren't frightened?

MARTIRIO. No. It's not the first time I've heard them.

AMELIA. We need to be careful. Could it have been the workers?

MARTIRIO. They don't arrive until six.

AMELIA. Maybe it was a rogue mule.

MARTIRIO. *(Muttering slyly.)* Yes, maybe so! A rogue mule.

AMELIA. We should warn the others!

MARTIRIO. No, no, don't say anything! It might just be my imagination.

AMELIA. Maybe so.

> *(Pause. AMELIA begins to exit.)*

MARTIRIO. Amelia!

AMELIA. *(From the doorway.)* What?

(Pause.)

MARTIRIO. Nothing.

(Pause.)

AMELIA. What were you going to say?

(Pause.)

MARTIRIO. I don't know, it's slipped my mind. It wasn't important.

(Pause.)

AMELIA. Maybe you should lie down for a bit.

ANGUSTIAS. *(Entering furiously, in great contrast to the stillness of the previous dialogue.)* Where's the locket of Pepe I had beneath my pillow? Which one of you has it?

MARTIRIO. Don't look at us.

AMELIA. Pepe's not a Saint Bartholomew medal.

(Enter PONCIA, MAGDALENA, and ADELA.)

ANGUSTIAS. Where's the locket?

ADELA. What locket?

ANGUSTIAS. One of you has hidden it.

MAGDALENA. You have the gall to insinuate such a thing?

ANGUSTIAS. It was in my room and now it's not.

MARTIRIO. You're sure it didn't escape into the yard last night? I hear Pepe likes to travel by moonlight.

ANGUSTIAS. This isn't a joke! Just wait till I tell him!

PONCIA. No need for that! I'm sure we'll find it before then.

(Glancing at Adela.)

ANGUSTIAS. I intend to find out which one of you has it!

ADELA. *(Looking at MARTIRIO.)* It's not me.

MARTIRIO. *(Slyly.)* Of course not.

BERNARDA. *(Entering with her staff.)* What's all this commotion in my house? And in the thick of the afternoon heat! The neighbor women must be standing with their ears glued to the wall.

ANGUSTIAS. They stole my locket of Pepe.

BERNARDA. *(Beside herself.)* Who? Who?

ANGUSTIAS. One of them.

BERNARDA. Which one of you was it?

(Silence.)

Answer me!

(Silence. To PONCIA.)

Search the rooms and check the beds.

[*Exit PONCIA.*]

This is what I get for not keeping you all on tighter leashes! But just you wait!

(To ANGUSTIAS.)

Are you sure about this?

ANGUSTIAS. Yes.

BERNARDA. You looked all over for it?

ANGUSTIAS. Yes, Mother.

(Everyone remains standing in awkward silence.)

BERNARDA. What poison you force a mother to swallow in her old age.

(To PONCIA.)

Did you find it?

PONCIA. *(Entering.)* Yes, here it is.

BERNARDA. Where did you find it?

PONCIA. It was . . .

BERNARDA. Out with it. Have no fear.

PONCIA. *(Incredulous.)* Beneath the sheets of Martirio's bed.

BERNARDA. *(To MARTIRIO.)* Is that true?

MARTIRIO. It's true!

BERNARDA. *(Rushing forward and striking her with the staff.)* You ought to be flogged, you troublemaking little trollop!

MARTIRIO. *(Enraged.)* Stop it, Mother!

BERNARDA. I'll stop when I'm good and ready!

MARTIRIO. I'll make you then! You hear me? Away from me!

PONCIA. Don't talk back to your mother!

ANGUSTIAS. *(Restraining BERNARDA.)* Enough! Please!

BERNARDA. You're not even capable of tears.

MARTIRIO. I'm not going to make you happy by crying.

BERNARDA. Why did you take the locket?

MARTIRIO. Can't I play a practical joke on my sister? Why else would I want it?

ADELA. *(Springing forward, full of spite.)* It wasn't a joke and you know it! You've never had a sense of humor. This came from somewhere else in that twisted heart of yours. Speak!

MARTIRIO. You shut your mouth and don't get me started, or I'll have these walls collapsing from shame!

ADELA. I'm sure there's no end to the sick stories you could make up!

BERNARDA. Adela!

MAGDALENA. Have you two lost your minds?

AMELIA. Your evil thoughts strike at us all.

MARTIRIO. Some are capable of far more evil deeds.

ADELA. Until their naked bodies are swept away by the river.

BERNARDA. Such filth you spout!

ANGUSTIAS. It's not my fault Pepe el Romano chose me.

ADELA. For your money!

ANGUSTIAS. Mother!

BERNARDA. Silence!

MARTIRIO. For your lands and your orchards.

MAGDALENA. That's exactly right!

BERNARDA. Silence I say! By god, I could see this tempest coming, but I didn't think it would erupt so soon. What a hailstorm of bile you hurl at my heart! Don't think I'm too old to chain you up in this house my father built. Not even the weeds will know what's going on. Now out of my sight!

(Exit the DAUGHTERS. BERNARDA sinks limply into a chair. PONCIA stands motionless with her back against the wall. BERNARDA reacts and stomps her foot defensively.)

They need to know the back of my hand! I must keep reminding myself of that.

PONCIA. May I speak?

BERNARDA. Speak. I'm sorry you had to hear this. That's the problem with an outsider in the midst of a family.

PONCIA. I can't take back what I've seen.

BERNARDA. Angustias will need to marry immediately.

PONCIA. Yes, you need to get her away from here.

BERNARDA. Not her, him!

PONCIA. Him too. Good thinking.

BERNARDA. It's not thinking. These things don't require thought. I command, that's all.

PONCIA. You think he'll agree to go away?

BERNARDA. *(Standing.)* What's going through that head of yours?

PONCIA. Nothing. I'm sure he'll marry Angustias!

BERNARDA. Go on. I know you well enough to see the knife you're hiding behind your back.

PONCIA. Since when does giving fair warning amount to murder?

BERNARDA. You wish to warn me about something?

PONCIA. I'm not interested in making accusations, Bernarda. I'm just saying: open your eyes and you'll see for yourself.

BERNARDA. See what?

PONCIA. You've always been clever. You see the evil in people from miles away. Often I was convinced you could read minds. But children are another story, and you have a blind spot when it comes to yours.

BERNARDA. Are you referring to Martirio?

PONCIA. Well, Martirio . . .

>   *(With curiosity.)*
>
>   Why do you think she hid that locket?

BERNARDA. *(Attempting to excuse her daughter.)* She says it was a joke. What else would it be?

PONCIA. *(Scornfully.)* So you believe her, just like that?

BERNARDA. *(Vehemently.)* It's not about believing. It's the way it is!

PONCIA. Fine, it's your business. But if this were happening at the neighbor's house, what would you think then?

BERNARDA. Here comes the knife.

PONCIA. *(Cruelly.)* No, Bernarda. What I'm trying to say is that something really big is brewing here. I don't want to blame you, but you've never let your daughters live their own lives. Martirio is a hopeless romantic on the inside, say what you will. Why didn't you let her marry Enrique Humanes? Why did you send a message telling him to stay away the day he was supposed to come to her window?

BERNARDA. *(Angrily.)* And I'd do it all over again! My blood will not be mixed with the likes of the Humanes clan as long as I live! His father was a field-worker!

PONCIA. This is what comes of all the airs you put on.

BERNARDA. I put on airs because I can. You can't because you know very well where you came from.

PONCIA. *(Hatefully.)* You don't have to remind me. I'm getting too old for this. I've always appreciated your help.

BERNARDA. *(Exploding.)* You could have fooled me!

PONCIA. *(Swallowing her hatred.)* Martirio will get over all of this soon enough.

BERNARDA. And if she doesn't she'll have me to contend with. At any rate this doesn't strike me as the "really big thing" you insist is brewing here. Nothing is brewing here. You only wish it were! And if anything ever does happen, rest assured it will never leave these walls.

PONCIA. I'm not so sure about that. There are people in this town who can read secret thoughts from awfully far away.

BERNARDA. Wouldn't you just love to see me and my daughters with no other option but the brothel!

PONCIA. None of us can know what end awaits us.

BERNARDA. I know mine! And that of my daughters! The brothel is reserved for the likes of a certain woman I once knew.

PONCIA. *(Furiously.)* Bernarda, show some respect for the memory of my mother!

BERNARDA. Then stop taunting me with your evil thoughts!

(Pause.)

PONCIA. I should just stay out of this.

BERNARDA. Exactly. You should do your work and keep your mouth shut. That's all that's required of servants.

PONCIA. But I can't. Don't you think Pepe would be better off with Martirio or . . . yes, with Adela!

BERNARDA. No, I don't.

PONCIA. *(Purposefully.)* Adela. She's the one who belongs with el Romano.

BERNARDA. Things never happen the way we wish.

PONCIA. But it's not easy for them to resist their instincts. It just doesn't seem natural for Pepe to be with Angustias, not to me nor to anyone else. Who knows how this will end!

BERNARDA. Here we go again! You're determined to plant malicious thoughts in my head, but I refuse to play your game. I'd end up scratching your eyes out.

PONCIA. I'm sure I'd survive!

BERNARDA. Fortunately my daughters respect me and have never defied my authority!

PONCIA. True enough, but if you ever give them free rein, they'll be gone in a second!

BERNARDA. I'll drag them back screaming and hollering!

PONCIA. You could outlast them, I'm sure of that!

BERNARDA. I've got some fire left in me!

PONCIA.   I don't know how things got to this point! A woman of Angustias' age, so taken with her fiancé! And he seems equally overwrought. Yesterday my elder son told me that he came down the street with his plow at four thirty in the morning and they were still talking.

BERNARDA.   At four thirty in the morning!

ANGUSTIAS.   *(Entering.)* That's a lie!

PONCIA.   That's what I was told.

BERNARDA.   *(To ANGUSTIAS.)* Speak!

ANGUSTIAS.   Pepe's been leaving at one o'clock for over a week now. God strike me down if I'm lying.

MARTIRIO.   *(Entering.)* I also heard him leaving at four.

BERNARDA.   But did you see him with your own eyes?

MARTIRIO.   I didn't want to peek. Don't you talk to him through the window overlooking the alley?

ANGUSTIAS.   No, we talk through the window in my bedroom.

(ADELA appears in the doorway.)

MARTIRIO.   So . . .

BERNARDA.   What's going on here?

PONCIA.   Better find out! Whatever the case, Pepe was at one of your windows at four in the morning.

BERNARDA.   And you're certain of that?

PONCIA.   Nothing is certain in this life.

ADELA.   Mother, don't listen to someone who would ruin us all.

BERNARDA.   I'll find the truth! If people in this village want to bear false witness against me, they'll have the fight of their lives. Meanwhile, you all keep your mouths shut. The neighbors will spread any filthy rumor they can to ruin us.

MARTIRIO.   I don't like lying.

PONCIA.   Something's going on, that's for sure.

BERNARDA.   Nothing's going on. I was born with my eyes wide open, and I'll keep them open and vigilant till the day I die.

ANGUSTIAS. I have a right to know what's happening.

BERNARDA. You have a right to do nothing but obey. I give the orders around here.

(To PONCIA.)

And you, mind your own business. I don't want anyone moving without my permission!

MAID. *(Entering.)* There's a crowd of people at the top of the street and all the neighbors are gawking from their doorways!

BERNARDA. *(To PONCIA.)* Go find out what's happening, quick!

([Exit PONCIA.] The DAUGHTERS rush to exit.)

Where do you think you're going? It's just like you to disgrace your father's memory by leering through windows like common trash. To the patio, all of you!

(Exit ALL. Confused shouting is heard in the distance. MARTIRIO and ADELA return and listen apprehensively from the doorway.)

MARTIRIO. You better be glad I didn't say anything else.

ADELA. I could have said a few things as well.

MARTIRIO. Like what? Wanting isn't the same as doing!

ADELA. I saw my chance and I took it. You wanted to do the same but were incapable.

MARTIRIO. This can't go on, Adela.

ADELA. I will have him all to myself!

MARTIRIO. I won't allow it.

ADELA. *(Imploring.)* Martirio, please!

MARTIRIO. Never!

ADELA. His intentions are decent!

MARTIRIO. I've seen how decently he paws at you!

ADELA. I didn't mean for this to happen. I feel like I'm being dragged by a rope.

MARTIRIO. Then you will hang!

(MAGDALENA and ANGUSTIAS peek in. The sound of the disturbance in the street grows.)

PONCIA. *(Entering.)* Bernarda!

BERNARDA. *(Entering.)* What is it? What's going on?

PONCIA. Librada's daughter, the unmarried one, had a baby and no one knows with whom.

ADELA. A baby?

PONCIA. And to hide her shame she killed it and buried it beneath some stones, but a dog dug it up and dropped it on her doorstep like a message from God. Now they want to kill her. They're dragging her down the street and men are pouring out of the olive grove, screaming and yelling like demons.

BERNARDA. Good, let them come with their rods and hoes, let them come and kill her!

ADELA. No, not kill her!

MARTIRIO. Yes, and let's all go watch!

BERNARDA. This is the price she pays for trampling common decency.

(In the street a woman screams amid the sound of great tumult.)

ADELA. No, let her go! Don't go out there!

MARTIRIO. *(Staring at ADELA.)* She must pay for what she did!

BERNARDA. *(From the doorway.)* Finish her off before the police get here! Plug that sinful womb with burning coal!

ADELA. *(Clutching her abdomen.)* No! No!

BERNARDA. Kill her! Kill her!

—CURTAIN—

Act 3

(Four white walls with a bluish tinge surround the inner patio of Bernarda's house. It's nighttime. The set should be as simple as possible. The doors, illuminated by the light from inside, cast a soft glow over the scene. At center stage stands a table with a kerosene lamp, at which BERNARDA and her DAUGHTERS are dining. PONCIA serves them. PRUDENCIA sits a few spaces away. When the curtain rises there's a long silence punctuated by the sound of silverware clinking on plates.)

PRUDENCIA.   Time for me to get going. It's been a long visit.

   (She stands to leave.)

BERNARDA.   Can't you stay a little longer? We never see each other.

PRUDENCIA.   Have they sounded the final rosary bells?

PONCIA.   Not yet.

   (PRUDENCIA sits.)

BERNARDA.   How's your husband doing?

PRUDENCIA.   Same as always.

BERNARDA.   We never see him either.

PRUDENCIA.   You know how he is. Ever since he fought with his brothers over the inheritance, he never goes out the front door. He uses a ladder to go over the wall of the backyard.

BERNARDA.   A true man. How's his relationship with your daughter?

PRUDENCIA.   He still hasn't forgiven her.

BERNARDA.   Good for him.

PRUDENCIA.   I don't know what to say about that. It's hard on me.

BERNARDA.   A disobedient daughter is not a daughter. She's an enemy.

PRUDENCIA.   I try to stay out of it. I take consolation in church, but now that I'm losing my vision I'm afraid I'll have to stop coming so the little ones won't take advantage of me.

   (A violent thud shakes the walls.)

   What was that?

BERNARDA.   The stallion. He's penned up and knocking against the walls.

   (Shouting.)

   Lasso him and take him out to the yard!

   (Under her breath.)

   It's breeding season.

PRUDENCIA.   Are you going to mate him with the new mares?

BERNARDA.   Tomorrow morning.

PRUDENCIA.   You've done a fabulous job expanding your livestock.

BERNARDA. It hasn't been easy.

PONCIA. *(Interrupting.)* She's got the finest herd in these parts! Too bad prices are down.

BERNARDA. Would you like a bit of cheese and honey?

PRUDENCIA. I don't have room for anything else.

(Another thud shakes the walls.)

PONCIA. Jesus!

PRUDENCIA. I felt that one in my chest.

BERNARDA. *(Standing furiously.)* Do I have to say things twice around here? Take him out where he can thrash against the hay!

(Pause, as if talking to the stable boys.)

Then put the mares in the stable, but let him out before he brings the house down!

(She returns to her seat at the table.)

For crying out loud!

PRUDENCIA. You're the man of the house now.

BERNARDA. It's true.

(ADELA stands.)

Where do you think you're going?

ADELA. I need a drink of water.

BERNARDA. *(To PONCIA.)* Bring a pitcher of fresh water.

(To ADELA.)

You may sit.

(ADELA sits.)

PRUDENCIA. When is Angustias' wedding?

BERNARDA. In three days.

PRUDENCIA. You must be happy!

ANGUSTIAS. Delighted!

AMELIA. *(To MAGDALENA.)* You've knocked over the salt.

MAGDALENA. I don't think our luck can get any worse.

AMELIA. I wouldn't bet on that.

BERNARDA. Stop that chattering!

PRUDENCIA. *(To ANGUSTIAS.)* Did he already give you a ring?

ANGUSTIAS. Take a look.

(She extends her hand toward PRUDENCIA.)

PRUDENCIA. Lovely. Three pearls. In my day pearls were associated with tears.

ANGUSTIAS. Things are different now.

ADELA. I'm not so sure. Things always mean the same. Engagement rings should have diamonds.

PRUDENCIA. That does seem more proper.

BERNARDA. Pearls or no pearls, it doesn't matter: things are what you make of them.

MARTIRIO. Or what God wills of them.

PRUDENCIA. I hear the furniture is lovely.

BERNARDA. Sixteen thousand is what it cost me.

PONCIA. *(Interrupting.)* The best is the mirrored wardrobe.

PRUDENCIA. I've never seen one of those.

BERNARDA. We always kept clothes in a chest.

PRUDENCIA. What matters is that all will turn out well in the end.

ADELA. You never know.

BERNARDA. There's no reason it shouldn't.

(Bells ring in the far distance.)

PRUDENCIA. The final bells.

(To ANGUSTIAS.)

I'll come another time so you can show me your dress.

ANGUSTIAS. Whenever you like.

PRUDENCIA. Good evening to you all.

BERNARDA. Goodnight, Prudencia.

DAUGHTERS. *(In unison.)* God keep you.

(Pause. Exit PRUDENCIA.)

BERNARDA. That's it, dinner's over.

(They all rise.)

ADELA. I'm going to walk to the front gate to stretch my legs and get a bit of fresh air.

(MAGDALENA sits down in a low chair against the wall.)

AMELIA. I'll go with you.

MARTIRIO. Me too.

ADELA. *(Containing her hatred.)* I'm not going to get lost.

AMELIA. It's nice to have company at night.

(Exit ADELA, MARTIRIO, and AMELIA. BERNARDA sits and ANGUSTIAS clears the table.)

BERNARDA. I'll tell you again: I want you to talk to Martirio. What happened with the locket was a joke, and you need to put it behind you.

ANGUSTIAS. You know she doesn't love me.

BERNARDA. No one knows what others feel on the inside. I don't pretend to understand the heart, but I want a calm façade and family harmony. Do you understand?

ANGUSTIAS. Yes.

BERNARDA. Good.

MAGDALENA. *(Drowsily.)* And anyway, you're leaving us any day now!

(She drifts off.)

ANGUSTIAS. None too soon.

BERNARDA. How late did you talk last night?

ANGUSTIAS. Until twelve thirty.

BERNARDA. What does Pepe have to say?

ANGUSTIAS. He seems distracted. He always talks as if his mind is elsewhere. If I ask him what's wrong he says, "We men have our worries."

BERNARDA. Then don't ask him. And when you get married, even less so. Speak when he speaks and look at him when he looks at you. That way you'll avoid ugly surprises.

ANGUSTIAS. I have a feeling, Mother, that he's hiding many things from me.

BERNARDA. Don't try to figure them out, don't ask him about them, and by all means, never let him see you cry.

ANGUSTIAS. I should be happy and I'm not.

BERNARDA. That's neither here nor there.

ANGUSTIAS. Sometimes I stare at Pepe through the window bars and his face dissolves as if disappearing in a dust cloud kicked up by cattle.

BERNARDA. That's your mind playing tricks on you.

ANGUSTIAS. I hope so!

BERNARDA. Is he coming tonight?

ANGUSTIAS. No. He went to the capital with his mother.

BERNARDA. So we'll all get to bed early. Magdalena!

ANGUSTIAS. She's asleep.

(Enter ADELA, MARTIRIO, and AMELIA.)

AMELIA. The night is so dark!

ADELA. You can't see two steps in front of you.

MARTIRIO. A good night for thieves. And others who need hiding places.

ADELA. The stallion was in the middle of the yard. Pure white! He seemed twice his normal size, filling the blackness.

AMELIA. It's true. It was startling, like something from a vision!

ADELA. The stars are as big as fists.

MARTIRIO. I thought she was going to break something, the way she was craning her neck to look at them.

ADELA. Don't you like looking at the stars?

MARTIRIO. I'm not concerned with the sky. I have enough to deal with beneath this roof.

ADELA. If that's what you find interesting.

BERNARDA. She's got her interests just like you've got yours.

ANGUSTIAS. Goodnight.

ADELA. You're going to bed already?

ANGUSTIAS. Yes. Pepe's not coming tonight.

(*Exit.*)

ADELA. Mother, why do people pray to Santa Barbara when they see lightning or a falling star? You know:
Santa Barbara divine,
written in Heaven so fine,
with paper and holy wine.

BERNARDA. The ancients understood many things that we've forgotten.

AMELIA. I close my eyes to avoid seeing the stars.

ADELA. Not me. I love watching something that's been rooted in place for so long rush forward all full of fire.

MARTIRIO. Such things have no bearing on our life.

BERNARDA. And it's better not to think about them.

ADELA. But the night's so lovely! I'd love to stay up late and enjoy the coolness of the fields.

BERNARDA. But it's time for bed. Magdalena!

AMELIA. She's already dreaming.

BERNARDA. Magdalena!

MAGDALENA. (*Irritated.*) Leave me be!

BERNARDA. Get to bed!

MAGDALENA. (*Standing grumpily.*) A girl can't get any peace around here!

(*Exit grumbling.*)

AMELIA. Goodnight.

(*Exit.*)

BERNARDA. You two as well, go.

MARTIRIO. Why didn't Angustias' fiancé come tonight?

BERNARDA. He's on a trip.

MARTIRIO. (*Glancing at ADELA.*) Ah!

ADELA. Goodnight.

(*Exit.*)

(MARTIRIO drinks a sip of water and exits slowly, looking toward the door that leads to the yard. Enter PONCIA.)

PONCIA. You're still up?

BERNARDA. Enjoying the silence. And the absence of the "really big thing" you insist is brewing here.

PONCIA. Bernarda, let's drop it.

BERNARDA. Nothing happens in this house without my permission.

PONCIA. Nothing happens on the outside. That's true. Your daughters live like cups in a china closet. But neither you nor anyone else can see through to their hearts.

BERNARDA. My daughters have nothing to be ashamed of.

PONCIA. That's your business. You're their mother. I'm just a servant and that's plenty for me.

BERNARDA. You're not so talkative tonight.

PONCIA. I know my place and I'm happy with it. That's all.

BERNARDA. The issue is you have nothing to report. If there were any weeds growing in this house you'd be sure to bring sheep from all around to chew on them.

PONCIA. There's plenty I'm not saying.

BERNARDA. Does your son still see Pepe here at four in the morning? Are the neighbors still saying evil things about us?

PONCIA. They're not saying anything.

BERNARDA. Because they can't. There's no meat on that bone anymore. This is what my vigilance has accomplished.

PONCIA. Bernarda, I don't want to talk about it because I don't trust your intentions. I'll just say that you shouldn't be so confident.

BERNARDA. I'm very confident!

PONCIA. Lightning could strike at any moment. A sudden shock could stop your heart.

BERNARDA. Rubbish. I have guarded against all possibilities.

PONCIA. Good for you.

BERNARDA. Yes, good for me.

MAID. *(Entering.)* I'm done with the dishes. Is there anything else, Bernarda?

BERNARDA. *(Standing.)* No. I'm going to bed.

PONCIA. What time shall I wake you?

BERNARDA. Don't wake me. I intend to sleep long and hard tonight.

(Exit.)

PONCIA. She can't handle the ocean so she just turns her back and pretends it's not there.

MAID. That pride of hers is as good as a blindfold.

PONCIA. I can't do anything about it. I tried to head things off, but I'm too frightened now. You hear that silence? That's the sound of storms brewing in every room. And when the sky opens up it's going to sweep us all away. I've said all I can say.

MAID. Bernarda thinks no one is a match for her. She doesn't understand the power a man has among five single women.

PONCIA. It's not all Pepe el Romano's fault. It's true he had a thing for Adela last year and she was crazy about him, but it's up to her to understand her place and not incite him. A man will always be a man.

MAID. Some say he's been speaking to her for many nights.

PONCIA. It's true.

(Whispering.)

And they do more than speak.

MAID. Who knows what will come of all this.

PONCIA. I'd like to cross the sea and leave this besieged castle behind.

MAID. Bernarda is trying to move up the wedding. Maybe nothing will come of it after all.

PONCIA. Things are too far gone. Adela is determined to get her way, and the others are constantly spying on her.

MAID. Martirio too?

PONCIA. She's the worst, that one. A well of venom. She knows el Romano will never be hers so she'd sink the whole ship if she could.

MAID. Evil, all of them!

PONCIA. Women without men, that's all they are. It's made them forget they're sisters. Shhh!

(Siting up in her seat to listen.)

MAID. What is it?

PONCIA. *(She stands.)* The dogs are barking.

MAID. Someone must have passed by the front gate.

(Enter ADELA in a white petticoat and bodice.)

PONCIA. Didn't you go to bed?

ADELA. I need a drink of water.

(She drinks from a glass at the table.)

PONCIA. I figured you were asleep.

ADELA. My thirst woke me. Aren't you two going to bed?

MAID. In a bit.

(Exit ADELA.)

PONCIA. Time for bed then.

MAID. Finally. Bernarda hasn't let me rest all day.

PONCIA. Take the candle with you.

MAID. The dogs are going crazy.

PONCIA. They may keep us awake.

(Exit PONCIA and the MAID. The set is now almost completely dark. Enter MARÍA JOSEFA, cradling a lamb in her arms.)

MARÍA JOSEFA.
> My little lamb, my little boy,
> let's be off to the shore.
> I will nurse you full of joy,
> and the tiny ant will guard his door.
>
> Bernarda, face like a dog.
> Magdalena, face like a frog.
> Little lamb.
> Baaa, baaa.
> To the gates of Bethlehem we'll scram.

(*She laughs.*)

> Neither of us desires to sleep.
> The door will open just a crack.
> We must run away to the beach
> and slip inside the coral shack.
>
> Bernarda, face like a dog.
> Magdalena, face like a frog.
> Little lamb.
> Baaa, baaa.
> To the gates of Bethlehem we'll scram.

(*MARÍA JOSEFA wanders off singing. Enter ADELA, who looks around silently and disappears through the door to the yard. Enter MARTIRIO through another door. She remains center stage, searching clumsily for ADELA. She wears a petticoat and a small black shawl over her shoulders. Enter MARÍA JOSEFA in front of her.*)

MARTIRIO.   Grandmother! Where are you going?

MARÍA JOSEFA.   Are you going to open the door for me? Who are you?

MARTIRIO.   How did you get out here?

MARÍA JOSEFA.   I escaped. But who are you?

MARTIRIO.   Go back to bed.

MARÍA JOSEFA.   You're Martirio, now I see. Martirio, face like a martyr. So when are you going to have a child? I had this one.

MARTIRIO.   Where did you get that lamb?

MARÍA JOSEFA.   I know it's just a lamb. But why can't a lamb be a child? Better to have a lamb than nothing at all. Bernarda, face like a dog. Magdalena, face like a frog.

MARTIRIO.   Shhh, don't raise your voice.

MARÍA JOSEFA.   It's true, everything's so dark. Because my hair is white you think I can't bear children, but I can: one child after another. This one will have white hair and he'll produce another one, and that one yet another, and they'll all have hair like snow, and we'll be like the waves, one after another after another. Then we'll all sit down and we'll all have white hair and we'll be froth upon the sea. Why is there no sea froth here? I see only the blackness of grief.

MARTIRIO.   Shhh, shhh.

MARÍA JOSEFA. When my neighbor had a child I'd take her chocolate, and then she'd bring me some, and so it went always, always, always. You'll have white hair, but the neighbors won't come. I have to go, but I'm afraid the dogs will bite me. Will you help me leave the countryside? I don't like the country. I want houses, but open houses where the women lie in their beds with their little ones and the men sit outside in their chairs. Pepe el Romano is a giant. You're all smitten with him. But he's going to gulp you down because you're just grains of wheat. No, not grains of wheat. Tongueless frogs!

MARTIRIO. *(Vehemently.)* Come now. Go back to bed.

(Pushing her.)

MARÍA JOSEFA. Very well, but then you'll let me out, right?

MARTIRIO. Of course.

MARÍA JOSEFA. *(In tears.)*
My little lamb, my little boy,
let's be off to the shore.
I will nurse you full of joy,
and the tiny ant will guard his door.

(MARTIRIO closes the door from which MARÍA JOSEFA emerged, shutting her inside, and moves toward the door to the yard. She hesitates, then takes two more steps.)

MARTIRIO. *(Whispering.)* Adela.

(Pause. MARTIRIO reaches the doorway and raises her voice.)

Adela!

(Enter ADELA, her hair disheveled.)

ADELA. What do you want with me?

MARTIRIO. Leave that man alone!

ADELA. Who are you to tell me what to do?

MARTIRIO. That is no place for a decent woman.

ADELA. Wouldn't you just love to occupy it!

MARTIRIO. *(Raising her voice.)* The time has come to speak. This can't go on.

ADELA. This is just the beginning. I've taken charge now, with all the resolution and capability you lack. I've had enough of the death beneath this roof. I'm leaving to claim what's mine, what belongs to me.

MARTIRIO. That soulless man out there came for another woman. You've crossed the line.

ADELA. He came for the money, but his eyes have always been on me.

MARTIRIO. I won't allow you to snatch him away. He will marry Angustias.

ADELA. You know as well as I do he doesn't love her.

MARTIRIO. Yes.

ADELA. You know because you've seen the truth: he loves me.

MARTIRIO. *(Desperately.)* Yes.

ADELA. *(Drawing closer.)* He loves *me*. He loves *me*.

MARTIRIO. Stab me with a dagger if you like, but stop saying that!

ADELA. That's why you can't bear the thought of us together. You don't care if he embraces a woman he doesn't love, and neither do I. He could be with Angustias forever, but a single glimpse of him wrapping his arms around me is poison to your soul because you love him too. *You love him too.*

MARTIRIO. *(Dramatically.)* Yes! Do you want me to shout it from the rooftop? Slice my breast open like a bitter pomegranate? Yes, I love him!

ADELA. *(Embracing MARTIRIO in a fit of emotion.)* Martirio, oh Martirio, it's not my fault!

MARTIRIO. Don't touch me! You won't get me to shed one tear for you. My blood is no longer yours. I'd like to look upon you as a sister, but all I see is another woman.

(She pushes ADELA away.)

ADELA. So be it. If I must drown, I'll drown. Pepe el Romano is mine, and he's taking me to the reeds at the river's edge.

MARTIRIO. It won't happen!

ADELA. I can't bear the horror of this house after tasting the sweetness of his mouth. I'll be whatever he wants me to be. The whole village can rise up against me. Let the self-appointed guardians of decency come after me and sear me with their fiery fingertips. I'll stand before them all and don the adulteress' crown of thorns.

MARTIRIO. Stop it!

ADELA. Yes. Yes.

(Whispering.) Let's go back to bed, let's let him marry Angustias. I don't care anymore. But I'm going to go away and live by myself in a little shack where he can come and see me any time he likes, whatever his pleasure.

MARTIRIO. That will never happen as long as I have a drop of blood left in my body!

ADELA. You have no power over me, you little weakling. I could bring a runaway horse to its knees with the strength of my little finger.

MARTIRIO. Lower that grating voice of yours. I'm choking on the evil spilling from my heart.

ADELA. They teach us to love our sisters. But God must have forgotten me in the shadows, because I see you now as never before.

(A whistle sounds. ADELA rushes toward the door, but MARTIRIO blocks her way.)

MARTIRIO. Where do you think you're going?

ADELA. Get away from the door!

MARTIRIO. Just try getting through!

ADELA. Out of my way!

(They struggle.)

MARTIRIO. *(Shouting.)* Mother! Mother!

ADELA. Get your hands off me!

(Enter BERNARDA in a petticoat and black shawl [and her staff].)

BERNARDA. Calm down, calm down. By god, if I had a lightning bolt I'd smite you both!

MARTIRIO. *(Pointing to ADELA.)* She was with him! Look at the straw in her petticoat!

BERNARDA. That's the bed of a sinful woman!

(She rushes furiously toward ADELA.)

ADELA. *(Standing her ground.)* I've had it with this prison house!

(She grabs the staff from her mother and breaks it in two.)

That's what I think of the tyrant's rod. Don't take another step toward me. I take orders from no one but Pepe.

(Enter MAGDALENA.)

MAGDALENA. Adela!

(Enter PONCIA and ANGUSTIAS.)

ADELA. I am his.

(To ANGUSTIAS.)

Get it through your head, then go out to the yard and tell him. He will rule over this whole house. You'll find him out there, raging like a lion.

ANGUSTIAS. My god!

BERNARDA. The shotgun! Where's the shotgun?

(BERNARDA rushes out. Enter AMELIA in the background, a look of terror on her face as she cringes against the wall. Exit MARTIRIO, following BERNARDA.)

ADELA. No one can stop me now!

(She makes a move to exit.)

ANGUSTIAS. *(Grabbing her.)* You're not going anywhere with your thieving little body, so triumphant! You've brought shame on our whole house!

MAGDALENA. Let her go so we'll never have to look at her again!

(A gunshot sounds.)

BERNARDA. *(Entering.)* Go look for him now.

MARTIRIO. *(Entering.)* That's the end of Pepe el Romano.

ADELA. Pepe! Oh god! Pepe!

(She rushes offstage.)

PONCIA. You killed him?

MARTIRIO. No! He got away on his horse!

BERNARDA. It was my fault. A woman's aim is worthless.

MAGDALENA. So why did you say that?

MARTIRIO. To spite her! I would have poured a river of blood over her head!

PONCIA. Damn you, child.

MAGDALENA. You're possessed!

BERNARDA. No, it's good she said it!

(A dull thud shakes the stage.)

Adela! Adela!

PONCIA. *(At the door.)* Adela, open the door!

BERNARDA. Open up! You can't hide your shame behind walls!

MAID. *(Entering.)* We've woken the neighbors!

BERNARDA. *(In a low growl.)* Open up or I'll break this door down!

(Pause. Total silence.)

Adela!

(BERNARDA steps away from the door.)

Bring a hammer!

(PONCIA pushes against the door and enters. She screams and rushes back onstage.)

What?

PONCIA. *(Raising her hands to her throat.)* May we never come to such an end!

(The DAUGHTERS recoil in horror. The MAID crosses herself. BERNARDA lets out a cry and steps forward.)

PONCIA. Don't go in there!

BERNARDA. No, I won't! Pepe, you may have escaped into the darkness of the forest, but one day you'll fall. Take her down! My daughter has died a virgin! Take her to her room and dress her as such. And not a word from anyone! She has died a virgin! Send word for the bells to toll twice at sunrise.

MARTIRIO. So fortunate she was to get what she wanted.

BERNARDA. And I won't tolerate any crying. Death must be faced head on. Silence!

(To one daughter.)

Silence I say!

(To another.)

You can cry when you're alone! We'll all drown in a sea of mourning. The youngest daughter of Bernarda Alba has died a virgin. Does everyone hear me? Silence, I say! Silence!

—CURTAIN—

APPENDIX 1

Variations from García-Posada's Text

My approach to the Spanish text is fairly conservative. I have occasionally supplemented Lorca's stage directions to add an entrance or an exit, always indicating the interpolation in square brackets. The minimal additional variations from García-Posada's text are explained in the table below.

Play	Spanish text (page numbers from OC, vol. 2)	I read as	Translation	Comments
The Audience	Señora (pp. 281, 325–26)		Mother	I have translated the *Señora* (Lady) of Tableau 5 as Mother to distinguish her from the *Damas* (Ladies) of Tableau 4.
The Audience	Director, Hombre 1 (p. 281)		Director (Enrique), Man 1 (Gonzalo)	I have supplied the personal names by which the characters are known.
Blood Wedding	Tu padre sembró mucho y ahora lo recoges tú. (p. 448)	Tu abuelo sembró mucho y ahora lo recoges tú.	Fruit of all the seed your grandfather sowed.	I believe this was a slip on Lorca's part, as the father produced only two children (the Groom and his slain older brother). The alteration brings the text in line with what the mother says about the grandfather, "a man who left a child on every corner."
Blood Wedding	¿Te ha disgustado? (p. 450)	¿Te has disgustado?	Are you upset with us?	This is an editorial error, which García-Posada corrects in his Akal edition.

210

Appendix 1

Play	Spanish text (page numbers from OC, vol. 2)	I read as	Translation	Comments
Blood Wedding	Pero mucho más hermoso si estuviera dormido. (p. 460)	Pero mucho más hermoso si estuvieras dormido.	But you'd be much more handsome if you were asleep.	This boils down to a difference between the polite and familiar forms. Lorca's Andalusian accent may have tricked him into suppressing the final *s* in writing.
Yerma	Mi hijo está sentado detrás de la ermita esperándome. (p. 523)	Mi hijo está sentado detrás de la ermita esperándote.	My son is sitting behind the shrine, waiting for you.	This is an editorial error. The sense is clearly "you" (*te*), as the passage goes on to confirm.
The House of Bernarda Alba	Le tienen miedo a nuestra madre. (p. 595)	Le tiene miedo a nuestra madre.	She's afraid of our mother.	The plural verb form is illogical as the subject is clearly Adelaida.
The House of Bernarda Alba	Pues ¿no estaba dormida? (p. 605)	Pues ¿no estabas dormida?	So you weren't asleep?	See last comment under *Blood Wedding*.

APPENDIX 2

Professional Debuts of Lorca's Major Plays

Title	Opening Date	Venue	Company / Director	Source
The Butterfly's Evil Spell	22 March 1920	Teatro Eslava, Madrid	Gregorio Martínez Sierra	Vilches de Frutos and Dougherty 1992a, p. 23
Mariana Pineda	24 June 1927	Teatro Goya, Barcelona	Margarita Xirgu	Vilches de Frutos and Dougherty 1992a, p. 37
The Shoemaker's Prodigious Wife	24 December 1930	Teatro Español, Madrid	Margarita Xirgu	Vilches de Frutos and Dougherty 1992a, p. 47
Blood Wedding	8 March 1933	Teatro Beatriz, Madrid	Josefina Díaz	Vilches de Frutos and Dougherty 1992a, p. 73
The Love of Don Perlimplín and Belisa in the Garden	5 April 1933	Teatro Español, Madrid	Pura Ucelay	Vilches de Frutos and Dougherty 1992a, p. 79
Yerma	29 December 1934	Teatro Español, Madrid	Margarita Xirgu	Vilches de Frutos and Dougherty 1992a, p. 97
Doña Rosita the Spinster	12 December 1935	Teatro Principal, Barcelona	Margarita Xirgu	Vilches de Frutos and Dougherty 1992a, p. 105
The House of Bernarda Alba	8 March 1945	Teatro Avenida, Buenos Aires	Margarita Xirgu	Vilches de Frutos and Dougherty 1992a, p. 113

Appendix 2

Title	Opening Date	Venue	Company / Director	Source
The Audience	19 May 1984	Theatr Studyjny, Łódź, Poland	Pawel Nowicki	Aszyk 1986, p. 279
The Dream of Life	19 May 1984	Theatr Studyjny, Łódź, Poland	Pawel Nowicki	Aszyk 1986, p. 279

FOR FURTHER READING

All references cited in the introductory materials, plus others that readers may find helpful, can be found in the bibliography below, which uses a modified MLA format (the year of publication follows the author). The critical literature on Lorca is vast, so I have been necessarily selective. For those who can read Spanish, Fernández Cifuentes 1986 and Doménech 2012 offer the most compelling global approaches to Lorca's theater, while Plaza Chillón 1998 and 2001 provide a superb account of his staging techniques. English-only readers who wish to explore Lorca further would do well to start with the following:

- On the literary and historical context of the period: Brown 1972, Edwards 1985, Shaw 1972, and Soufas 2007.
- On Lorca's life and legacy: J. L. Anderson 2009, Badcock 2016, Castilla and Magán 2012b, Doggart and Thompson 2010, Durán and Colecchia 1991, Edwards 2009, Eisenberg 1991, Gibson 1973, Gibson 1989, Govan 2012, Kassam 2015, Kolbert 2003, London 2001, O'Donnell 2016, Stainton 1999, and Tremlett 2012.
- On global and comparative approaches to Lorca's theater: Allen 1974, Álvarez-Altman 1983, A. A. Anderson 1986, Blum 2005, Burton 1983, Delgado 2008, Dolan 1980, Edwards 1980, Edwards 2003, Gilmour 1992, Godoy 2008, Greenfield 1986, Klein 1991, McDermott 1991, Nolan 2007, Rosslyn 2000, Smith 1992, Smith 1998, Soufas 1996, and Wright 2007.
- On *The Audience*: A. A. Anderson 1992, A. A. Anderson 1997, A. A. Anderson 2017, De Witte 2017, Figure 1983, Jerez-Farrán 2000, Jerez-Farrán 2001, Martínez Nadal 1974, Monegal 1994, and Rubia Barcia 1988.
- On *Blood Wedding*: A. A. Anderson 1987, R. Anderson 1974, Basterra 2003, Edwards 1997, D. Fox 2017, C. L. Halliburton 1968, Herrero 1987, Jones 2016, Lima 1995, D. López 1977, MacMullan 1993, Miller 1988, Palley 1967, Silverman 2009, Smith-Kleiner 1996, Soufas 1983, Soufas 1987, Stavrakopoulou 2015, and Walsh 1991.
- On *Yerma*: R. Anderson 1982, Badenes 2015, Baumgarten 1974, Cannon 1960, Cannon 1962, Correa 1962, Falconieri 1967, L. Halliburton 1983, Hearn 1993, Jiménez-Vera 1991, Knapp 1991, Lima 1991, Lott 1965, Martín 1985, Morris 1972, Nordlund 1995, Parr 1971, Skloot 1966, Sullivan 1972, and ter Horst 1980.
- On *The House of Bernarda Alba*: Barrick 1980, Blake 2010, Cabrera 1978, Cappuccio 1993, Edwards 2000, A. Fox 2011, Galerstein 1985, Godoy 2004, Gómez 2010, Greenfield 1955, Jiménez-Vera 1974, Lima 2001, Morris 1989, Newberry 1976, Oxford 2012, Podol 1995, Poeta 1999, Poeta 2001, Rodríguez 1981, Seybolt 1982, Sharp 1961, Soufas 1991, Spires 1978, and Taylor 1989.
- Helpful critical guides are provided by Bonaddio 2007, Colecchia 1979, and Ortúzar-Young 2002. See the various chapters in Bonaddio for overviews and assessments of other categories of Lorca's work (poetry, drawings, music, etc.).

Select Bibliography

Aguilar Piñal, Francisco. 1986. "La honra en el teatro de García Lorca." *Revista de Literatura*, vol. 48, no. 96, pp. 447–54.
Allen, Rupert C. 1974. *Psyche and Symbol in the Theater of Federico García Lorca:* Perlimplín, Yerma, Blood Wedding. U of Texas P.
Alvarado, Esther. 2014. "El hombre que no desapareció tras Lorca." *El Mundo*, 25 August, www.elmundo.es/cultura/2014/08/25/53fa03e5ca4741cd6c8b4579.html.
Álvarez-Altman, Grace. 1983. "The Empty Nest Syndrome in García Lorca's Major Dramas." *García Lorca Review*, vol. 11, no. 2, pp. 149–59.
Anderson, Andrew A. 1982. "¿De qué se trata *Bodas de sangre*?" *Hommage à Federico García Lorca*, edited by Michèle Ramond, U of Toulouse, pp. 53–64.
———. 1986. "The Strategy of García Lorca's Dramatic Composition, 1930–1936." *Romance Quarterly*, vol. 33, no. 2, pp. 211–29.
———. 1987. "García Lorca's *Bodas de sangre*: The Logic and Necessity of Act Three." *Hispanófila*, vol. 30, no. 3, pp. 21–37.
———. 1992a. "'Un dificilísimo juego poético': Theme and Symbol in Lorca's *El público*." *Romance Quarterly*, vol. 39, no. 3, pp. 331–46.
———. 1992b. "*El público, Así que pasen cinco años* y *El sueño de la vida*: tres dramas expresionistas de García Lorca." Vilches de Frutos and Dougherty 1992b, pp. 215–26.
———. 1997. "'Una desorientación absoluta': Juliet and the Shifting Sands in García Lorca's *El público*." *Revista Hispánica Moderna*, vol. 50, no. 1, pp. 67–85.
———. 2017. "Approaching Lorca's *Viaje a la luna*: Structural Patterns, Symbolic Concatenation, and *El público*." *Hispanic Review*, vol. 85, pp. 1–21.
Anderson, Jon Lee. 2009. "Lorca's Bones." *The New Yorker*, 22 June, www.newyorker.com/magazine/2009/06/22/lorcas-bones.
Anderson, Reed. 1974. "The Idea of Tragedy in García Lorca's *Bodas de sangre*." *Revista Hispánica Moderna*, vol. 38, pp. 174–88.
———. 1981. "Christian Symbolism in Lorca's *La casa de Bernarda Alba*." *Homenaje a Antonio Sánchez Barbudo: ensayos de literatura española moderna*, edited by Benito Brancaforte et al., Department of Spanish and Portuguese, U of Wisconsin, pp. 219–30.
———. 1982. "The Idea of Tragedy in García Lorca's *Yerma*." *Hispanófila*, vol. 25, no. 74, pp. 41–60.
Arango L., Manuel Antonio. 1984. "Símbolos sociales en *La casa de Bernarda Alba* de Federico García Lorca." *Cuadernos Americanos*, vol. 5, no. 256, pp. 111–21.
Aristotle. 1961. *Poetics*. Translated by Francis Fergusson, Hill and Wang.
Aszyk, Ursula. 1986. "Federico García Lorca y su teatro en Polonia." *Cuadernos Hispanoamericanos*, vol. 433, no. 36, pp. 270–80.
Badcock, James. 2016. "Remains of Federico García Lorca 'Hidden at the Bottom of a Well.'" *The Telegraph*, 13 April, www.telegraph.co.uk/news/2016/04/13/remains-of-federico-garca-lorca-hidden-at-the-bottom-of-a-well/.
Badenes, José I. 2015. "Until Death Do Us Part: Matrimony, Casti Connubii, and the Catholic Church in Federico García Lorca's *Yerma*." *Christianity and Literature*, vol. 65, no. 1, pp. 51–67.
Barga, Corpus. 1935. "Tragicomedia: *Yerma* y la política." *Diario de Madrid*, 6 January.

Barrick, Mac E. 1980. "'Los antiguos sabían muchas cosas': Superstition in *La casa de Bernarda Alba*." *Hispanic Review*, vol. 48, no. 4, pp. 469–77.

Basterra, Gabriela. 2003. "The Grammar of Fate in Lorca's *Bodas de sangre*." *Journal of Romance Studies*, vol. 3, no. 2, pp. 49–68.

Baumgarten, Murray. 1974. "'Body's Image': Yerma, the Player Queen, and the Upright Posture." *Comparative Drama*, vol. 8, pp. 290–99.

Bejel, Emilio. 1978. "Las funciones dramáticas de *La casa de Bernarda Alba*." *Explicación de Textos Literarios*, vol. 6, no. 2, pp. 183–86.

———. 1979. "*Bodas de sangre* y la estructura metafórica." *García Lorca Review*, vol. 7, pp. 73–85.

Belamich, André. 1985. "*El público* y *La casa de Bernarda Alba*, polos opuestos en la dramaturgia de Lorca." Doménech 1985a, pp. 77–92.

Blake, Thomas. 2010. "Bernarda Alba and Frogs with No Tongues." *MP Journal*, vol. 3, no. 1, pp. 23–38.

Blum, Bilha. 2005. "'¡Silencio, he dicho!' Space, Language, and Characterization as Agents of Social Protest in Lorca's Rural Tragedies." *Modern Drama*, vol. 48, no. 1, pp. 71–86.

Bonaddio, Federico, editor. 2007. *A Companion to Federico García Lorca*. Tamesis.

———. 2010. *Federico García Lorca: The Poetics of Self-Consciousness*. Tamesis.

Brown, G. G. 1972. *A Literary History of Spain: The Twentieth Century*. Ernest Benn.

Burton, Julianne. 1983. "The Greatest Punishment: Female and Male in Lorca's Tragedies." *Women in Hispanic Literature: Icons and Fallen Idols*, edited by Beth Miller, U of California P, pp. 259–79.

Cabrera, Vicente. 1978. "Poetic Structure in Lorca's *La casa de Bernarda Alba*." *Hispania*, vol. 61, no. 3, pp. 466–71.

Cannon, Calvin. 1960. "The Imagery in Lorca's *Yerma*." *Modern Language Quarterly*, vol. 21, pp. 122–30.

———. 1962. "*Yerma* as Tragedy." *Symposium*, vol. 16, pp. 85–93.

Cappuccio, Brenda. 1993. "Twisted Systems and Sisters: A Structuralist Analysis of *La casa de Bernarda Alba*." *Hispanic Journal*, vol. 14, no. 1, pp. 37–46.

Castilla, Amelia, and Luis Magán. 2012a. "El amor oscuro de García Lorca." *El País*, 9 May, cultura.elpais.com/cultura/2012/05/09/actualidad/1336592315_908655.html.

———. 2012b. "Lorca's Last Love Letter." *El País in English*, 16 May, elpais.com/elpais/2012/05/16/inenglish/1337182573_261333.html.

———. 2012c. "Querido Juan, es preciso que vuelvas a reír." *El País*, 9 May, cultura.elpais.com/cultura/2012/05/09/actualidad/1336592881_755639.html.

Cavanaugh, Cecelia J. 1995. *Lorca's Drawings and Poems: Forming the Eye of the Reader*. Bucknell UP.

Chauncey, George. 1994. *Gay New York: Gender, Urban Culture, and the Making of the Gay Male World, 1890–1940*. Basic Books.

Colecchia, Francesca. 1952. "El teatro de García Lorca visto a través de su drama poético *Yerma*." *Estudios*, vol. 1, no. 3, pp. 9–17.

———, editor. 1979. *García Lorca: A Selectively Annotated Bibliography of Criticism*. Garland Publishing.

Correa, Gustavo. 1962. "Honor, Blood, and Poetry in *Yerma*." Translated by R. Allen, Jr., *Tulane Drama Review*, vol. 7, no. 2, pp. 96–110.

Cortez, Beatriz. 2001. "Sadomasoquismo y travestismo en *El público* de Federico García Lorca: un reto al heterosexismo compulsivo." *Hispanófila*, vol. 133, pp. 31–42.

Crispin, John. 1985. "*La casa de Bernarda Alba* dentro de la visión mítica lorquiana." Doménech 1985a, pp. 171–185.

Delgado, Maria M. 2008. *Federico García Lorca*. Routledge.

Dewell, Michael, and Carmen Zapata, translators. 1993. *Federico García Lorca: Three Plays*. Farrar, Straus and Giroux.

De Witte, Ben. 2017. "Dramatizing Queer Visibility in *El público*: Federico García Lorca in Search of a Modern Theatre." *Modern Drama*, vol. 60, no. 1, pp. 25–45.

Díez de Revenga, Francisco Javier. 1991. "Interrelación de elementos líricos y dramáticos en *Yerma* de Federico García Lorca." *Lenguaje y Textos*, vol. 1, pp. 91–92.

Dobos, Erzsébet. 2006. "Máscaras y biombos. La búsqueda de identidad en *El público*, de García Lorca." *La metamorfosis en las literaturas en lengua española*, edited by Gabriella Menczel and László Scholz, Eötvös József Könyvkiadó, pp. 107–112.

Doggart, Sebastian. 2010. "The Lorca Fiesta: Celebrating the Centenary in Newcastle." Doggart and Thompson 2010, pp. 19–27.

Doggart, Sebastian, and Michael Thompson, editors. 2010. *Fire, Blood and the Alphabet: One Hundred Years of Lorca*. Manchester UP.

Dolan, Kathleen. 1980. "Time, Irony, and Negation in Lorca's Last Three Plays." *Hispania*, vol. 63, no. 3, pp. 514–22.

Doménech, Ricardo, editor. 1985a. La casa de Bernarda Alba *y el teatro de García Lorca*. Cátedra.

———. 1985b. "Símbolo, mito y rito en *La casa de Bernarda Alba*." Doménech 1985a, pp. 187–209.

———. 1986. "Realidad y misterio: notas sobre el espacio escénico en *Bodas de sangre, Yerma* y *La casa de Bernarda Alba*." *Cuadernos Hispanoamericanos*, vols. 433–34, pp. 293–310.

———. 2008. *Teatro español: autores clásicos y modernos, homenaje a Ricardo Doménech*. Edited by Fernando Doménech. Fundamentos.

———. 2012. *García Lorca y la tragedia española*. 2nd ed. Fundamentos.

Dougherty, Dru. 1986. "El lenguaje del silencio en el teatro de García Lorca." *Anales de la Literatura Española Contemporánea*, vol. 11, nos. 1–2, pp. 91–110.

Durán, Manuel, and Francesca Colecchia, editors. 1991. *Lorca's Legacy: Essays on Lorca's Life, Poetry, and Theatre*. Peter Lang.

Edmunds, John, translator. 1997. *Federico García Lorca: Four Major Plays*. Oxford UP.

Edwards, Gwynne. 1980. *Lorca: The Theatre beneath the Sand*. Marion Boyars.

———. 1985. *Dramatists in Perspective: Spanish Theatre in the Twentieth Century*. St. Martin's Press.

———. 1997. "*Bodas de sangre* in Performance." *Anales de la Literatura Española Contemporánea*, vol. 22, no. 3, pp. 375, 469–91.

———. 2000. "Productions of *La casa de Bernarda Alba*." *Anales de la Literatura Española Contemporánea*, vol. 25, no. 3, pp. 699–728.

———. 2003. *Lorca: Living in the Theatre*. Peter Owen.

———. 2009. *Lorca, Buñuel, Dalí: Forbidden Pleasures and Connected Lives*. I. B. Tauris.

Eisenberg, Daniel. 1991. "Lorca and Censorship: The Gay Artist Made Heterosexual." *Angélica: Revista de Literatura*, vol. 2, pp. 121–45.

Elizalde, Ignacio. 1986. "La metáfora en la estructura poética de *Bodas de sangre*." *Crítica semiológica de textos literarios hispánicos*, edited by Miguel Angel Garrido Gallardo, Consejo Superior de Investigaciones Científicas, pp. 665–78.

Falconieri, John V. 1967. "Tragic Hero in Search of a Role: *Yerma*'s Juan." *Revista de Estudios Hispánicos*, vol. 1, no. 1, pp. 17–33.

Feal, Carlos. 1984. "El sacrificio de la hombría en *Bodas de sangre*." *MLN*, vol. 99, no. 2, pp. 270–87.

Fernández Cifuentes, Luis. 1984. "*Yerma*: anatomía de una transgresión." *MLN*, vol. 99, no. 2, pp. 288–307.

———. 1986. *García Lorca en el teatro: la norma y la diferencia*. U of Zaragoza.

Fernández-Montesinos, Manuel. 1991. *Federico García Lorca en la Residencia de Estudiantes*. Tabapress.

Figure, Paul. 1983. "The Mystification of Love and Lorca's Female Image in *El público*." *Cincinnati Romance Review*, vol. 2, pp. 26–32.

Fox, Arturo A. 2011. "*La casa de Bernarda Alba* y la tradición de la tragedia." *A Confluence of Words: Studies in Honor of Robert Lima*, edited by Wayne H. Finke and Barry J. Luby, Juan de la Cuesta, pp. 141–63.

Fox, David. 2017. "The Wilma's *Blood Wedding* Is a Marriage of Compromises." *Philadelphia Magazine*, 3 November, www.phillymag.com/ticket/2017/11/03/review-wilmas-blood-wedding-marriage-compromises/.

Friedman, Edward, et al., editors. 2012. *Aproximaciones al estudio de la literatura hispánica*. McGraw-Hill. [First edition published by Random House in 1983.]

Galerstein, Carolyn. 1985. "The Political Power of Bernarda Alba." *Drama, Sex and Politics*, edited by James Redmond, Cambridge UP, pp. 183–90.

García Lorca, Federico. 1996. *Obras completas*. Edited by Manuel García-Posada, Galaxia Gutenberg/Círculo de Lectores, 4 vols. (Abbreviated as *OC*.)

García-Posada, Miguel. 1985. "Realidad y transfiguración artística en *La casa de Bernarda Alba*." Doménech 1985a, pp. 149–70.

Gibson, Ian. 1973. *The Death of Lorca*. J. Philip O'Hara.

———. 1989. *Federico García Lorca: A Life*. Pantheon.

———. 2009. *Lorca y el mundo gay*. Planeta.

Gil, Ildefonso-Manuel. 1973. "Algunas críticas aparecidas en la prensa diaria con ocasión de los estrenos de obras dramáticas de Federico García Lorca." *Federico García Lorca*, edited by Ildefonso-Manuel Gil, Taurus, pp. 471–92.

Gilmour, John. 1992. "The Cross of Pain and Death: Religion in the Rural Tragedies." *Lorca: Poet and Playwright*, edited by Robert Havard, U of Wales P, pp. 133–55.

Godoy, Juan M. 2004. "The Voice from the Closet: The Articulation of Desire in *La casa de Bernarda Alba*." *Pacific Coast Philology*, vol. 39, pp. 102–11.

———. 2008. "*Bodas de sangre*, *Yerma* y *La casa de Bernarda Alba*: la articulación del deseo homoerótico desde el armario." *Letras Peninsulares*, vol. 21, no. 2–3, pp. 235–48.

Gómez, Michael A. 2010. "*La casa de Bernarda Alba*: A Nietzschean Reading." *Bulletin of Hispanic Studies*, vol. 87, no. 2, pp. 221–239.

Gómez Torres, Ana María. 1997. "Historia de una recepción teatral: los estrenos de *El público* de Federico García Lorca." *Revista de Literatura*, vol. 59, no. 118, pp. 505–19.

González del Valle, Luis. 1971. "*Bodas de sangre* y sus elementos trágicos." *Archivum*, vol. 21, pp. 95–120.

———. 1972. "Justicia poética en *Bodas de sangre*." *Romance Notes*, vol. 14, pp. 236–241.

Govan, Fiona. 2012. "New Search Underway for Civil War Grave of Poet Lorca." *The Telegraph*, 6 January, www.telegraph.co.uk/news/worldnews/europe/spain/8997854/New-search-underway-for-civil-war-grave-of-poet-Lorca.html#.

Graham-Luján, James, and Richard L. O'Connell, translators. 1955. *Three Tragedies of Federico García Lorca*. New Directions.

Grande Rosales, María Angeles. 1999. "*El público*: la verdad de las máscaras." *Imprévue*, vol. 1, pp. 95–122.

Greenfield, Sumner M. 1955. "Poetry and Stagecraft in *La casa de Bernarda Alba*." *Hispania*, vol. 38, no. 4, pp. 456–61.

———. 1986. "Lorca's Tragedies: Practice without Theory." *Siglo XX/20th Century*, vol. 4, nos. 1–2, pp. 1–5.

Guerrero, José Antonio. 2009. "La madre de Lorca, una maestra ejemplar." *ABC*, 17 July, www.abc.es/20090717/cultura-libros/madre-lorca-maestra-ejemplar-20090717.html.

Gullón, Ricardo. 1990. "Radiografía de *El público*." *Estudios en homenaje a Enrique Ruiz-Fornells*, edited by Juan Fernández Jiménez et al., Asociación de Licenciados y Doctores Españoles en Estados Unidos, pp. 279–94.

Halliburton, Charles L. 1968. "García Lorca, the Tragedian: An Aristotelian Analysis of *Bodas de sangre*." *Revista de Estudios Hispánicos*, vol. 2, pp. 35–40.

Halliburton, Lloyd. 1983. "An Aristotelian Analysis of *Yerma*." *García Lorca Review*, vol. 11, no. 2, pp. 161–69.

Hearn, Melissa. 1993. "Patriarchal Myth of the Virgin in García Lorca's *Yerma*." *West Virginia University Philological Papers*, vol. 39, pp. 138–43.

Hernández, Mario. 1979. "Cronología y estreno de *Yerma*, poema trágico de García Lorca." *Revista de Archivos, Bibliotecas y Museos*, vol. 82, pp. 289–315.

———. 1991. *Line of Light and Shadow: The Drawings of Federico García Lorca*. Translated by Christopher Maurer. Duke UP.

Herrero, Javier. 1987. "The Dance of Death: The Moon as Hunter." *Selected Proceedings of the Thirty-Fifth Annual Mountain Interstate Foreign Language Conference*, edited by Ramón Fernández-Rubio, Furman U, pp. 193–209.

Iborra, Juan Ramón. 2016. "La otra muerte de Lorca." *El Cultural*, 19 June, www.elcultural.com/revista/letras/La-otra-muerte-de-Lorca/38336.

Jerez-Farrán, Carlos. 2000. "Towards a Foucauldian Exegesis of Act V of García Lorca's *El público*." *Modern Language Review*, vol. 95, no. 3, pp. 728–43.

———. 2001. "Transvestism and Sexual Transgression in García Lorca's *The Public*." *Modern Drama*, vol. 44, no. 2, pp. 188–213.

———. 2004. "Viejos mitos, nuevos significados: una visita al sepulcro de Julieta en *El público* de García Lorca." *Bulletin of Hispanic Studies*, vol. 81, no. 2, pp. 173–99.

Jiménez-Vera, Arturo. 1974. "Violence in *La casa de Bernarda Alba*." *Rivista di Letterature Moderne e Comparate*, vol. 27, pp. 45–49.

———. 1991. "The Role of Spanish Society in *Yerma*." Durán and Colecchia 1991, pp. 147–58.

Johnston, David. 1993. "Las terribles aduanas: The Fortunes of Spanish Theatre in English." *Donaire*, vol. 1, pp. 18–24.

Jones, Chris. 2016. "Lookingglass' *Blood Wedding* Can't Get By on Good Looks Alone." *Chicago Tribune*, 13 March, www.chicagotribune.com/entertainment/theater/reviews/ct-blood-wedding-review-ent-0314-20160313-column.html.

Josephs, Allen, and Juan Caballero. 1986. "Introducción." *Bodas de sangre*, by Federico García Lorca, 2nd ed., Cátedra, pp. 13–80.

Karageorgou-Bastea, Christina. 2003. "Amat y Lorca de viaje a la luna." *Letras Peninsulares*, vol. 16, no. 1, pp. 261–76.

Kassam, Ashifa. 2015. "Federico García Lorca Was Killed on Official Orders, Say 1960s Police Files." *The Guardian*, 23 April, www.theguardian.com/culture/2015/apr/23/federico-garcia-lorca-spanish-poet-killed-orders-spanish-civil-war.

Kidd, Michael. 2004. "Translator's Notes." *Life's a Dream*, by Pedro Calderón de la Barca, translated by Michael Kidd, U of Colorado P, pp. 41–70.

Klein, Dennis A. 1991. Blood Wedding, Yerma, *and* The House of Bernarda Alba: *García Lorca's Tragic Trilogy*. Twayne.

Knapp, Bettina L. 1991. "García Lorca's Yerma: A Woman's Mystery." Durán and Colecchia 1991, pp. 135–46.

Kolbert, Elizabeth. 2003. "Looking for Lorca." *The New Yorker*, 22 December, pp. 64–75.

Lacomba, José M. 1978. "*El público* de García Lorca: estreno mundial." *Sin Nombre*, vol. 9, no. 1, pp. 77–90.

Lima, Robert. 1991. "Towards the Dionysiac: Pagan Elements and Rites in *Yerma*." Durán and Colecchia 1991, pp. 115–34.

———. 1995. "Blood Spilt and Unspilt: Primal Sacrifice in Lorca's *Bodas de sangre*." *Letras Peninsulares*, vol. 8. no. 2, pp. 255–59.

———. 2001. "Missing in Action: Invisible Males in *La casa de Bernarda Alba*." *Bucknell Review*, vol. 45, no. 1, pp. 136–147.

London, John. 2001. "Federico García Lorca." *Censorship: A World Encyclopedia*, edited by Derek Jones, Routledge, pp. 906–7.

López, Daniel. 1977. "Predestination in Federico García Lorca's *Bodas de sangre*." *García Lorca Review*, vol. 5, pp. 95–103.

López, Ianko. 2016. "Laura García Lorca: 'Los restos de Lorca sólo atañen a su familia.'" *Vanity Fair*, 13 April, www.revistavanityfair.es/actualidad/articulos/laura-garcia-lorca-federico-garcia-lorca-fundacion-centro-lorca-dali-bunuel/22181.

Lott, Robert E. 1965. "*Yerma*: The Tragedy of Unjust Barrenness." *Modern Drama*, vol. 8, pp. 20–27.

Lucas, Antonio. 2016. "Huellas inéditas del último amor de Lorca." *El Mundo*, 8 May, www.elmundo.es/cultura/2016/05/08/572e191ee5fdea9c1a8b45e1.html.

MacMullan, Terence. 1993. "Federico García Lorca's Critique of Marriage in *Bodas de sangre*." *Neophilologus*, vol. 77, no. 1, pp. 61–73.

Martín, Eutimio. 1985. "Yerma o la imperfecta casada." Doménech 1985a, pp. 93–121.

Martínez Nadal, Rafael. 1974. *Federico García Lorca and* The Public: *A Study of an Unfinished Play and of Love and Death in Lorca's Work*. Schocken Books.

Maurer, Christopher. n.d. "Biografía." *Fundación Federico García Lorca*, www.garcia-lorca.org/Federico/Biografia.aspx.

———. 2007. "Poetry." Bonaddio 2007, pp. 16–38.

Maurer, Christopher, and Andrew Anderson, editors. 2013. *Federico García Lorca en Nueva York y La Habana: cartas y recuerdos*. Galaxia Gutenberg/Círculo de Lectores, 2013.

Mayhew, Jonathan. 2009. *Apocryphal Lorca: Translation, Parody, Kitsch*. U of Chicago P.

McDermott, Patricia. 1991. "Death as a Way of Life: Lorca's Dramatic Subversion of Orthodoxy." *Leeds Papers on Hispanic Drama*, edited by Margaret A. Rees, Trinity and All Saints College, pp. 125–52.

Millán, María Clementa. 1986. "*Poeta en Nueva York* y *El público*, dos obras afines." *Insula*, vol. 41, nos. 476–77, pp. 9–10.

———. 1995. "Aportaciones al teatro europeo de vanguardia: *El público* de Federico García Lorca." *De Baudelaire a Lorca: acercamiento a la modernidad literaria*, edited by Manuel Losada-Goy et al., Reichenberger, pp. 811–18.

Miller, Norman C. 1988. "Lullaby, Wedding Song, and Funeral Chant in García Lorca's *Bodas de sangre*." *Gestos*, vol. 3, no. 5, pp. 41–51.

Monegal, Antonio. 1994. "Un-Masking the Maskuline: Transvestism and Tragedy in García Lorca's *El público*." *MLN*, vol. 109, no. 2, pp. 204–16.

Morris, C. B. 1972. "Lorca's Yerma: Wife without an Anchor." *Neophilologus*, vol. 56, pp. 285–97.

———. 1989. "Voices in a Void: Speech in *La casa de Bernarda Alba*." *Hispania*, vol. 72, no. 3, pp. 498–509.

Muller, John P., and William J. Richardson. 1982. *Lacan and Language: A Reader's Guide to Écrits*. International Universities Press.

Muñoz Cáliz, Berta. 2004. "El teatro crítico español durante el franquismo, visto por sus censores." Doctoral thesis, U of Alcalá.

Nandorfy, Martha, editor. 2003. *The Poetics of Apocalypse: Federico García Lorca's Poet in New York*. Bucknell UP.

Newberry, Wilma. 1976. "Patterns of Negation in *La casa de Bernarda Alba*." *Hispania*, vol. 59, no. 4, pp. 802–9.

Nieva de la Paz, Pilar. 2008. "Identidad femenina, maternidad y moral social: *Yerma* (1935), de Federico García Lorca." *Anales de la Literatura Española Contemporánea*, vol. 33, no. 2, pp. 373–94.

Nolan, Lisa. 2007. "A Politics of the Body: José Antonio Primo de Rivera's Fascism and Federico García Lorca's Benjaminian Response." *Modern Drama*, vol. 50, no. 1, pp. 1–24.

Nordlund, David E. C. 1995. "Lorca's Social Pathology and Juan's Twisted Authority in *Yerma*." *Hispanic Journal*, vol. 16, no. 2, pp. 421–31.

Núñez Jaime, Víctor. 2016. "Federico García Lorca: a las afueras de Granada." *Laberinto*, 13 August, www.milenio.com/cultura/laberinto/Laberinto-Federico_Garcia_Lorca-A_las_ afueras_de_Granada-Victor_Nunez_Jaime_0_791321000.html.

O'Donnell, Peter. 2016. "Federico Garcia Lorca: Madrid, Memories, Salvador Dali and Luis Bunuel [*sic*]." *The Australian*, 6 August, www.theaustralian.com.au/life/travel/federico-garcia-lorca-madrid-memories-salvador-dali-and-luis-bunuel/news-story/3f27e44cf2d7a 45243a50ccba9bb4c86.

Ortega, José. 1981. "Conciencia social en los tres dramas rurales de García Lorca." *García Lorca Review*, vol. 9, no. 1, pp. 64–90.

Ortúzar-Young, Ada. 2002. "Federico García Lorca." *Modern Spanish Dramatists: A Bio-Bibliographical Sourcebook*, edited by Mary Young, Greenwood Press.

Oxford, Jeffrey. 2012. "Cultural and Literary Ethos as Represented in García Lorca's *La casa de Bernarda Alba*." *The Woman in Latin American and Spanish Literature: Essays on Iconic Characters*, edited by Eva Paulino Bueno et al., McFarland, pp. 101–14.

Paco, Mariano de. 2002. "El teatro en las revistas de vanguardia: *Los Cuatro Vientos*." *Monteagudo* (tercera época), n. 7, pp. 115–24.

Palley, Julian. 1967. "Archetypal Symbols in *Bodas de sangre*." *Hispania*, vol. 50, no. 1, pp. 74–79.

Parr, James A. 1971. "La escena final de *Yerma*." *Duquesne Hispanic Review*, vol. 10, pp. 23–29.

Pinto V., Patricia. 1972. "El símbolo del agua y el motivo de la sed en *Yerma*." *Boletín del Instituto de Filología de la Universidad de Chile*, vols. 23–24, pp. 283–304.

Plaza Chillón, José Luis. 1998. *Escenografía y artes plásticas: el teatro de Federico García Lorca y su puesta en escena (1920–1935)*. Fundación Caja de Granada.

———. 2001. *Clasicismo y vanguardia en La Barraca de F. García Lorca, 1932–1937 (de pintura y teatro)*. Comares.

Podol, Peter L. 1995. "*La casa de Bernarda Alba* in Performance: Three Productions in Three Media." *Estreno*, vol. 21, no. 2, pp. 42–44.

Poeta, Salvatore. 1999. "Poetic and Social Patterns of Symmetry and Contrast in Lorca's *La casa de Bernarda Alba*." *Hispania*, vol. 82, no. 4, pp. 740–49.

———. 2001. "Federico García Lorca as Elegist and/or Tragedian: The Case of *La casa de Bernarda Alba*." *Letras Peninsulares*, vol. 14, no. 3, pp. 367–78.

Quinto, José María de. 1986. "Sobre el verdadero estreno en España de *La casa de Bernarda Alba*." Ínsula, nos. 476–77, pp. 8, 26.

Rodrigo, Antonina. 1975. *García Lorca en Cataluña*. Planeta.

Rodríguez, Alfred. 1981. "Bernarda Alba, Creation as Defiance." *Romance Notes*, vol. 21, no. 3, pp. 279–82.

Romero, Héctor R. 1983. "La frustración de Yerma: un replanteamiento." *García Lorca Review*, vol. 11, no. 2, pp. 203–10.

———. 1986. "El protagonista y la estructura dramática: dos elementos inseparables en la dimensión trágica de *Bodas de sangre*." *Mester*, vol. 15, no. 1, pp. 38–46.

Rosslyn, Felicity. 2000. "Lorca and Greek Tragedy." *Cambridge Quarterly*, vol. 29, no. 3, pp. 215–36.

Rubia Barcia, José. 1988. "*El público*, Naked and Unmasked." "*Cuando Yo Me Muera . . .*": *Essays in Memory of Federico García Lorca*, edited by C. B. Morris, UP of America, pp. 233–57.

Ruiz Ramón, Francisco. 1992. "García Lorca (1898–1936) y su universo dramático." *Historia del teatro español: siglo XX*, 9th ed., Cátedra, pp. 173–209.

Sáenz, María Ascensión. 1997. "Rebelión en la escena: *El público* contra la audiencia." *Romance Languages Annual*, vol. 9, pp. 681–84.

Sáenz de la Calzada, Luis. 1976. *La Barraca: teatro universitario*. Revista de Occidente.

Sánchez, Jordi. 2006. "Federico García Lorca ou la tragédie vitale faite théâtre (*Bodas de sangre*, *Yerma* et *La casa de Bernarda Alba*)." *Théâtre, tragique et modernité en Europe (Xixe et Xxe siècles)*, edited by Muriel Lazzarini-Dossin, Peter Lang, pp. 199–215.

Sánchez García, Remedios. 2012. "Teatro para el pueblo o despertar al dormido: a propósito del compromiso lorquiano con 'La Barraca.'" *Anuario de Estudios Filológicos*, vol. 35, pp. 201–13.

Santos Sánchez, Diego. 2009. "El teatro de Lorca y la censura franquista: *La casa de Bernarda Alba*." *Theatralia*, vol. 11, pp. 113–26.

———. 2011. "*Mariana Pineda*'s Struggle against Censorship." *Bulletin of Hispanic Studies*, vol. 88, pp. 931–44.

Seybolt, Richard A. 1982. "*La casa de Bernarda Alba*: A Jungian Analysis." *Romance Quarterly*, vol. 29, no. 2, pp. 125–33.

Sharp, Thomas F. 1961. "The Mechanics of Lorca's Drama in *La casa de Bernarda Alba*." *Hispania*, vol. 44, no. 2, pp. 230–33.

Shaw, Donald L. 1972. *A Literary History of Spain: The Nineteenth Century.* Ernest Benn.
Silverman, Renée M. 2009. "The Lyric Performance of Tragedy in Federico García Lorca's *Blood Wedding.*" *South Atlantic Review*, vol. 74, no. 3, pp. 45–63.
Skloot, Robert. 1966. "Theme and Image in Lorca's *Yerma.*" *Drama Survey*, vol. 5, pp. 151–61.
Smith, Paul Julian. 1992. "Lorca and Foucault." *The Body Hispanic: Gender and Sexuality in Spanish and Spanish American Literature*, Clarendon Press, pp. 105–37.
———. 1998. *The Theatre of García Lorca: Text, Performance, Psychoanalysis.* Cambridge UP.
———. 2000. "Yerma y los médicos: García Lorca, Marañón y el grito de la sangre." *Federico García Lorca, Clásico Moderno (1898–1998)*, edited by Andrés Soria Olmedo et al., Diputación de Granada, pp. 21–33.
———. 2010. "Lorca's Legacy: Writing in the Institution." Doggart and Thompson 2010, pp. 31–42.
Smith-Kleiner, Felicia. 1996. "The Cultural Process of Adaptation: *Bodas de sangre.*" *Hispanic Journal*, vol. 17, no. 2, pp. 285–307.
Soria Olmedo, Andrés. N.d. "El escritor y su tiempo: teatro." *Fundación Federico García Lorca*, www.garcia-lorca.org/Federico/Obra.aspx?Sel=Teatro.
Soufas, Christopher. 1983. "Interpretation in/of *Bodas de sangre.*" *García Lorca Review*, vol. 11, no. 1, pp. 53–74.
———. 1987. "*Bodas de sangre* and the Problematics of Representation." *Revista de Estudios Hispanicos*, vol. 21, no. 1, pp. 29–48.
———. 1991. "Dialectics of Vision: Pictorial vs. Photographic Representation in Lorca's *La casa de Bernarda Alba.*" *Ojáncano: Revista de Literatura Española*, vol. 5, pp. 52–66.
———. 1996. *Audience and Authority in the Modernist Theater of Federico García Lorca.* U of Alabama P.
———. 2007. *The Subject in Question: Early Contemporary Spanish Literature and Modernism.* Catholic UP.
Spires, Robert C. 1978. "Linguistic Codes and Dramatic Action in *La casa de Bernarda Alba.*" *American Hispanist*, vol. 3, no. 23, pp. 7–11.
Stainton, Leslie. 1999. *Lorca: A Dream of Life.* Farrar, Straus and Giroux.
Stavrakopoulou, Anna. 2015. "*Blood Wedding* by Federico García Lorca (Review)." *Theatre Journal*, vol. 67, no. 2, pp. 326–28.
Sullivan, Patricia. 1972. "The Mythic Tragedy of *Yerma.*" *Bulletin of Hispanic Studies*, vol. 49, pp. 265–78.
Taylor, Diana. 1989. "Interiority and Exteriority in García Lorca's *La casa de Bernarda Alba.*" *Estreno: Cuadernos del Teatro Espanol Contemporáneo*, vol. 15, no. 1, pp. 19–22.
ter Horst, Robert. 1980. "Nature against Nature in *Yerma.*" *The World of Nature in the Works of Federico García Lorca*, edited by Joseph W. Zdenek, Winthrop College, pp. 43–54.
Thompson, Michael. 2010. "Introduction." Doggart and Thompson 2010, pp. 9–16.
Torrente Ballester, Gonzalo. 1968. *Teatro español contemporáneo.* 2nd ed. Guadarrama.
Tremlett, Giles. 2012. "Name of Federico García Lorca's Lover Emerges after 70 Years." *The Guardian*, 10 May, www.theguardian.com/culture/2012/may/10/name-garcia-lover-emerges.
Venuti, Lawrence. 1993. "Translation as Cultural Politics: Regimes of Domestication in English." *Textual Practice*, vol. 7, no. 2, pp. 208–23.

Vilches de Frutos, María Francisca, and Dru Dougherty, editors. 1992a. *Los estrenos teatrales de Federico García Lorca (1920–1945)*. Tabapress.
———, editors. 1992b. *El teatro en España: entre la tradición y la vanguardia (1918–1939)*. Tabapress.
Villena, Luis Antonio de. 2014. "Los novios de Federico." *El Mundo*, 25 August, www.elmundo.es/cultura/2014/08/25/53fa12b9ca4741d76c8b4573.html.
Wahnón, Sultana. 1995. "La recepción de García Lorca en la España de la Posguerra." *Nueva Revista de Filología Hispánica*, vol. 43, no. 2, pp. 409–31.
Walsh, John K. 1991. "A Genesis for García Lorca's *Bodas de sangre*." *Hispania*, vol. 74, no. 2, pp. 255–61.
Wright, Sarah. 2007. "Theatre." Bonaddio 2007, pp. 39–62.
Ynduráin, Francisco. 1985. "*La casa de Bernarda Alba*: ensayo de interpretación." Doménech 1985a, pp. 123–47.